WEB WEALTH

HOW TO TURN THE WORLD WIDE WEB INTO A CASH HOSE FOR YOU AND YOUR BUSINESS ... WHATEVER YOU'RE SELLING!

Dr. Jeffrey Lant

Published by JLA Publications
A Division of Jeffrey Lant Associates, Inc.
P.O. Box 38-2767
Cambridge, MA 02238
(617) 547-6372
http://www.worldprofit.com
e-mail drjlant@worldprofit.com

WEB WEALTH

HOW TO TURN THE WORLD WIDE WEB INTO A CASH HOSE FOR YOU AND YOUR BUSINESS ... WHATEVER YOU'RE SELLING!

Dr. Jeffrey Lant

Dedication

There's no question to whom this book, of all books, should be dedicated: George Kosch and Sandi Hunter, my associates in Worldprofit, Inc., the home of my own Web malls. George and Sandi are among the brightest and most decent folks I have ever met... just the kind of people I most admire: intelligent, hard-working, ultra dependable, down-to-earth, with a sometimes wicked good humor... both blessed with the kind of vision that has turned Worldprofit into a major Internet content provider. I can't thank you both enough for what you do every single day! I know I don't just speak for myself in this admiration either but for the thousands of people you have worked with in our malls, all of whom benefit every day from your skill, technical knowledge and infectious enthusiasm for the profit-making possibilities of the Web. My life is better because you're both in it!

Copyright 1997, Dr. Jeffrey Lant
ISBN 0-940374-37-4

Contents

Introduction

Why I wrote this book, what's in it, how to use it, what you should know about the author

I know two things about the World Wide Web. It's the most significant development in marketing in this century... and it's a tool that most people are misusing, failing to get the maximum benefit.

These two facts caused me to write this book. I wrote it for one reason: so that businesses worldwide, businesses of any kind or type, could make maximum profit from the World Wide Web. If that's what you want, you're definitely in the right place!

In this book, you'll come to see just why you and your business must get a site on the Web... and you'll learn how to avoid the problems that are handicapping so many businesses with their Web presence.

With this book in hand you'll solve the Problem of the 4 Pesky Ps:

- putting your Web site in the wrong PLACE, the place where you don't make money. On the Web the old real estate addage of "location, location, location" applies. Why not? When you're on the Web, you're running a retail store, and you've got to be as concerned about location as any other retail store owner must be.

- PAYING too much for it. Web sharks will take you for not just hundreds, but thousands of dollars to put you on the Internet, tempting you with big traffic numbers. The truth is, if you pay too much, it's much harder to make your investment back in a reasonable time, much harder to move into the profit column fast. In this book, I'll show you how to get your own Web site... with fax-on-demand capacity — for only about a buck a day... AND not in some backwater, either... but in a place where the traffic increases substantially ever single day!

- making the wrong PRESENTATION of your products and services. Whose silly idea was it anyway to think you could dump whatever you wanted on the Web and get it to magically attract people? Your Web site isn't a bulletin board... it's a retail store. As such, presentation, as any retailer can tell you, is everything. If you're going to sell on the Web, which really means if you're going to make money on the Web, you've got to be 100% client-centered in your presentation. You can't bore people into buying what you're selling. In this book you'll find out just what you've got to do!

- poorly PROMOTING your site. To my astonishment, lots of people think that the Web promotes itself. "Put up a bunch of stuff about my business," they reason, "and millions, yea tens of millions, of people will trip over themselves rushing to it. My future's secured. Tra la!" Where do these nutty ideas come from anyway? When you're on the Web to make money, you're in the promotion business. Not just sometimes. Not just when you feel like it. But every single day. Why? Because when you stop promoting your Web site, you sign its death certificate.

In this resource — utterly characteristic, hard-hitting, opinionated, insistent and action-oriented like everything I write — these major problems, and many others, are systematically dealt with so that you can turn the Web into a continuing source of both immediate and long-term profit.

Read that paragraph again. This book isn't about the beauties of the Web... or how much fun you can have on the Web... or the delights of having worldwide penpals... or how easy it is to find some piece of recherché information. No way! THIS BOOK IS ABOUT MAKING MONEY ON THE WORLD WIDE WEB FOR YOU AND YOUR BUSINESS. If this is the mission you want to accomplish, get into the cockpit with me. We're about to take off.

What's In This Book

This resource is divided into 11 chapters. Chapters 1-6 are of general interest and should be read by everyone. Chapters 7-11 are designed for people in specific kinds of businesses as noted or who wish to achieve selected objectives, often in conjunction with my own aggressively marketed Internet company and malls, Worldprofit.

Chapter 1 begins by detailing the reasons why you *will* be on the Web if you want to run a profitable business. Right now the world of business is being divided into two new parts: there are those who are determined to take advantage of the new Internet technology to make maximum profits... and there are the others.

These "others" don't understand that a business without a Web site is a business that's dying the death of a thousand cuts, little by little ceasing to be competitive, a business casualty waiting to happen. This chapter explains why you must be on the Web to maintain a competitive footing and develop new income sources. The more skeptical you are about the Web, the closer you should read this crucial chapter. It may well change your life and your prosperity level.

Chapter 2 takes up the crucial matter of your place on the Internet. Already thousands of business people have discovered that merely posting a Web site isn't the answer to their problems. No way! They've found that they can get a site and spend a lot of money on presentation... but fail ignominiously. In this book, I deal with the reasons why it is *not* a good idea for you to post a free-standing Web site and why the real question is determining just which mall you're going to be in.

In Chapter 3, you discover the crucial secrets of "netvertising," that is how to create a client-centered Web site that takes full advantage of the unique Internet environment. (Note: I use the terms "home page" and "Web site" interchangeably.) Right now too many Web sites are nothing more than one-dimensional space ads. That's wrong and severely retards the profitability of your Web site while inconveniencing the maximum number of people (including yourself)! A netvertised Web site enables you to provide your prospects with all the information they need so that they either emerge as supremely well qualified prospects or as immediate buyers. Your netvertised Web site enables you to achieve both these crucial objectives with efficient celerity and so increase your profits while lessoning your work load.

Once you've got a home page, you're in the promotion business. Indeed, promotion is one of the key elements for your success on the Web. Thus Chapter 4 takes up the essential matter of how to promote your home page *within* the Internet environment. When you've got a home page, you need to create a *systematic* promotional program both on and off the Internet. In this chapter, and throughout this book, you'll learn that a day without promotion is a day when your Web site suffers.

Chapter 5 continues the discussion on promotion by providing one detailed suggestion after another about how to promote your home page off the Internet. These suggestions are designed to give you maximum traffic for minimum expense. Take a look at the marketing communications you're using right now: your business card, stationery, brochures, flyers, media kits, shipping labels, *etc., etc., etc.* Do you have a URL (Universal Resource Locator, that is, Web site address) AND prime benefit for visiting that site on each? By the time you finish this chapter you'll understand that every single one of these things — and all the other things you use to connect with prospects and customers — is a tool that can be used to increase your Web site traffic and thus your profit — without costing you an arm and a leg.

In Chapter 6, we deal with fax-on-demand technology and how you can put that to work as part of your client-centered marketing program. To my astonishment, lots of business people still haven't heard of fax-on-demand, much less starting using it. This is crazy! Nowadays when people call me to secure information on the many activities I'm involved with, the first thing I say is "Have you got a fax?" If the answer is yes (and it generally is nowadays), I say, "Dial (403) 425-6049 on your fax phone. Touch <number> on your telephone number pad and that information will be faxed back to you immediately." Before they ring off, I get necessary follow-up information (prospect name, address, phone, fax). I then go back to work... and the prospect makes the call... on his own dime, mind. Whether you're running a local or international business, selling products or services, fax-on-demand should be in your future.

Chapter 7 is particularly for local service businesses. Lots of people have the crazy notion that the Internet is only for businesses selling nationwide or worldwide. WRONG! As this chapter points out in detail, every *local* service business should be on the Internet. It doesn't matter what kind of service business you're running or where you offer services, the Internet assists by enabling you to post every important thing about what you're selling and how you do business so that your prospects can access it instantaneously — whether you're open or not. Remember, one of the greatest things about the Internet is that it NEVER CLOSES. Human that you are, you may occasionally like to get out of the office. The Web remains working, working, working for you FOREVER.

Are you in network marketing? Millions of people are. That's why in Chapter 8, I take up the question of how to grow your network marketing organization on the Web. After you've implemented the suggestions in this chapter, you'll be able to leverage faster organizational growth and larger monthly commission checks by integrating the Web into your promotional program. When you're on the Web, you can make money without having to pester your Aunt Sally to buy what you're selling!

If you're a periodical publisher, particularly a publisher selling advertising space, you'll want to pay particular attention to Chapter 9. Smart publishers have already transferred at least a portion of their operations to the Internet. No wonder! On the Internet publishers have neither paper, printing nor postage expenses!!! This chapter shows you how to expand your publishing empire by creating an Internet division. Using this chapter you'll turn your Web presence into a significant competitive advantage and new profit center.

As I said from the beginning, this entire book is about making money on the Internet. But Chapter 10 is about making REALLY BIG MONEY on the Internet. As Microsoft CEO Bill Gates has adamantly said, the Web will make thousands and thousands of new millionaires. One group that will so profit is the entrepreneurial mall owners/content providers who associate themselves with the malls at Worldprofit by developing their own lucrative specialized mall properties. This chapter shows you how to join their number and use the Internet to develop very profitable mall properties in my own fast-growing mall complex.

There are basically three ways to make money with us at Worldprofit: one is to have your own Web site or sites in one or more of our malls, using the guidelines of this resource to turn them into continuing profit centers. Chapter 10 presents the second way to make money: by developing your own mall property. In Chapter 11, I present the third way — by becoming a Worldprofit Dealer and referring new Web site advertisers to us in return for a commission on all sales. Do you have a house mailing list, ship packages, write articles, have your own newsletter or other publication, or do workshops and seminars nationwide? Do you reach, one way and another, lots of business people? Then you can pick up lots of extra money simply by distributing Worldprofit sales information and helping people benefit from my malls. This chapter tells you how to cash in.

How To Use This Book

Like all my books this one is action-oriented. I didn't write this to be a "good read" (although I hope it's that). I wrote it to give you a money-making tool... to provide both insight in and ways to develop new sources of wealth through the marketing, communications and business phenomenon that is the Internet.

Because the World Wide Web is itself so new (can you remember just how recently you didn't even have the phrase in your vocabulary?), much of what is in this book is new... indeed, most of it cannot be found elsewhere. That's as it should be. I'm not on this planet to reheat someone else's dinner. As such, you cannot read this resource just once and expect to extract all the gold from it. Read it once to get a good overview. Then go back, pen in hand, and get the benefit of this book by applying the ideas to the development of your own Web presence and empire.

People often write to me after finishing one or another of my books to say that when they've finished any given portion more of it's highlighted and scribbled on than not. Good. I hate fluff. I want each section, each idea, each paragraph to ignite a light bulb in your head... and start a flurry of action in your office to capitalize on these thoughts.

Because this is an activist's book, I offer no apologies on all that you have to do to make these ideas work. Building value is work... and if you're smart you can use this book to build your own Web ponderosa... or even indeed your own Internet imperium.

Like all humans I've known moments when I felt I'd been born too late. That all the great deeds had already been done... the great ideas already thought... even the great books already written. We all feel that way from time to time. But since the advent of the Internet no such thoughts trouble me, because I know that we are living — right now — in one of the great, one of the epochal periods of history. Using the resources of the Internet you can, right now, put your products, your services, your cause, your ideas in a marketplace that can be accessed, with a few key strokes, by tens of millions of people worldwide. Millions whose numbers are growing right this minute.

Each of us now has the ability to touch the lives of millions... and to reap the benefits that come when they acquire our products and services to enrich and transform their lives. In short, we can do what a legion of kings throughout the ages could not do... and all without leaving the comfort of our computer keyboard. If this startling power doesn't touch your soul, your blood runs thin indeed.

The World Wide Web has given you a chance and a choice. Right now fortunes are being made thanks to the Web and the foundations of far greater numbers of fortunes. Typically some people scoff at the Web, that it hasn't in an instant realized its full potential. But I ask you, how would you like the definitive judgement on you to have been rung out when you were only — two or three. How would you have felt if people had said, "He's not as handsome as he could be..." or "she's not as intelligent as she might be"... when you were only 1000 days old or so? Think not of any small deficiencies in this medium... think of how startling the growth and how astonishing its power. Rejoice that you were here to see it... and to take advantage of it. For you have been given a chance that comes only once to a generation... the chance to set yourself upon a high road and to move, if you're smart and determined, far faster and much farther than you could before the transfiguring event made such quick advancement possible.

The generation of 1945 had this chance at the end of World War II. Those who acted intelligently then created an epoch of glorious wealth and security for themselves. They rode the tiger... and it made the smart ones people of power and substance.

Now we have the chance to do the same — thanks to the Internet. Yes, you and I both have a chance.

But you have to make a choice. Right now people in every business in the land, and soon every business in the world, are being confronted with a choice. Whether they want to choose or not, they must decide whether to participate in this revolution. Just as all the women in the kingdom where Cinderella lived had to try on the glass slipper to see if it fit, all of us have to decide whether we'll allow ourselves to prosper from this astounding communications and business transformation.

There are those right now who have decided, with resounding certainty, to reject the Internet and deride its development and potential. They have decided to keep on doing things the way they've always done things. Such obstinacy might make sense in a placid era of miniscule changes. But it makes no sense at all at a time when the rules of the game have entirely changed and where success depends on understanding the changed environment and coping successfully within it. These rejecting ones had better be happy hearing the sound of their own voices... because they have determined that in the future no one else will listen to them.

Then there are those — with you, I trust, among them — who are seizing this moment to create out of the raw material of cyber-space the site where you are the lord of the land. That is what a Web site is. Or will you go beyond just a site, to create your own Internet imperium from wence your word will go out to touch the lives of millions around the world, motivating them to respond? For what else is your own mall than a satrapy at the crossroads of the world's richest trade routes where you, with the greatest finesse, are enriched with every single trade, connection and transaction?

Oh, yes, you have a chance now… and a choice. And whether you will or no, the choice will be made. You see, as in all the great events on the planet, you cannot escape history. Whatever choice you make, however you approach this event, the event is bigger than you are. It will shape you and your course on this orb whether you want it to, or not. Under these circumstances, isn't it best to discern how most to profit? What other choice makes any sense at all?

Profit or oblivion? More and better? Or less and less and less?

J. Lant At Your Side As Counselor And Friend

The Internet has been called The Information Highway. It sounds good… but it's a severely inadequate phrase. The Internet is not a highway taking you securely from Point A to Point B, a sort of cyber version of the Via Appia where all roads lead to Rome. Wouldn't that make life easy? You open up your computer on any given day, put yourself on the Internet and cruise to your profitable destination. Hah!

But the Internet is not a highway. It's infinite space where, here and there, colonies have been established, some anaemic, some flourishing, some imperial, others provincial. Where rogues and highwaymen, every bit as colorful and dangerous as the ones who used to relieve 18th century gentlemen of their purses at gun point, do their damnednest to take your resources. The Internet is full of missionaries, some holy, others demented, and zealots eager to impose their will in the service of an Undoubted Greater Good. You'll find selfless explorers and selfish exploiters. It is much, much more complicated than a highway.

Many have rushed into this environment confident that they knew the way, despite the fact that they have plunged into little known or even uncharted infinity. The fact that so many of these people have failed to make good is unsurprising. Remember how many pioneers failed to find gold in California… or get the good land in the Oklahoma land rush… or to buy real estate at just the right moment in the 1980's. Still, people will plunge ahead spurred by ambitious ignorance.

That is why a guide is called for. *I am that guide.*

I am a guide who insists you think the journey through before you make it. That you consider who you are, what you want, the resources you have and the tool that is the Internet *before* you rush into it. I am a guide who knows that everything in life is uncertain… but who does everything, both for himself and for you, to minimize those uncertainties and increase the likelihood that we will reach our objective — in this case to use the Internet as a certain wealth-building tool.

In this book, you prepare for our journey… but as you'll see, our journey together doesn't stop when this book stops. Certainly not. For you see, I am not just an armchair observer of the Internet scene… I am daily enmeshed in the great work of developing its infinity and forcing profit from it. Today we start an alliance which can, properly developed, bring us both increasing profit for the rest of our lives and through the major Internet growth cycles yet to come.

You should therefore know who I am and what I bring to the table.

An Unrelenting Marketer

What I am is an activist. A man who understands that life is there for the taking, so long as one is prepared to do what is necessary to mold it to his will. Every single day I work on achieving any one of a number of objectives, those that must be completed today… those that are in the process of being completed this week… others that must be done by the end of the month or the end of the year… and still others that are in the process of being accomplished over decades. In short, every single day is a day to make progress towards both very short term objectives and those being laboriously pursued over the course of many years.

Many skills and attributes need to be brought into the reckoning to achieve these objectives but my marketing skills, and the attributes that drive them, are some of the most important of all.

You will see much evidence of these skills and attributes in this resource. We will talk much about establishing objectives, assessing resources, learning to see advantages where others see only difficulties. I shall push you and prod you, perhaps irritate and, I hope, inspire you… but most of all, I intend to make you get up and take the necessary steps towards success.

The Internet is, after all, only a tool. It is an astonishingly powerful and influential tool but like all tools it is worth nothing until you set to work using it.

Over the course of the years, I have created and used many tools to build my own empire. Behind me now are my own publishing company, two internationally syndicated columns, a newsletter, magazine, catalog, card-deck, Internet malls and a complicated international Web of deals, contracts, understandings and enterprises. None of this just happened. None of this was just given to me. None of it was effortless. None of it was inevitable. All of it took time, trouble, and treasure. All of it makes me stronger and further success easier and more likely.

Developing your own profitable foothold on the Web is going to take you time, trouble, and treasure, too. But you have one inestimable advantage today that I didn't have when I began: my experience is completely at your disposal, at your fingertips. Thus, you should be able move with greater speed and certainty to accomplish your objectives. This is no mean advantage.

I have approached this book determined to provide all I can to ensure your success on the Internet. Make sure that you, too, are willing to do everything you can to help yourself. Don't just dip into this book. Tear into it. Understand what I'm saying. See how it applies to yourself. Let my ideas stir your ideas. And then implement both to achieve success.

Before we rip into the meat of this volume, I want to say thank you for letting me share one of the most important journeys of your life, for indeed entrusting me with the opportunity to help shape that journey for you. I am not unaware of the very great honor you do me. In a lifetime an epochal event like the introduction and initial development of the World Wide Web comes but once. You will never forget the people who make this journey with you… they are special indeed. Thank you for making me one of them!

September, 1996
Cambridge, Massachusetts

WHY YOU <u>WILL</u> BE ON THE WEB

Before we go another step together, I think it would be worthwhile if I presented the reasons why — sooner or later — you'll be on the Web. The worst possible reason for doing so is because everybody else is doing it. As you've already seen, lots of people are rushing onto the Web without thinking very much (or at all) about it. That's dumb. There are good solid reasons why you should be on the Web, however. Here they are.

■ *You Run A Service Business Of Any Kind*

Lots of people who run local service businesses think the Web has nothing to offer them. They think that because their clientele is local and that they're small, the Web doesn't make sense for them. But they're wrong!

If you run any kind of service — from dog walker to window washer to day care provider — the Web is in your future. While I've got a whole chapter later on about the connection between the Web and your flourishing service business, here are a few key points right now.

Just think for a minute of how you run your service business.

- You are constantly being called and asked for "information" about how you work, what you charge, where you're located, what your hours of business are, specific details relating to the service you provide, right?
- You run ads, have brochures, distribute business cards to get more business, right?
- You have an answering machine with an outgoing message on it, right?
- You have a customer mailing list and regularly send customers and prospects information about what you've got available, right?
- You're constantly searching for new business. Right? Right? Right!

If you've been nodding your head through these questions, the Web is in your future. Here's why.

– You're constantly called for "information", (often at times you really don't feel like providing it!)

Most service businesses are small, often just a handful of people, frequently as few as one (I know!), micro in size, home-based in site. There's always too much to do in terms of providing the service... and not enough hands to do it. Therefore, regrettably, marketing is often relegated to a back burner, done as an afterthought. Providing the service can be fun; handling the marketing is a chore. Isn't that about the size of it?

When you're on the Web, things are different. Instead of handling your marketing when you can get around to it, when you may or (more frequently) may not be at your best, on the Web you can always concentrate on providing just what the prospect needs to know about you and why he should do business with you.

When you've got a Web home page, you can answer — just as you want to answer, as precisely, thoroughly and genially as you like — every single question that every single prospect wants to know. And if you miss one, you can go back to add the information later, as it occurs to you to do so. Try this with a brochure that's already gone to press!

Now when a prospect calls you at 9:30 p.m. (as one of mine did last night and the night before… and the night before that) and starts asking weary ol' you a string of questions about how you do business, all you've got to say is, "Do you have access to the Internet?" If the answer is yes, after you get her name, address and phone number (you'll still want to follow up later, of course), you can tell her how to access all the information she needs RIGHT NOW. While you're taking a well deserved rest, prospects can be reading everything they need to know about your service business and how you work… on their own time, getting prepared to get down to brass tacks with you later.

Note: Right now, there are people (imagine!) who still don't use the Web because they hate computers. However, in the not so very distant future, the Web will be accessible (and much faster, too, than through today's modems) via your television set. Trial groups are already under way (some are taking place in Massachusetts as I write) with selected families to work out the bugs, so the advent of the Web onto your television set is just around the corner. When this happens, instead of saying, "Can you access the Web?", all you'll say is, "Turn on your television and do thus and so." Oh, yes, you're certainly going to have to be on the Web!

– *You run ads, have brochures, distribute business cards.*

Like most service business owners and employees, you no doubt distribute a lot of ads, flyers, brochures, business cards, and all the rest of the endless stream of things which say, in effect, "Here I am. Call me." The Web isn't going to end this bother, but it is going to change it.

Say you're a roofer. You spend most of your days in season up top cavorting amongst the shingles and tiles. While you're up there, prospects may well be responding to your ads and other marketing materials. You have to play phone tag with them and otherwise stop what you're doing to complete the sales sequence. Well, instead of taking their calls at odd times and places, now you can use your marketing communications to do this:

- tell the prospect what you do
- the benefits they get from you, and
- how to get all the details on the Web.

Thus,

"Need roofing, siding, remodeling for house, barn, garage? FREE estimates. <Phone.> <e-mail.> Get all the details — 24 hours — at http://www.goodroof."

Now every time you create and distribute any kind of marketing communication, you're not merely asking prospects to call you, you're telling them how to access complete details whenever they want them. And, remember, this enables you to provide the necessary information in sufficient detail so that the bulk of prospect questions are answered!

– You have an answering machine with an outgoing message.

Most service providers haven't yet figured out that the outgoing message on their answering machine constitutes a marketing communication and should be used in the same client-centered fashion as anything else they've invested in to bring in prospects and move them to complete the sale. The problem is that most people take the name — "answering machine" — literally. It answers. It takes a message. That suffices. How jejune.

No, an answering machine — particularly an answering machine in the Age of Web — must do much more. It must...

- provide one or more client-centered benefits
- capture the name, address, phone number and e-mail of the caller, and must
- direct that caller to your Web site (and/or the fax-on-demand emanating from it) where he can get all the information he needs... at the moment he most wants to get it.

Note: I've introduced here the concept of "fax-on-demand" technology. This is still, for most businesses, a foreign concept, unfortunately so. We are all familiar with the concept of faxing information to others. With fax-on-demand technology, people fax the information to themselves you want them to have. They get on their fax machine, dial the provided number, and indicate, by pushing the correct number on the number pad of their touch-tone phone, which document they want. This service is available when you've got a Web home page. Thus, even if a person doesn't have access to the Web, if he has a fax, he can access your information 24 hours a day.

Now, then, here's the answering machine message for Charlie the Copywriter: "You've reached Charlie the Copywriter. You want marketing communications that get you more prospects and help you make more sales. I can help. For complete details on how you get client-centered marketing communications, use this 24-hour fax-on-demand number (403) 425-6049 document 99. Also access complete details on the World Wide Web at http://www.charliehelps. Don't forget to leave your name, address, phone, fax and e-mail and as much information as you can about your project. You'll hear from me within two hours."

Is this what your answering machine sounds like, or does it more resemble a businessman's I called the other day which said, "I'm not here. Leave me a message, and I might return it if you're lucky"? I kid you not...

– You've got a customer mailing list.

For some strange reason, lots of people think that mailing, mailing, mailing to their prospects and customers makes sense. Maybe it makes them feel like they're "marketing," or maybe they just like the ego satisfaction that comes from spreading their name around town. What do you think?

My objective, remember, is to cut expenses, increase profits. That's the game. In this connection, the Web weighs in helpfully, because it enables you to keep contacting customers and prospects at the least possible price.

Find out from your customers if they have e-mail... if they have access to the Web. Why? Because once you know that, you can

- immediately cut your postage and printing bills
- develop an e-mail newsletter or other marketing communications
- hit them, hit them and hit them again with your client-centered messages — all for far less money than it costs you now to do your regular mailings.

Imagine being in the position to send out monthly, weekly, even daily (if you're the eagerest beaver) information on client-centered benefits you've got available, including special offers, sales, close-outs, reasons to act now.

These "marketing blurbs" don't have to be long, either. They can be just a paragraph, so long as they're a client-centered paragraph making the benefits very clear to the prospects and providing them with the complete details they need for taking immediate action... like completing the order form you've so considerately provided and faxing it back for immediate service!!!

• Using intra-Web promotion to get more leads

One of the great things about the Web is that — if you've positioned your home page properly — you don't have to do all the promotion of your business yourself.

Think for a minute how you promote your service business now. If you want new customers, you've got to do all the marketing yourself, right? There are no fairy godmothers magically presenting you with clients.

But on the Web things are different. When you're on the Web you've got to consider both external *and* internal promotion. This matter of internal promotion needs a few words.

The crazy idea exists in some quarters that merely plopping yourself down on the Web with some marketing verbiage is going to make money for you and your business. But consider...

The Web is infinite inner space. Just because you've got a site somewhere in it doesn't necessarily mean very much at all. Think, for example, if you owned a star in a galaxy far, far away. Sure, it would be yours. However, what would it matter if no one knew you were out there and nobody ever visited except, Captain Kirk-like, some centennial probe from the Enterprise? Get the point? Just because you're in there, doesn't mean your home page makes sense or will get traffic.

Amazingly, a lot of people just don't get this. They think that just because there are mega millions of people with access to the Web that these people are bound to hit all the Web sites and, so hitting, to buy the stuff they encounter, willy, nilly. Just reading this ought to show you how incredibly stupid this notion really is.

There are, after all, billions of planetary bodies in outer space. Yet the vast majority of them go on with their lives entirely unconnected to everything else that's happening in the universe. Why should the infinite *inner* space of the Web be any different?

That's why going it alone just doesn't make any sense for the average service business, and why, odds are, it won't make any sense for you, either.

The solution to this problem is to link up with a mall. And not just any mall, either, but a mall where the order of business is promotion, promotion, promotion — both inside and outside the Web.

We'll be discussing this mall concept again later. For now, however, it's important for you to understand that once you're in a promotionally minded mall, run by people who understand that one principal aspect of their jobs is doing everything they can to boost the mall traffic, you'll get traffic to your site you otherwise wouldn't have gotten. That is, you'll benefit from what you do to increase your own traffic... and you'll benefit from what the mall promoters are doing to bring traffic to the mall and, by extension, to your site. Thus you derive marketing advantages that are inconceivable from the way you currently promote your business. As I said, I'll have more to say about this later! What should be clear, service provider, is that you're gonna be on the Web.

■ *You Sell Any Product Or Service <u>Nationwide</u> (Or Would Like To)*

Are you the kind of get-ahead, progressive thinking business person who wants to make more money but is constantly bumping your head against the reality that there are "only so many hours in the day"? Have you got a product or service that more people could benefit from? Have you got the fire in your belly that makes you keen to do whatever is necessary to bring it to their attention?

Well, then, the Web is in your future.

Consider the problem that all of us ambitious business types face daily. There are, what, 290 million or so Americans nowadays? And, in your organization, how many people are there to serve them? 500? 100? Maybe just you? It seems an unequal proposition at best, right? Yes, for most business people, in most circumstances. This is why so many of these people end up accepting their limits, saying, in effect, "Yes, I've got something that'll help people. But there's just no way I can get to them. So I guess I'll just have to settle for less."

Yikes! I call that depressing, don't you? Increasing the number of people you can sell to, increasing the profit you make from them, why, that's the game! And it's a game the Web enables you to play better and win continually.

Start by reviewing your operations. Do you do any of the following:

- answer prospect questions on the phone
- meet with prospects to get them to buy what you're selling
- mail information packages about your product/service
- produce a prospect/customer newsletter, or
- run space ads, card deck ads, yellow pages ads, *etc.*?

Very likely, you've said yes to more than one of these questions.

Now, think of how much time and money this all takes. You've probably always considered this drudgery and expense a necessary component of your job. Fortunately, "necessary components" change as technology advances. With the advent of the Web, technology has made a quantum leap!

The first thing the Web makes you do is understand that the dimensions of the game itself have changed. It is no longer necessary to accept either the way you currently do business... any geographical limitations... or the numbers of people with whom you currently do business. Properly understood, the Web dramatically increases your horizons. It changes the game entirely and it significantly augments the resources on your side, adding as it does a powerful connecting and efficiency ally to what you do.

Now you can...

- post every single question prospects ever ask you along with your precise, detailed answers. Now you don't ever again have to be rushed or brusque with a prospect who is asking question after question. As soon as you've established that the person either has access to the Web and/or a fax, you will direct them to it — and to answers which are never less than complete and perfect.

- provide thoughtful and complete information about every single product and service you sell. There's hardly a business in the land that provides complete information about EVERYTHING they sell. Most survive by providing more information about their major products and thumbnail sketches about the rest. Moreover, if you deal with new personnel (a daily occurrence in my life), you're lucky if you can get any useful information at all. With the Web all this changes. You can give each product/service its due, providing all the information about each that prospects need to know to feel comfortable about making their purchase.

- talk directly to every single kind of person you wish to sell to. Now there is no excuse for writing generic marketing copy. You can speak directly, candidly, helpfully to every single targeted marketing group you aim to deal with. Marketing, as every book on the subject tells you, is about addressing the specific wants of specific groups of people. Unfortunately, these days business people are too rushed to do that. That's why there is so much generic marketing copy about. The marketer casts his net as broadly as possible in the hope of catching someone, instead of doing what he ought: speaking as specifically as possible to specific groups of people, letting them know he has just what they want. And then reformulating his marketing message to the next specific group of people... and the next... and the next. When you work on and through the Web, you can finally become the marketer you ought and need to be, directing your specific message to the specific groups who need to have it.

What's more, you can change everything with lightning speed as today's fast-moving world necessitates equally fast-moving response.

Now the game becomes doing whatever you can, through rigorously client-centered prospect advertising, to increase the number of prospects you deal with... and fully integrating the Web into how you handle the continuing increase in prospect traffic. You'll be running your business the way it's supposed to be run

- with the greatest possible geographical territory
- in the greatest possible number of hours in the day, days in the year
- with greater speed and efficiency.

In short, even if you're running the tiniest micro business based in rural Alabama, you're still running a completely national business, able to generate prospects nationwide and to serve them with speed, accuracy, efficiency and complete client-centeredness. Oh, yes, the Web is in your future!

■ *You Sell Any Product Or Service Worldwide (Or Would Like To)*

Having been brought up in America's Heartland, our national provinciality is no surprise to me. I cut my teeth on it. Away from a few enclaves on both coasts, America is predominantly inward-looking, nationalistic, isolationist. This is, of course, one reason why any attempt to send American military personnel overseas to be of assistance always becomes such a gut-wrenching debate. When you're in Indiana, what difference does Bosnia really make to your life anyway?

The practical effects of this isolation are immense. Businesses that logically need have no boundaries, impose such boundaries on themselves. Sales which ought to be made don't get made because some business person somewhere has artificially set the boundaries of where, when and how he'll do business.

When you're on the Web, however, this kind of self-imposed cap to growth is immediately challenged. To be on the Web is to give your business the possibility of going from a self-restricted concern to one with international interests. I know. When my prospect leads come in from the Web every day, a significant percentage of them are from people in many other countries. Why? Because I invite them to contact me… and because I can make money through my association with them. Why should you be any different?

Ask yourself one single question: is there any reason, any reason whatsoever, why you cannot offer what you sell in other countries? Now think! Maybe there's a real reason you cannot do so. But if the reasons you come up with are those resulting simply from a lack of knowledge ("I don't know anything about how to export what I make"; "I can't understand any foreign languages"), then there's really no excuse for you to fail to boost your business by developing an international sales component. Learning a few new things along the way doesn't strike me as nearly so difficult as staying an ostrich with head in the sand avoiding what needs to be done to make money internationally.

In fact, international trade has never been easier than it is right now:
* you can generate qualified prospect leads from the Web;
* you can post in your home page any peculiar conditions of doing business abroad (such as higher shipping costs, the cost of insurance, *etc.*);
* you can get immediate payment on a credit card. (You get authorization on an order from Norway on a credit card just as fast as an order from Kansas), and
* as English is the international commercial language, you'll ordinarily find no difficulty in either understanding or framing business communications from people in other countries and if you do, countries have consulates with business attachés whose job is to assist you.
* shipping companies like DHL, UPS, and Federal Express all have international divisions where you can, as necessary, get the help you need, including customs forms and other technical assistance.

In short, trading abroad has never been easier than it is right now. The Web was the last necessary component to fall into place.

Up until now the question was, how do I identify people in Canada, Switzerland, Singapore who are interested in what I'm selling? Because of the practical difficulty and expense of advertising overseas, such markets were necessarily dominated by only the most well-known companies, those with international recognition and sales operations. The Web has changed all that.

Now by prominently posting your client-centered benefits (as you see, these are all-important and constantly worth stressing) you will say to people not just in the United States but around the world, "Here's what you get from us — whoever you are, wherever you are!"

The kinds of prospects you'll generate are just the kinds you want

- better educated
- computer literate
- more prosperous
- generally English speaking
- with credit cards or the means of expediting payment.

In short, a huge new cadre of buyers!!!

Do you want to tap into this body of buyers? Of course you do. And that, friend, is why *you're* going to be on the Web!

■ *You Have A Catalog Of Any Kind*

The Web is catalog heaven, as L.L. Bean, the giant catalog house, can attest. Unfortunately, the vast majority of catalogers haven't yet discovered this. As anyone receiving mail can confirm, over the last few years the number of catalogs has exploded. There are, it seems, catalogs on virtually everything, even catalogs of catalogs! Come to my office, and you'll see on any given day sprawling stacks of them, littering the floor. It may look like I never review them, but in truth I go through them as fast as possible. The stack, however, never diminishes as new ones flood in.

I suspect, however, that the dramatic expansion in the traditional catalog business is over. There are practical reasons for this. The first is the substantial increase in paper costs. It now costs at least 50% more to produce a catalog than it did just a year or so ago, with increased paper costs being a major culprit. Seconded by substantially increased postage costs, producing a catalog is today much less attractive than it was not so long ago. These increased costs have caused catalogers not only some sleepless nights, but also constant meetings at which the necessary question of cost reduction is ardently considered.

Smart catalogers are in the business of constantly assessing just where they can cut expenses to remain competitive. Bar coding, zip plus four and other postal savings get implemented. Catalogers buy large quantities of paper to hedge against future price increases. The size of the catalog gets trimmed, with less remunerative items being rigorously reduced. Swap deals get made where one trades mailing lists with other catalog houses. New deals get cut with providers, who are asked to lower their profit margins or face the elimination of their goods from the catalog. One does, in short, what one can.

That's where the Web comes in.

When you've got a home page on the Web, you've got a mammoth store. Into that store you can put all the graphics and all the descriptions of all the merchandise you carry. In short, you can put your catalog on line. When you do, think of what you save

- 100% of the paper cost
- 100% of the production cost, and
- 100% of the postage cost.

If I walked into the offices of some catalog company executives today and said that they could save 100% of their paper, production and postage costs and add that profit to their bottom line, there would probably be incredulity. They'd think I was mad. Then, if they didn't let their first impression remain, they'd start paying real close attention to what I was saying... after which I bet they'd dance a jig in the streets and even invite me to a three-martini lunch.

The Web, as you surely must know by now, necessitates a change in your thinking. To a catalog house, paying exorbitant prices for paper, production and postage seems — just now — entirely natural. While they try to make adjustments to changing circumstances, they have probably never allowed their minds to play with the possibility that the troubling weights attached to each foot can be more than adjusted for comfort — they can be eliminated. Such a stretch of mind, they might say, would be beyond possibility, a clear impossibility in the natural world.

But that's where the Wizard of Web comes in. The Web dramatically challenges our thinking about what is possible, causing us to reconsider the fundamentals of the way we do business, of where we should invest our money, of what constitutes a necessary constraint and of what is just a needless fetter from the past.

Now there isn't a catalog in the world that wouldn't be better off on the Web, assuming a few necessary conditions

- association with a reasonably priced, unrelentingly promoted mall. Catalogs, remember, ordinarily have no way of promoting themselves except through the catalog itself and, perhaps, some space ads asking people to acquire a free issue. Thus under ordinary operation, as you reduce mailed circulation, you reduce impact and sales. The key word here is "ordinary." The Web, remember, changes the game — but only if one pays a reasonable amount to upload catalog pages... and only if the catalog becomes associated with a mall which is vigorously and continually promoted.
- the company is set up to take orders 24 hours a day and to ship worldwide. The Web, remember, is never closed, and business is universally generated.

The ability to take credit cards on the Web and to process them on the Web is currently in its infancy. There are still a few bugs to work out. This problem will, however, be solved shortly. Many people currently do not like to leave credit card information on the Web fearing that it is not secure, as some media stories about unfortunate incidents have reported. For obvious reasons, many people are working as fast as they can to solve this problem, understanding that when people feel secure about leaving a credit card on line, the facility of transacting business worldwide will be monumentally enhanced. Long before the next edition of this book is out, the problem of Internet credit card security will have been solved. (Don't forget, my *Worldgram* newsletter will keep you informed of developments if you provide me with an e-mail address.)

For the moment, however, you can ask people who wish to purchase from your catalog to do the following

- fax in the order
- e-mail in the order
- call in the order
- mail in the order.

This situation is not yet perfect, but, really, it's hardly so very bad, either. That's why, if you've got a catalog, you will be on the Web!

■ You Are The Prime Supplier Of Any Product. (Now Is Your Opportunity To Sell Worldwide!)

Nobody knows how many people are prime suppliers of products — but it numbers in the tens of millions; people who have created something of value and who own all or partial rights to sell it and profit accordingly. I am one of these people. Over the course of the last twenty years or so, I've created over 200 products to which I own ALL rights; this book is one of them. Every single day I hear from people around the world who have developed one thing or another and want to know more about how they can sell it. Among other ways, I turn them on to the Web.

Up until the advent of the Web, prime suppliers all too often thought provincially. Like a kid with a kool-aid stand, they seemed to think that small sales territories made the most sense. Well, I'm a guy with bigger horizons than that. Even when I was just 10, I created a newspaper that flourished in part because I signed up all the local kids in my neighborhood as commission sales reps and benefited as they sold issues of the paper (with their names prominently displayed) to their parents, family and friends!

Now you've got a different job. Because you can use the Web universally to expand your sales territory, you need to think most carefully about who can benefit from what you've got. You need to brainstorm to decide the greatest number of people, not the fewest, who would be better off because of what you're selling. Now there is absolutely no reason to limit your sales territory and every reason to think just how you can make what you've got enticing to the largest possible number of prospects worldwide.

Write down

- every kind of person who might like your product
- why they'll be better off because of it
- where these people are located
- anything else that's pertinent about these people that may impact on their ability to purchase what you're selling now.

At the end of this exercise, ask yourself whether these constitute the broadest conceivable markets for the benefits you have available. Remember, it takes time to shake off archaic thinking and to embrace the thrilling potential of dramatically expanded international markets! Thus, you may have to return to this brainstorming exercise more than once until you feel comfortable that you've truly identified *everyone* who can benefit from what you've got.

A bit of advice: this brainstorming process never actually ends. Despite the fact that I've been doing all this for many years now, I constantly find myself coming up with new markets for my goods and services as I review periodicals, read the work of other specialists, and generally pump people for information. The truth is, there are actually millions of markets worldwide; the trick is positioning what you've got to make it appear that it was developed just for any individual market you're approaching... while you're simultaneously doing the same thing for dozens, hundreds, thousands, or even tens of thousands of other markets. In this mad dance of intensely focused positioning, the Web is the best possible partner to have. Which is why, prime product producer, you're certain to become a part of it!

■ *You're The Distributor Of Any Product. (Now Is Your Opportunity To Promote Yourself Worldwide.)*

If there are millions of people who have developed products, there are even more — many more — who represent these products as independent distributors. Unfortunately, all too often their incomes are minimal. The real money, as most smart entrepreneurs know, is not in being an independent distributor, sales rep or subsidiary agent; the real money's in creating your own enterprise and getting a horde of such reps working to create wealth for you. Why, even as a 10 year old, I'd managed to figure that out! I started life as an entrepreneur with a corner lemonade stand in Downers Grove, Illinois when Ike was president. I quickly discovered that business life with me as chief cook, bottle washer, and everything else wasn't as glamorous as may at first have appeared. It was better, infinitely better, to organize all the neighborhood children and have them peddle newspaper subscriptions for me. Having learned that at an early age, I have never forgotten the lesson. You shouldn't either.

But, you argue, who wants all the trouble of

- inventing the product
- manufacturing the product
- stocking the product
- shipping the product
- keeping the product up to date
- dealing with regulatory and other legal hassles
- finding, training and maintaining personnel, and
- all the hundreds of other problems that necessarily come when you're the head honcho?

Good point. It *is* a lot of bother keeping it all straight.

That's where the Web comes in.

Up until now, most independent distributors, sales reps and agents worked locally, often with assigned local territories. Their incomes were necessarily capped. They could make a living, sometimes a very good living, but it was necessarily a restricted living.

The Web has changed all that.

Now your territory, even if you're only an independent distributor, is the entire world of people with access to the Web. The only constraint is the number of such people with access... and the number who can be motivated, one way and another, to visit your client-centered site to learn about the benefits you've got.

To make this experience profitable, of course, there are things you must do:

- make your message as benefit-rich as possible. Throughout this resource, I'll keep hammering home my message of client-centered benefits. If you review the marketing communications of most companies engaging independent distributors, you'll find them heavily focused not on the prospect, but on the company. "Look how great we are!" This, of course, is marketing suicide, whether you're on the Web or running a classified ad in a local newspaper. People don't want to know how great you are; they want to know how great they'll be because of what you've got to offer. Yet no matter how many times I say this, the vast majority of companies continues to turn out me-centered marketing communications that just don't cut the mustard, much less bring home the bacon.

- be clear who you want to attract. Because the Web has such a gigantic audience and because it's also an audience that's attracts a large percentage of young people (who probably don't have the kinds of skills and resources you're looking for), it's imperative that, in any marketing communications you present as part of your home page, you're clear about just who you're looking for. Don't mince any words, either. If you need someone with $5,000 to purchase your product, say so. It's no good beating around the bush. Client-centered candor is most appropriate on the Web and helps avoid subsequent problems caused by lack of clarity.

- put your home page in a vigorously marketed mall. Getting the message? Going it alone on the 'net is senseless unless you are willing to spend a ton of money to promote your site. As anyone knows who has spent ten minutes with the average American capitalist, gigantic egos are never wanting in the executive suites. But that doesn't mean that intelligence is part of the package. On the Web this has meant that some of the world's best-known corporate names have rushed off to create free-standing Web sites without giving much thought to how those sites would be promoted. That's why some of these same well-known names have had very abbreviated careers on the Web. They got on. Waited for lightning to strike. When it didn't, they said, "This doesn't work," and went back to doing things the old-fashioned way, thereby doing the proverbial nose cutting and face spiting.

Just as in traditional forms of advertising, message is 10% of success, promotion is 90%. Thus an essential element of promotion on the Web is positioning yourself in an unrelentingly promoted mall which is dedicated, first, to attracting the kinds of people you want to sell to, and, second, to engaging in continual promotion to bring these people to the mall and, then, by extension to you.

When these conditions are in place, any independent distributor of any product can leap-frog over the restrictions that necessarily come from having a small territory with restricted earnings potential. Think what this means to you!

Properly positioned on the Web, even the tiniest distributor running his/her business from a back bedroom is now running an international business with worldwide prospects, sidestepping the bothersome details that bedevil headquartered executives while capitalizing on all the benefits that come from a well-managed company with valuable life-changing products. I think that's fabulous!

Note: Once you've created a client-centered home page bristling with benefits, once you've positioned that home page in a vigorously promoted mall attracting the kinds of people you want to sell to, you can benefit still further by continuing to identify other go-ahead malls. You can link all these malls together, directing all traffic to your home page, through what's called a hyper-link. This enables you to direct traffic throughout the Internet to your site while actually maintaining just one complete client-centered home page.

Independent distributor, do you see now why you're certain to be on the Web?

■ *You're In Any Network Marketing Company*

All people in network marketing are of course independent distributors, so this point is just an extension of the one above. However, because the Web constitutes a marketing paradise for network marketers, it's worth saying a few special words to them.

Right now, most people in network marketing (which I still persist in calling MLM, multi-level marketing, a perfectly good phrase) are advised to practice "warm marketing." That is, they are advised to focus on recruiting members of their inner circles, such as family, friends, neighbors, co-workers, *etc.* These people in turn are advised to do the same, and so on *ad infinitum*.

In practice, this means that people in MLM will almost always fail. Why? For the following reasons:

- There are significant costs involved in getting involved in any network marketing company, including the cost of products, sign-up and other fees, marketing materials, mailing costs, *etc.*
- Most people never recruit more than 2 people into any given network marketing opportunity they're in.
- The commission returned from what these people buy is rarely sufficient to cover the expenses, thus ensuring that the network marketer actually loses money and so gets discouraged and drops out — looking for an easier way to make money.

There is little incentive for the companies to assist in solving this problem. They, after all, make money on *everything* that's sold, from diet pill to marketing brochure. If you drop out, if the people you recruit drop out without making any money, that's unfortunate to be sure (in an ideal world they'd surely like you to remain and keep generating profit). However, your failure is hardly catastrophic for the company, since you've already helped them make money!

This is why for the vast majority of people MLM is such a revolving door of inflated hopes destroyed by stark reality.

Does it need to be this way? It does not, as I've shown in my book on the subject **Multi-Level Money**. The Web can help change things... but it must be worked properly. This means...

- developing client-centered marketing copy stressing the benefits of what you're selling. Most MLM companies produce shameful marketing communications that do nothing more than extol the virtues of the company. This dog won't hunt! You've got to stress client-centered benefits, and if the company won't produce such materials you must provide them yourself; (or else get an entity like my International Copywriting Center to do so).

- avoiding the temptation to place your home page in an isolated location. Lots of people in MLM who have gone on the Web have placed their message in places where no one is going to find it. As you now know, to get a home page and to place it in isolation is pointless.

- placing your home page in a reasonably priced, intensely promoted mall. Reread this line, because every word is important! It's no good going into a mall that's overpriced... and it's no good going into a mall that's not intensely promoted. You benefit by doing what promotion you can... but you benefit more from the continuing promotion the mall — and every advertiser in it — does.

- getting members of your downline to take home pages in other sections of the mall. Have you ever visited a Web mall yourself? Did you read every single home page? Go through every single section? Doubtful. Large malls can have literally thousands of home pages in them. It would take days to read through them all. That's why you need to strategically place your downline members in those malls you've determined get a sufficient volume of the kind of traffic you want. You need a downline member in every single mall category that makes sense given the people you are selling to and given your ability to focus your benefit-centered message for just these people. In other words, go where the people you want to attract are and focus your message accordingly. The Internet enables you to do that, network marketer, and that's why you'll be on the Web!

– You Publish Anything With Advertisers

The last few years have been rocky for lots of publications and the future promises to be rockier still. As I write we've already seen major increases in paper and postage prices and there's even a whiff of recession in the air. Yes, the "R" word has returned to plague us! As a result, lots of publications have seen their advertising revenues plummet, with the downward trend far from over. Enter the Internet.

Why are publishers moving to the Web? It's easy to see why...
- there are no paper costs
- there are no production costs
- there are no postage costs
- information can be uploaded and made accessible immediately
- outmoded information can be changed immediately
- new information can be added immediately, and
- (once positioned in a mall that helps bring in traffic) the publication benefits from

a kind of promotion that doesn't exist in the print world where it's every man (or magazine) for himself.

There's one more big reason, too: the possibility of doubling existing ad revenues.

Right now, publishers make money in basically two ways: by selling subscriptions and, more importantly, by selling advertising. As such, the Web is of the utmost value to them.

Consider, what does an advertiser want? More responses. What can the Web supply? More responses. What the publisher needs to do is make an arrangement whereby the advertisers that run in his print publications also get access to the Internet at reasonable cost through him. How can this be done?

- To start with, by assessing malls to find out if they reach the kinds of people his advertisers want to reach. As I have already stressed, it makes no sense for most people to purchase an isolated home page. Of course, you could argue that any given publication does have the means at hand to promote a home page. That's true. However, the people it would be promoting to are the same people who get the actual print publication. In short, there's no additional benefit this way. A publisher needs to place his home page in an inexpensive, well trafficked mall that brings *new* prospects to his advertisers!

- Once such a mall has been found (I think you know where I suggest publishers begin their search), each publisher can start telling his advertisers, "Look, I can give you an option whereby you just run in our print publication with an audience <so large.> That's Option A. Or, I can give you an option whereby you'll get the same ad on the World Wide Web for just <amount.> That's Option B. Or I can give you Option C, where you get both Options A and B."

Obviously, the key is to buy space on the Internet at a low rate... and to make the surcharge to existing advertisers attractively priced so that they'll want to take either Option B or C, thereby giving themselves additional circulation and the publisher a new revenue source FROM THE SAME CUSTOMER!

Are publishers doing this now? They are just beginning to, although many publishers have not yet taken this sensible action. Why? For several reasons. Until recently the only option was establishing a disconnected home page that did not benefit from overall mall promotion. Malls were either rather thin on the ground or else failed to provide the necessary conditions for success being either overpriced or underpromoted, or both. Besides, all too often print publishers, being myopic, chose, ostrich-like, to bury their heads in the sand and pretend that if they ignored the Internet, this troubling phenomenon might go away. After all, print publishers like and understand print publishing; the Internet could be construed by such people as a threat, rather than a means of augmenting their revenues.

Get-ahead publishers are waking up to the fact, however, that the Internet has now advanced to the point where they can benefit from it:

- the cost of mall space has never been lower
- good malls are being aggressively promoted, which brings publishers and their advertisers additional traffic they could not supply themselves
- mall owners have the means of uploading all the ads from their advertisers and thereby producing more prospects (and thus a higher likelihood of ad renewal) for them, and

- thus the Internet now offers print publishers an additional revenue source from the same advertisers and their ads. All they have to do is sell Option B or C and let the advertisers know that, for a reasonable surcharge, they will be significantly better off.

What happens if publishers don't get this message? Well, the get-ahead publishers who do see the benefits of selling both traditional and Web advertising will start nibbling away at the advertisers of those who don't get the message, saying in effect "Yes that publication is all very well, but I can give you traditional space advertising and Web advertising — for the same price. Advertiser, you'll be better off with us!"

Advertisers aren't stupid. Enough of them will get the message that they can do better being both on the Web in an intensely promoted mall as well as in traditional space ads than having such ads only. As more of more of them get it, the pool of advertisers happy with traditional advertising means will constantly shrink. Net result? One publication after another that fails to get the message and adapt accordingly will go out of business, publisher snarling all the while about that "damned Internet." But after this chapter, that won't happen to you, will it, publisher? Because you're going to be on the Web!

Last Words

So, who will be on the Web? As *USA Today* has emphatically written, "*Every* business will have a Web site!" Or, better, every business that wants to make money. There will be business grumblers, of course. You can already hear them, working overtime to think up reasons why they'll pass on the Web. But the Web is like Old Man River, it just keeps rolling along. I, for one, prefer to keep on rolling along with it, profiting accordingly. Et tu, Brute?

Chapter 2

WHY YOU MUST BE ASSOCIATED WITH A MALL TO SUCCEED ON THE WEB!

Did you ever watch "Star Trek"? About every week Captain Kirk and crew bumped into another world existing entirely unto itself, generally worlds without outside contact. Clearly those worlds made no attempt to lure a steady stream of visitors! No, they certainly weren't in the marketing and promotional business!

Now, that may be okay for a television series, but it is most assuredly not all right when you've got to make a living! No, to do that you've got to have a steady stream of prospect leads.

Now consider the Internet. While Kirk and company navigated through outer space, the Internet is inner space. It's an infinite communications medium accessed through your computer, which constitutes a window into infinity. We communicate within this medium through home pages, that is defined islands of text and graphics on the World Wide Web. But, remember, each island is just like any one of the distinct worlds on "Star Trek." No matter how large, it's a decidedly finite speck in an unfathomably infinite expanse.

You already know that on "Star Trek" visitors to these distant worlds are few and far between; (how many times did even Kirk get back to most of the places he visited, after all?) Well, the same is true for most of the home page sites on the Web. Without an ambitious, unrelenting promotional campaign, visitors to any given home page will be few; without this promotion only rarely will visitors drop in, much less drop in and buy — which, remember, is the objective!

It's obvious to me that the vast majority of people who currently have home pages on the Internet were never told these home truths. They couldn't have been... or they wouldn't have set up isolated home pages connected to nothing. But that's precisely what so many millions of people have (stupidly) done... and continue to do!

Instead, these cyber-lemmings got caught up in the hype about the 30, 40 or even 60 million people with access to the Internet and the suggestion (so often made by Web-sharpsters) that all one had to do to make money on the 'net was to take a home page and break out the rocking chair, sitting back and waiting for the money to roll on in. (Psst, want to trade Manhattan island for a few mirrors and calico shreds?)

Well, as everybody's mother knows, if it sounds too good to be true, it probably isn't. Which is true, in spades, on the Web.

Consider...

    1) The Internet's space is infinite.

2) 60 million people may well have access to the Web. (After all over 100,000,000 Americans will use a computer this year, and more and more of them are getting access to the Web, not to mention the millions who access it everywhere else.) But the key to this concept is "access." They're not on it every day, and they're not constantly "surfing the net." Like all space voyagers, even if they do a little exploring, most of the time they go back to their favorite places — just like you and I do.

3) About 60,000,000 people with access to the Web aren't going to visit the disconnected, isolated home pages that they've never heard about and which have not been seriously promoted. A few will drop in from time to time, but these visits will be about as rare as Spock coming by for dinner. When was the last time *that* happened to you?

What I'm saying here is BE CAUTIOUS. Know what you're getting into and precisely how it works. In short, do the exact opposite from the vast majority of people who are currently on the Web, more and more of whom are waking up to discover that, sure, they own their own private world, but because of that world's isolation and detachment, it's going to stay just that — private, no money maker, a waste.

If You Persist In Going It Alone

I must be clear with you: the best thing is, obviously, not being in this position at all. As the title of this chapter (to say nothing of the resounding text that follows) makes perfectly clear, I do not think that the vast majority of people on the Internet can succeed (which means one and only one thing: to make money) by going it alone, by operating outside a mall. Thus, to me the crucial question is: which mall should one affiliate with, which one is best run, most promoted, most likely to reach the kinds of people in the kinds of numbers you need to make your experience on the Web profitable? That's the question you need to consider.

However, either say that

1) you already have a free-standing home page and want to do what you can to make it a going concern, or

2) you (with just a touch of masochism) like to sing "I'll do it my way," going ahead to establish that free-standing site, damn the consequences. (By the way, I'm not one of those people who like this Sinatra classic. Every time I listen to the words, it strikes me that the sentiments are those of a selfish and cynical individual, both silly and pathetic, rather like Sinatra himself. Be warned!)

So, you want to go it alone, either establishing a new or promoting an existing (but not so far productive) home page. Very well. I strongly disagree with your decision. Still, here's what you must do both inside the Internet and without.

Going Solo: Promotion Outside & Inside The Internet

These days you see Web promotional devices all over the place. Indeed, I'm wearing one as I write: my worldprofit.com t-shirt. Bright yellow with our green globe logo, it's one of dozens of devices used to bring traffic to home pages.

In considering the matter of home page promotion, I start from the proposition that the marketing resources of most home page proprietors are decidedly limited. Thus you need to be especially canny in determining just what to do to attract the kinds of people you need to attract.

— Step 1: Decide Who You Want Visit Your Home Page

As in all marketing, prospect identification is crucial. Sure, there may be 60,000,000 people with access to the Web, but of these just who are you looking for? Be precise. This clarity offers several benefits. In the first place, it will help you focus your home page. If you know just who you want to visit, you'll arrange the benefits and message of your home page accordingly. Further, if you know just who you want to visit (specifically, mind), you'll be able to find the places — both on the Internet and outside — where you can reach these people... and shape your marketing message just so.

— Step 2: Decide How Many You Need To Visit

One of the first things I did when I got on the Internet was to determine just how many visitors I wanted each month. Indeed, I even wrote an extensive special report on the subject, not just saying how many I planned to have... but how (anticipating another step) I planned to get them there.

I am a firm believer (as you know if you've read my other books and special reports) on setting a precise numerical objective and a date for reaching it. And not just setting it, either, but posting it, too, where you can see it; in short, *contracting* with yourself for reaching that objective.

The mind is a marvelous thing, particularly when it is gnawing at the problem of how to achieve a specific thing by a specific date. Over the course of many years now, I've had ample opportunity to review the lives of thousands of people, both successful and also-rans. It is clear to me that those who succeed don't just have goals (goals are a dime a dozen) — they have a *written* objective and an achievable *plan*.

Just before starting to write this morning (so early, it's pitch black outside), I received a fax from a person who just doesn't understand this concept. He's always prattling on about what he wants to achieve in his life, but when pressed he can't tell you either when or how this "goal" will be made. As a result, his individual actions, each day, week in, week out, have an irritatingly random quality about them. If you point this out to him, he gets plenty irritated citing one "reason" after another why his plans have been derailed. Of course, not one of these "reasons" is ever his fault or responsibility. I despise such people. And I do everything I can to avoid them. Do the same. Ensure that you don't duplicate their self-defeating behavior by failing to set precise numerical quotas for yourself and for being equally clear about how and when you'll achieve them.

How many people do you want to visit your home page this week? This month? This year? Write it down!

But, you wail, I don't know how to guesstimate these numbers. I don't know whether 500 a week is realistic... or 10,000. Well, friend, when you first begin to set traffic estimates, you probably won't know. You'll have to estimate, monitor and revise. Here's a good rule of thumb to assist.

Try to break even on the cost of your home page within six months of a one-year contract. To do this...

- add the cost of your home page *and* the cost of following up all prospect leads by phone, mail, fax, *etc.*
- calculate the cost of advertising and promoting your home page
- track how many Web prospects it takes to make a sale
- determine how many sales you need to cover all your costs.

On a one-year home page contract (a good testing period), you should break even in six months and have six months of profit. This is entirely reasonable.

Be strict with yourself about monitoring everything... all your expenses, all your prospect leads, all sales emanating from your site on the Web. Unless you do this you make precise future planning impossible. Remember, while guesstimating results is acceptable the first year, in subsequent years you should be making reasonable forecasts.

P.S. If you've worked hard to create a client-centered home page with compelling benefits and you've put yourself in an aggressively promoted mall reaching the kinds of people who can benefit from what you're selling, you're going to break even well before six months have elapsed... so, cat, you'll be even deeper in cream.

— Step 3: Decide When You Plan To Reach Your Objective

Stating an objective without stating the time you want to reach it is like baking a cake without flour. It's just not going to work. You need to be clear not only on what you're striving to achieve, but just when you plan to reach it. I call this "Mind Channeling", and it's a crucial success technique.

Using the rule of thumb in Step 2, you could say, "My objective is to draw enough traffic to my site within six months to break even, so that my profit begins not later than day 180. To do this, I shall do what's necessary to attract the traffic, to get prospects to identify themselves with all the information I need to follow up, to follow up promptly, and to close prospects in sufficient numbers to reach my objective."

— Step 4: Understand Your Marketing Options

But how should you reach your prospects?
There are two general ways to reach Web prospects

- *inside the Web,* and

- *outside the Web.*

You've got to use both.

• Promoting your home page inside the Web

However you count them, the number of people with access to the Web is astronomical — and growing all the time. Not all of course are prospects for what you're selling, for your home page... just like taking 60,000,000 random people worldwide wouldn't be prospects for any particular store you might be running.

The goal is to identify just those people who might be interested in what you've got and establish an unrelenting campaign to tell them about what you've got for them — not just once, but in an ongoing way.

Here's how you do this inside the Web. You must

- identify all the intra-Web promotional devices that exist
- review them to see if they offer you any promotional opportunities. That is, do they get to the kinds of people you want to connect with?
- add those that do to your permanent contact list. Remember, you're not just going to want to use these promotional devices once, you're going to want to use them on a regular basis and must prepare accordingly.
- write a signature file that's really a promotional message
- learn how to "play" the newsgroups for maximum effect
- identify all the search computers and discover how to get your home page listed and what you should say in that listing
- capture all the e-mail addresses you can
- properly store them
- learn how to create an e-mail mailing list so that you can regularly dispatch client-centered messages about your home page and what you're selling to these people.

In Chapter 5, I'll be sharing detailed specifics on these things. The point you've got to remember now is that once you've got a home page you must do ALL these things ALL the time. Just as you wouldn't take on running a store without intending to master marketing (although, ridiculously, people do this all the time), so you must master marketing on the Web. And you must master marketing both internally and externally, just as you would with any store you'd run. You've got to get people outside your store in… and once they're in, you've got to sell them the maximum amount you can while they're there. That's the game… and you must become expert at it.

• Promoting your home page outside the Web

Very well, what can you do *externally* to get as many people to your site as possible? Since I intend to spend an entire chapter (#6) on this subject, what we do now is just preliminary. But pay close attention: the more you soak your brain in promotional ideas, the faster you become profitable!

To begin with, remember that promotion can be both ridiculously expensive and time-consuming. That's why you've got to keep your objective in mind at all times: bringing in maximum traffic in the shortest period of time for the least possible expense. Reread this line. Memorize it. This is your mantra:

- maximum traffic
- shortest period of time
- least possible expense.

If you deviate from any one of these three key elements, you're asking for trouble.

Now, remembering these crucial points, you should begin your marketing by brainstorming all the ways you have available for promoting your home page that don't take a lot of either time or money. These include putting the chief benefit for visiting your Web site and your URL/Web site address on every single marketing communication that leaves your office, including:

- outgoing answering machine message
- business letterhead
- business cards
- envelopes
- shipping labels
- brochures
- cover letters
- annual reports
- media releases
- flyers
- video cassette text and labels
- audio cassette text and labels
- special reports
- space ads and other paid advertising.

Get the drift?

You can easily develop an appropriate template for each of these that you can use and reuse. To a considerable extent, marketing is and always has been a numbers game. *Every time* you spend a dollar on any marketing communication or device, ask yourself whether you cannot — for a little extra money, or even none at all (how much, for instance, does it cost you to include the chief benefit of visiting your Web site and your URL address as part of your outgoing answering machine message, for instance?) include your Web address.

Note: don't just include your URL number naked and unadorned. Always make sure to include a benefit that people get when they visit your home page. Remember, a URL is like a phone number, and phone numbers per se don't cause anyone to leap in the air saying, "I want that!" Thus, instead of providing just the number always say, "Visit our home page on the Internet and get <benefit.> Here's how to access it <details>" Remember, always push the <u>benefit</u>... only then does the means of acquiring that benefit (your URL) become important.

As time allows, start doing a search for sensible places to advertise your home page; when you look at any advertising source ask yourself whether it has the kinds of readers/listeners who'll benefit from what you're presenting in your home page.

Remember, if you're going to run a free-standing site, the entire burden of promoting your home page falls on you. If you want traffic, *you* are responsible for generating it! This means identifying all potential advertising sources that reach the kinds of people you want to visit your home page. You should be compiling a list of sources including

- name of source
- frequency of source
- cost of advertising in source
- closing date for advertising copy
- format source needs for the ad you're using, *etc.*

In short, you need to develop a list of sources and compile all the information you need about them for future reference. You should be punctilious about recording this information on your computer for easy access and use.

– Step 5: Drafting Your Plan

While the search for advertising sources never ends, as soon as you have a reasonable number, you should start drafting your overall plan. Remember, this is your roadmap to achieving your objective.

Plans go through defined stages:

- first, draft your plan. Provide, at any given moment, your best and most considered evaluation of how you'll reach the goal you've set for yourself, within the time and budget you have available.

- second, monitor the plan based on what happens, on the data you gather, on the results you achieve. The newer you are to planning, the more likely you are to make significant changes in your plan. Plans emerge naturally from data.

- third, change the plan as necessary to reflect current reality, what you've learned, what's taken place. Changes are possible, desirable, and unavoidable. That's natural. Remember, you're not a cement maker. You're a marketer.

- fourth, use a completed plan (and the experiences it's based on) as the basis for your next plan. This, because of the planning you've already done, should be far more precise and useful, so long as you don't forget steps 1-3 above. Planning is never the most fun to do, but if you follow these directions, your plan in Year II should be infinitely easier to create than the one you may have struggled with in Year I.

– Step 6: Post The Objective Your Plan Is Intended To Help You Reach

Once you feel good about both your objective (simultaneously challenging and realistic) and the plan that's going to achieve it for you, post the objective. Let it be the first thing you see in the morning, the last thing you see at night. Make sure the brain is constantly reminded about what you're trying to achieve. Remember, "Out of sight, out of mind." That's why your objective must be prominently placed!

– Step 7: Start Implementing Your Plan By Promoting Your Home Page ASAP

What's amazing to me is how many people have home pages but never do even the most elementary promotion of them. This is irresponsible — and dumb. Even if you don't have any money to purchase ads to promote your home page and draw visitors to it, you can start promoting your home page immediately.

- the next time you have to reorder your business cards, envelopes, or letterhead, add your Web site benefit and URL address.
- the next time you generate a letter on your word processor, ditto
- the next time you mail a media release, don't forget that URL,
- the next time you speak at a conference and develop a hand-out — feature your URL address.

Now think! Do you have a home page? Do you run out of shipping labels for your products and have to buy new ones? Do you see the connection between these two events? If not, you're in for a lot of needless pain when it comes to creating a profit-making home page! See for yourself...

While writing this book, I received an astonishing and all-too-typical fax from someone I know. In this communication, the writer told he that no one was visiting his home page. Alas and alack! A paragraph later he told he me was too "busy" to do any of the things I've been recommending in my articles for promoting a home page... like making sure the URL address (and, mind, a benefit for using it) are part of every single advertisement one uses. Was there *anything* I could suggest?

Well, I promptly put a flea in his ear and told him to get smart, get with the program, and follow the directions. In short, to shut up, stop moaning, and do the sensible things to promote his home page.

You do the same!

– Step 8: Assess Everything

I've been in the marketing business now a long, long time. One thing that's very clear to me about it is that most business people are winging it. They don't know which marketing methods and messages work because they are too self-centered and self-important to gather the necessary data that makes intelligent planning and forecasting possible.

You be different.

It is in the nature of the Internet that lots of people will visit your home page without you ever knowing they've visited... and without them taking any action to purchase anything. They come, they sniff, they leave. Accept that as a given and don't moan about it like so many people do. Remember, if you mail out 1000 circulars, the vast majority of them are going to end up in the trash. It's a sad reality of the marketing game. In the same way, most of the people visiting your home page won't benefit you either. So be it.

However, those that do take action will make your experience positive — if you not only get them to buy from you, but learn everything else they have to benefit you. This means

- getting from as many as possible their name, address, phone number, fax, e-mail address, *etc.*
- finding out whenever possible how they came to know about your home page, and
- recording this information for subsequent use in both reconnecting with the prospect and making intelligent marketing decisions.

When a person calls me from the Internet, or anywhere else for that matter, the first thing I want to know is how he/she heard about me. This information assists me in planning my later marketing moves. Should I repeat what I've done? Do more of it? Drop it altogether? The answers are not in the stars, but in what my prospects tell me — and tell you.

– Step 9: Work The Plan Daily. Remember "If it's to be, it's up to thee."

Once you've got your plan, work it. There are actually two crucial stages in the marketing process: planning and execution. Once you're happy with your plan (even if it's relatively imperfect), then work it. Look at the objective, promise that you'll achieve it, then begin implementing it.

There's a tremendous source of satisfaction that comes, each morning, from knowing that you are moving towards, however awkwardly, a defined objective. At the end of the day, you'll know whether you've come close. You can assess what worked... what didn't. You can make appropriate changes. You can brainstorm around a particular point. And at the end of the day you can go to bed feeling fulfilled... even if you may have fallen somewhat short of the objective. Why? Because by keeping the objective and your plan constantly in mind and by constantly evaluating every single thing you've done to achieve that objective, you'll constantly be learning how to evaluate data, which data are important, and how to use what you learn to achieve the objective.

– Step 10: Reward Yourself

As you achieve your traffic and income objectives, don't let them pass by without rewarding yourself and the people who have assisted you in reaching them. That would be wrong, wrong, wrong!

Significant milestones in your progress need to be appropriately marked. These include...

- the moment you hit 1/4 of your traffic/income objective
- the moment you hit 1/2 of the same
- the moment you hit 100% of your objective.

Successfully achieving objectives doesn't just happen — and it certainly doesn't just happen on the Web. Sure, there may be 60,000,000+ people on the Web with the numbers going up all the time... but when you've succeeded in directing a desired number of those people to your home page... and when you've made the kind of presentation that ensures that they buy in such numbers and such amounts to enable you to reach your profit objectives, then you deserve something special.

Note: don't wait for others to see what you've done, deduce its importance, and react properly. That's likely to disappoint. Learn to consider the rewards that you want for achievements... and give them to yourself.

Last Words On Going Solo On The Web

Does all this sound like a lot of work? It is, of course. And when you are riding solo on the 'net, all this work is on your shoulders. Whether there's going to be failure or success is 100% determined by YOU.

No wonder so many people on the Web fail.

- They have to evaluate the server to make sure it's right for them.
- They have write and design their own home page.
- They have to do every single thing to promote that home page and bring traffic to it, through both what they do on the Web and outside.

- They have to handle all the changes to their home page to keep it current.
- They have to stay abreast of and implement all the necessary changes in technology.

And on and on and on... all at the same time that they have dozens of other business-related activities to master and superintend.

Let's face it: most people on the Web — millions of people on the Web — are just not prepared for all this.

It's as if, having decided to start a publication, they had to

- think up the idea
- write every article in every issue
- print it
- promote it
- distribute it, *etc., etc., etc.*

Do you know any magazine owner in the world who does this — and makes money — and has any kind of life at all? I don't.

Thus, having read this chapter, you should be clear about one very significant point: that going it alone on the World Wide Web just doesn't make any sense for 99.9% of the people in the world. These people

- don't know how to create a profit-making home page
- don't have either the money or promotional vehicles at their disposal to promote their home page, and
- generally do not have the resources (including time, money and technical expertise) to keep abreast of the constantly changing technology, technology which enables both message and transmission to be brought more effectively to the attention of an ever-widening audience.

For these reasons, going solo on the Internet is one of the most stupid things you can possibly do in business — if making a profit is one of your objectives!

Why Getting Malled Is Preferable

One evening while writing this chapter, I finished a long day by watching a PBS "Nature" program with George Page. I always find such programs — dealing as they do with the constant internecine battles in nature — soothing, making my day, however difficult, look like a walk in the park. This particular program dealt with the island of New Guinea; a significant portion dealt with its marine life. One scene was particularly interesting to me. It showed a school of barracuda effectively working as a team to increase food intake and safety for all. I was impressed.

Humans use the word barracuda pejoratively and I, in my ignorance, thought that such fish must work alone. Not at all. Barracuda have found that — whatever their individual skills — their interests are best served by working together as a team, thereby enhancing positive results for all. This, fellow barracuda, is precisely what happens when you join the right Internet mall and work it properly... as I'm about to show you how to do.

What A Good Mall Should Do For You

Some Yahoos find the word "mall" as applied to the Internet hilarious. I don't see why. A home page, remember, is a store. Infinitely expandable. Open all the time. With an infinite visitor capacity. Now a store can be run solo... or it can be run as part of a mall, that is where a number of store owners band together, reckoning that they'll be better off if they all aggressively promote their own interests while simultaneously benefiting from the promotion other store owners are doing to increase traffic overall.

To make this concept work, however, several things must fall into place, involving the precise roles of both mall and home page/store owner.

The mall owner must:

- have available the necessary personnel and technical experience to assist home page owners make the best possible presentation both technically and from a marketing standpoint
- engage in strenuous ongoing promotion to ensure ever-increasing visitorship to the mall, and
- must stay abreast of both technical and marketing developments to ensure that the presentation of both the mall overall and each individual home page is always on the cutting edge, defying comparison to anyone.

By the same token the individual home page owner must

- do what is necessary to make his home page interesting, compelling, vital to prospects
- within the compass of his usually more limited marketing budget do everything he can to increase traffic, and
- must agree to work with the mall owner so that within his particular aspect of the mall, the message is always client-centered and up-to-date.

In short, there must be a significant partnership between mall owner and home page owner.

Learning How To Review Malls

To say that one should place one's home page in a mall is most decidedly not to say that any mall will do. Not by a long-shot. All malls are not equal. Malls can be

- overpriced (a common problem)
- underpromoted (again a common problem)
- run by slothful and disorganized personnel (a nightmare)
- inefficiently organized from the prospects' standpoint (which kills your traffic and makes the entire exercise futile).

Oh, no, all malls are not alike. Let's be clear: there are good malls and bad malls, superior malls, mediocre malls. There are malls that are good value for money... and malls where signing on the dotted line is like having your pocket picked. You've got to be able to differentiate between them, because selecting the right mall is critical to your success on the Internet.

What You Should Be Looking For In A Mall

Before you go looking for a mall, here's a list of the criteria you must look for...

- **domain ownership**

The site should be in the form "http://www.worldprofit.com". It should not go something like "http://www.anothermall/joes_page/yourfile.htm." Seeing a meandering phrase like this clearly indicates that you're dealing with a rank amateur. The mall owner has not really registered the site. He's simply setting up your file within someone else's domain called "anothermall.com". You can deduce several things from this:

- the mall and its owner are small potatoes
- traffic's probably a trickle, if that
- promotion's limited (a long-term problem for you)
- so are service and technical assistance personnel. (Do you really want to wait for help a couple of days or more when you've got something that needs to be changed on your home page?)

Another big problem: people on the Internet are speed freaks. They don't like to type in long, complicated URL addresses. They simply pass such sites by. And the more savvy they are about the Internet, the more likely this is to happen. After all, they know the drawbacks listed above, too.

- **mall staff able to get you off to a good start**

Your home page is going to have to be registered. Will the mall staff do this? How long does it take? Do they even know they're supposed to do it... or where to do it? They should also provide you with step-by-step guidance in the form of both a welcome package and periodic updates. Remember, things on the Internet develop quickly. How does the mall intend to let you know what's happening? Remember, the Web is a tool. Are you getting what you need from the mall to be able to use it effectively, both when you start and along the way?

- **immediate technical assistance when you need it**

You're not born knowing about the Internet and you're probably not going to take the time to read every single thing you ought to read to know everything about it before you get started. Moreover, if you're like me you just don't have the time to figure everything out yourself. Got a question? You want, like me, to pick up the phone and get an answer! Well, this means you've got to be able to get through to a Webmaster or mall manager. This person has got to have regular business hours (every other Saturday from 1-3:30 p.m. just won't cut it). Believe me, you're going to need this person so you can get straight answers to your questions about how to build your site, upload pages, handle graphics, add sound bites and, of course, integrate all the great new upgrades that continue to come down the pike.

Note: I spoke to a supposedly knowledgeable business guy the other day who bragged to me about how he'd gotten a home page for "next to nothing." Nah nah nah nah nah. Believe me, I'm thrilled to be able to burst the saliva bubbles of these kinds of nit-wits. "Is there technical assistance available for your home page?" No. "Do you know how to get to people who can help you? Do you know their hours? Do you even know if they can help you?" No. No. And, you guessed it, no again. Without breaking stride, I was able to show him that "next to nothing" means "next to disaster." Next!

• Low-priced Web site updates

Some malls may look like they charge a small price, but the fact is they lure you in with something that looks real fair… and then sock it to you on the updates and upgrades. Remember, your Web site is not set in cement. It's a store. And with any store, you're going to want to change things — maybe very often indeed. Do you really want to be hit with insultingly high prices every time you want to change your offer or fine tune the benefits of your main product? OF COURSE NOT!

As I write I'm looking at the very deceptive sales materials of a mall that claims to be like Worldprofit. It must have been written by a descendent of the spider who said, "Come into my parlor" to the fly. While the initial prices look competitive with ours… by the time you figure in all the add-ons and the costs that people will incur over a year when they upgrade and change their home pages, you're looking at costs that are more than four times ours. This way of rooking the customer is, alas, all too common on the Internet. And it's done by perfectly respectable business people who think that if they pat the dog, love their Significant Other, and occasionally honor most of the Ten Commandments that they're Heaven-bound indeed!

You've also got to be alert to the technical expertise of the mall staff. This may be tough for you to evaluate, especially if you have the kind of limited technical background of humanists like me. Nonetheless, if you're dealing with technical people who aren't technically adept you're buying into a very big problem for yourself, your home page, and your overall success on the Internet. Your technician must

- understand Web site and large mall architecture. This is a very complicated subject about which I have seen nothing written, despite its importance. You must understand large mall architecture to make a domain easy to navigate. This comes only with significant experience developing malls. Very few people in the world currently have this experience. Are you dealing with one who does… or with a person who thinks that all you need to do to make a mall work is to post information and hope that people find it on their own?
- coordinate page changes and advise on Web developments such as cgi scripts, java applets, video and audio so that you can use them to achieve your profit objectives
- be in a position to advise you on a regular basis about the vast changes on the Internet that occur on literally a daily basis. How does the technician keep abreast? How does this technician alert you to the changes and advise on how to use them to best advantage? (Caution: As far as we know, the "TechAdvance"

section of my *Worldgram* newsletter prepared by Worldprofit Mall Manager George Kosch is the only organized attempt by a mall to brief prospects and customers on Internet technical advances and translate them into useful, money-making tips. Other malls seem to have a "sink or swim" attitude which we at Worldprofit regard with horror and disgust. Be warned!)

Another very important technical point: the mall you're considering must make it easy for people to find you and your Web site, to get access, that is, to what you're presenting and selling. In this connection, find out whether the mall you're considering has a local search engine (such as we have at Worldprofit). Such a search engine enables prospects to type in key words and phrases to find just what they're looking for. It's just not good enough to lump everything together, cheek by jowl. People on the Internet want just what they want, when they want it, not an endless fishing expedition for which they have neither the time nor the patience. Creating such an internal mall search engine takes a high level of skill and expertise; it involves a mastery of the intricate links on the commercial domain. If you don't see it, if the mall you're considering doesn't have it, you're either dealing with people who

- don't know how to do it (bad, with implications for the general overall technical expertise of mall personnel)
- don't see the point of giving mall visitors an easy way of finding out what's there (very bad, a sure sign there are likely to be other lapses in client-centered behavior), or
- both (an indication you should run, not walk, in another direction!)

• Copywriting & design expertise

The mall you're considering must be a full-service mall. That is, its management must not only be able to post what you want... they must be able to create it for you, too — both in terms of copy and design.

One of the craziest notions going is that it simply doesn't matter what you post on the Internet, that anything will work. This is madness.

Do you believe it matters what your yellow pages ad says? Your cover letters? Your business brochure? How would you feel if some wizenheimer said to you, "Oh, you can put anything you want in that letter, in that brochure. It's all the same and won't make any difference to your response." Would you believe *that*?

Yet purportedly sensible business people, who understand that profit-making ads have necessary client-centered components, unthinkingly accept the argument that posting anything you want in an Internet home page makes sense.

One giant — and growing — problem of the World Wide Web is the amount of garbage that's in there now... and which is growing exponentially every single day. People are dumping whatever they can think of — yes, including the kitchen sink — into their home pages in the vane hope of snagging someone, *anyone*, who might just buy something, *anything*.

THIS IS RIDICULOUS!!!

When you're in business and using the Web to generate sales, nothing should go up as part of your home page that isn't as rigorously client-centered as every other marketing communication you're using.

In the next chapter, I'll be going into how to create a profit-making home page and so will address this important matter in detail. Here, however, I want to make sure that any mall you're considering offers

- a client-centered copywriter, someone who understands how to create a compelling, motivating home page
- a graphic artist. The Web, remember, is not just a means for dispensing text. It is also a visually exciting medium. This means you're going to need the services of a graphic artist. Does the mall you're considering have one?
- reasonable prices for these services. You must understand that on the Wild Web, prices are all over the map. A new frontier, people charge what the traffic will bear. Given the fact that much of this traffic is abysmally ignorant, those prices are ordinarily breathtakingly high from everything from page set up to graphic artists. Suggestion: if you're ever even thinking of signing up with another mall, call us first to check our prices. In virtually every case, you'll find them not just lower, but far lower than anyone else's.

Note: to check out the copywriting and graphics, there's nothing like a trip to the mall you're considering. Don't fail to make it. Go in and start examining not just one but a series of home pages. Look at them with the critical eye of someone whose home page might end up in this mall. Also look at them with the eye of a prospect who is seeing these home pages for the first time. Do these get you excited? Motivated? Put you in that critical buying mood?

- Is what you're seeing visually compelling? Is your eye drawn into the home page causing you to want to stay and read it? Is the home page easy to read? Or does it look "difficult", thus causing the brain to say, in effect, "This may be important, but it's going to take time and bother. I'll come back later"?
- Is the copy interesting, motivating, fast-moving?
- Does the copy have a pulsating beat, stressing client-centered benefits, and moving the prospect through these benefits as fast and efficiently as possible to that all important response device, be it on-line order form, 800 number, fax, *etc.*?

Remember, the purpose of the mall generally and each home page specifically is not just to look good, but to move the prospect towards responding.

- ## Does it have the right market focus for what you're offering?

Does the mall get to the kinds of people you're looking for? A mall, remember, is a collection of home pages/stores around a common theme. Mega-malls (like we have at worldprofit.com) are divided into submalls, each of which has a clear theme and market identification. This market identification helps everyone — mall manager, mall advertiser, mall visitor.

Good managers want you in the mall if you both represent and accentuate the theme. Mall visitors want to come in if you've got the theme they're interested in and will be happy to stay away if you don't.

Making it clear what you do and who you want saves everybody a lot of bother.

Ask the mall manager just who the mall is designed for... then go in and make sure that everything in the mall reinforces one single market identification. The mall should constantly be saying, stressing, reinforcing this line: "This mall is for you if this is you:_____."

At all times the prospect should be confirmed in his belief that he/she is in the right place. This is not only important now... but it's important for stimulating future visits. You see, the objective is not just to get the prospect to come once... but for the prospect to understand that what he/she wants is to be found in the mall over and over again in the future. This can only be done by having a clear-cut market identification and using every opportunity to reassure the prospect that he/she is in the right place... and will get more of the same upon returning.

Thus, when you look at a mall, scrutinize it carefully. Do you get the sense that the mall manager has dumped everything imaginable into this mall? Or do you get the sense that the mall has a clear theme? That prospects would know instantly if they were in the right place? Would they get the sense that new things in their area of interest were being regularly added? Or would a single look convince them that they were rather in a kind of cyber flea market, where there were mounds and mounds of stuff in no particular order?

Where would you rather be?

– marketing expertise

As should be clear to you by now, a mall without marketing expertise is a mall you should strenuously avoid.

One day at lunch years ago the eminent writer and historian Thomas Boyston Adams, descendant of two American presidents, told me that in his youth to make some extra money he sold watches for a Waltham, Massachusetts company.

"The first day on the job the owner looked me in the eye and said 'It's a lot easier to make watches than to sell watches.'"

So is it a lot easier to put up home pages on the Internet than to get prospects to visit, much less visit and buy. This is a point you must never forget. More to the point here, you must be sure the mall manager hasn't forgotten it either.

If I had to choose between a bad home page well promoted and a superior home page poorly promoted, I'd never hesitate: I'd take the former. Of course, in reality I'd want to make sure I had a good client-centered home page and rigorous prospect-centered promotion, but as you can see from my selection, I regard prospect-centered promotion as *the* crucial variable for success on the Internet.

That's why you've got to quiz the manager about the marketing expertise he and his team bring to the crucial matter of promoting your home page. When you do this, you may well be shocked.

The truth is, most mall owners are watch makers, not watch sellers. That is, in the terms of Mr. Adams' story, they have some idea how to put together a mall... but much less of an idea how to promote it and get increasing numbers of prospects to visit.

Reason? Too many malls are run by techies who may be adept at the technology... but whose marketing skills leave everything to be desired. This is a formula for disaster. You see, the kinds of skills that make one technically adept are not at all the kinds of skills one needs to be proficient from a marketing standpoint. The techies, by definition, love the technology and are totally fixated by it. However, the technology is nothing more than a series of features. As you already know, features per se don't sell products or services. Benefits do. The best marketers know this... and that's why they spend their time translating these features into benefits and hammering these benefits home to designated prospect groups so that they'll visit, so that they'll buy, so that they'll visit again to buy again.

Note: techies without marketers do not, as you can see, create effective malls. By the same token, marketers without techies also create weak malls that fail to reach their full potential. Lots of marketers have seen the potential of the Internet and rushed to establish malls by linking up with whatever technical people they can find. Unless both techie and marketer have a full grasp of the necessary collaboration and mutual identification of purpose that must exist between both technical and marketing experts, the mall will be out of balance, to the detriment of everyone, including the advertiser.

– extensive promotional program

Marketing expertise in a vacuum is, of course, useless. It's not enough to know that the mall manager or his personnel are adept at marketing. You've got to know just what they do.

In this connection, you should find out specifically what the mall management team is doing to bring the designated audience to the mall, thereby increasing your visitors and, in due course, your sales from these visitors.

Beware! When you start asking the mall management just what marketing they do, you'll find many become (however charmingly) evasive. There's good reason for this.

Far too many mall managers are hoping against hope that all they have to do is engage in a series of intra-Web promotional activities to generate the necessary traffic. They hope this for a very good reason: intra-Web promotional activities, as you already know, don't demand cash or a lot of time.

These mall managers go to the various search engines and to the news and special interest groups and merely post messages saying, in effect, "here's what we've got. Come and see it." Now, I'd be the last person in the world to tell anyone not to engage in every single promotional gambit that one can to improve traffic and response. But I'm equally clear that you cannot build significant traffic in a mall simply by leaving such messages at newsgroups and engaging in the other kinds of standard intra-Web promotional activities.

Thus, it's your job to discover whether this is, in fact, all the mall you're considering does. If so, escape while your money's still in your pocket.

One of the chief reasons for joining a mall is because, in effect, it takes a percentage of what every single advertiser pays and, on behalf of the interests of all, engages in strenuous outreach and promotion. Just how strenuous depends on the expertise, technical skills, and financial resources of the mall management team. Let me give you an idea of what can be done by listing some of the promotional devices we use at Worldprofit.

- quarterly 100,000 circulation Sales & Marketing Success Card Deck
- making sure the largest number of cards in this deck have a URL address directing readers of that card to particular home pages at Worldprofit
- running promotional cards in many other card decks with well over a million circulation a year
- national ad campaign. Placement of space ads in hundreds of publications in many countries providing details on what the malls contain and how to get access to them.
- extensive promotion in quarterly 140,000+ circulation Sure-Fire Business Success Catalog
- promotion through my two internationally syndicated columns, "Sure-Fire Business Success" and "Qwik-Smarts with Dr. Jeffrey Lant," now reaching over 1.5 million people monthly. Every single article concludes with a "Resource Box" inviting readers to visit the Worldprofit Mall Complex and providing them with complete details on how to do so.
- publication of Worldprofit details in all my books
- including Worldprofit address on all business letterhead, envelopes, shipping labels, *etc.*
- providing instructions on how all mall advertisers (of whom there are now thousands) can promote their home pages by including URL address and benefit of visiting their home pages in all marketing communications. (And we don't just tell them once, either; we constantly remind advertisers about what to do… right to the point that when they communicate with us by, say, using an envelope without their URL address on it… we send them an e-mail message telling them to "Get with the program!")
- twice-monthly promotion through *Worldgram* newsletter in which we promote not only the malls overall but specific Web sites within the malls,
- And, of course, by engaging in a strenuous intra-Web promotional program as outlined in Chapter 5.

Marketing, as you know, is a numbers game. Marketing on the Web is a numbers game that you must play both on the Web and outside.

Before you even consider placing your home page in any mall, ask some pointed questions about just how the management team handles overall mall promotion. Also make sure that they want you to do your part, too. Good mall management, you see, understands that the real strength of a mall comes not just from what it does… but from what it does in conjunction with all the advertisers. Silly management may give you the impression, or may even say, "You don't have to do anything," but that's naive at best, deceptive at worst. To succeed on the Web, of course you must do something — all the "somethings" advanced in this book. However when you've selected the right mall, you'll have the satisfaction of knowing that you're not working alone, but rather as part of a get-ahead, client-centered, aggressive management/promotional team that not only understands the importance of an unrelenting marketing program… but is working to implement one every single day.

– growing traffic

Is all this working? Are more people visiting every single day? On the good malls you don't have to wonder. You can know at a glance. Why? Because there's a counter in plain view, a counter that lets you know, minute by minute, how the traffic is growing — or not!

Want to see how a counter works? Go to worldprofit.com, and you'll find one right on the Main Menu. Come back in a couple of minutes, and you'll find the numbers are greater than when you came in! Those numbers are steadily rising not by chance or luck, but as the predictable result of an aggressive marketing campaign, a campaign which may well be responsible for your visit, too!

Now check out any other malls you may be considering. Chances are you'll look in vain for a traffic counter. Care to guess why? Well, it goes something like this, "If you've got it, flaunt it." When a mall doesn't post a counter, it's because they cannot stand the scrutiny that a counter necessarily entails. So don't even consider going into a mall without a counter. Odds are, its traffic is minuscule, as you can affirm by quizzing its management about its marketing program.

If the mall does have a counter, find out what time period it covers. At worldprofit.com we tell you how many visitors have come since a particular date. If you want to know what the average daily traffic is, all you've got to do is use your calculator and you'll know. (By the way, you'll notice at Worldprofit that the *rate* of traffic increase is constantly higher… which is just the way it should be given the extensive promotion we do and the constant increase in our advertisers, all of whom also work to increase the traffic to their individual home pages and thus, in due course, to the mall generally.)

While the absence of a counter almost certainly means meager traffic, the fact that there is a counter doesn't necessarily mean that there's much traffic. Use your noggin! There are malls which use a counter but that counter demonstrates nothing more that traffic is slight. While the absence of a counter is an almost certain indication traffic is limited, the existence of a counter may do nothing more than confirm the infrequency of visitors.

– continuing assistance with marketing

Earlier in this chapter I discussed the important of technical assistance. By the same token, your mall should offer continuing marketing assistance. Does it?

The mall management team must understand that having all advertisers master marketing is both crucial to the success of the mall and a part of their function.

In the Worldprofit *Worldgram* we provide basically two kinds of tips: those dealing with technical enhancements newly available to improve home pages and with marketing suggestions to improve visitorship and response rates. We provide these tips without cost and ensure that they are as detailed and specific as possible. You see, it's as much in our interest as in yours to ensure that home pages are as compelling as possible… and that traffic is as large as it can be, and as active.

When you ask other mall owners if they provide such a service, chances are you'll get a sputtering, incredulous response. No wonder. Most consider their job finished if they throw any amount of text up for the advertiser and toss out a few announcements in some on-line newsgroups. We couldn't agree less!

— organization of mall for maximum clarity

A mall is neither a jumble sale nor a garbage dump. Instead, it is an organized presentation to a defined group of prospects. These prospects, generally called visitors on the Internet, are constantly invited in to peruse, in the most clear and efficient manner imaginable, items of interest to themselves.

Just how this visit is organized for maximum effect must be well thought through by mall management before a single visitor comes through the counter. Yet at most malls has it been thought through successfully?

Most malls are organized on a stacking principle, simply adding new advertisers one on top of the other. It is easy to see why this happens. A computer screen offers limited space while the Internet itself is infinite. Most mall owners "solve" this problem by creating what amounts to one central data storage area. As new advertisers sign up, they are automatically placed on top of the prior advertisers, rather like one layer of snow falling upon another, covering up everything that has gone before. Such a "system" is, of course, highly detrimental to the advertisers who are buried. This is particularly true when the different advertisers are all trying to sell different, unrelated products and services, where an advertiser for baby furniture is placed before a financial planner but after a service for senior citizens. This kind of "organization" is a prescription for irritation, frustration and no second visits! In short, for disaster.

Now consider how we organize Worldprofit.

Instead of lumping network marketing in with native Americans in with home-based businesses in with business to business products/services, we separate them out by systematically exploiting one of the chief benefits of the Internet, the ability to go deeper and deeper into any given subject area by "clicking" into it with a mouse. This enables people who are interested in a particular area to focus on that subject and to leave all the millions of other things they're not interested in just then alone.

You must understand that Worldprofit, then, is a broadcasting conglomerate. At the main Worldprofit menu you will learn about all the channels that exist — the various malls. Each of these channels offers 24 hour programming and an infinite number of programs — the Web sites/home pages. Each channel is thematically coherent so that each program (home page) offered within that channel reinforces the basic theme. In other words, what we say is, "If you're interested in this particular subject... you'll find at Worldprofit in the mall on that subject, hundreds, even thousands of different angles on it. But you won't find anything within that channel/mall that isn't about what you're generally interested in." Thus, when you go to the Total Home & Garden Mall, everything's going to be about your home and garden, just as in the Better Health Mall everything's designed for the superior health of you and your family. Both prospects and advertisers like this kind of organization; after all, it makes their lives easier by focusing on just what they're interested in. And when they want to see something entirely different why, then, they go back to the main menu and select another mall where they'll find the same degree of visitor-centered clarity.

This is very different from most malls. In them the addition of new advertisers only compounds the problems; remember, they are merely in the business of stacking advertisers and their offers. At Worldprofit, however, there's no stacking. As existing malls move towards maturity, we add new malls on thematically unified subjects. Thus, at any given time, the malls that you see at Worldprofit are not all the malls that we are in the process of developing. Chances are very good that we're both brainstorming and developing another half dozen malls at any given time… malls that are at once new and old. They're new in subject matter and old in that they mirror the experiences we've already had about how to organize and promote theme malls successfully.

Within the individual theme malls, of course, we are subject to the same hazards of stacking advertisers that distinguish other mall owners. We understand that older advertisers do not wish to be constantly lowered in priority as new advertisers come in. We combat this problem in many ways, including

- rotation policy. We regularly rotate advertisers in each mall to ensure that no one is always on the top and no one always on the bottom… but so that all the prime spots in each mall are regularly shared amongst all the advertisers
- providing main menu positions in each mall. Any advertiser can purchase a main menu position at the prevailing rate. However, we often make such positions available without cost to advertisers in my card deck and to those who provide other services to Worldprofit. We reckon these positions are there to be used… and that it's better to award them to our advertisers for a variety of services rendered than to waste them by not using them at all.
- splitting malls as necessary. Malls have an optimum size, and once this size has been reached, exceeding it creates advertiser problems. That's why large malls must be subdivided.
- traffic and home page trouble-shooting. From time to time, one of our advertisers will call to express anxiety about what he perceives as low traffic. We could like so many mall owners take the standard "caveat emptor" approach, letting them know in one way or another that that's not our problem. But at Worldprofit we have a different objective. We want 100% of our advertisers to renew. That's our policy. To achieve it, we know that adjustments may well have to be made.

Upon reviewing an individual advertiser's situation, we may discover

- the copy in his home page is outmoded. You can't advertiser a Christmas special in July.
- his home page is no longer state of the art in terms of graphics and other enhancements. Remember, you can't attract customers with inferior tools when they've become used to them (as so quickly happens on the Internet).
- the presentation of benefits is not as sharp as it needs to be.
- the home page isn't coded so that the advertiser couldn't know if it's generating responses of not. Ordinarily when they add a code, they discover right away that the site really is generating traffic after all!

Our job is to advise on how to improve response and this may even include changing his position or offering various enhancements at cost, or even less.

We may also run a module about this company in our *Worldgram* asking subscribers to check out this Web site, pointing out the benefits of doing so. (This always increases traffic.)

You see, at Worldprofit our objective is to have a customer for life. This means constantly taking a pro-active stance and making it clear we share the advertiser's objective of turning the Internet into a predictable source of profit for his/her business.

— reasonable fees

As I write, I'm looking at an ad in *Catalog Age*. It's a publication read by people like me who publish catalogs and want to stay abreast of technical developments in the field. This obviously includes how to position your catalog on the Web to make money.

In this particular issue, there's a full-page ad by one of our competitors which dramatically illustrates why it pays to shop around before committing yourself to a company producing home pages and malls. "There is," pronounces the ad," a one-time set up fee of $50 per link per site, and a $750 minimum link charge per month, exclusive of set up fees." In other words, these people want well over $10,000 a year from you! Highway robbery!!!

To understand pricing on the Web, it helps to have some understanding of the rough and tumble world of the American frontier at the end of the nineteenth century or of the Klondike gold rush. In short, as far as Web pricing is concerned just about anything goes.

Regularly, I hear from people who have been charged thousands and thousands of dollars for a home page... who are paying high monthly charges for their site... and several dollars per prospect lead. This is unconscionable! Revolting! Unnecessary!

When I decided my next business development would be on the Web, I vowed to do here what I'd already succeed in doing in the card deck industry: I'd set the standard for the lowest prices with top quality service. When I started publishing my Sales & Marketing Success Card deck many years ago, the industry, as I have written elsewhere, was essentially a Venetian oligarchy. It was run by a few publishers — a very few publishers — who had set prices at very high levels and were quite content to leave things that way. The very last thing they wanted was a brash young capitalist reformer in their midst who said, "I'll drastically slash prices, increase the number of advertisers and make money while forcing you to completely change the way you run your business."Yet that is precisely what happened.

From Day I in the card deck industry, my prices were the lowest in the land, and years later they continue to be the lowest in the land. Not surprisingly, my deck is also the largest in the land. What's more, advertisers get service which is comparable to — or even better — than they can get from the high-priced decks. In short, you could call me the Richard Branson of the card-deck biz. Other deck owners didn't like what was happening (what they say about me is not printable), but the advertisers certainly did! <By the way, in case you miss the reference, Branson's the guy who launched Virgin Records and currently owns Virgin Atlantic Airlines, along with a lot of other stuff. In fact, not so much older than I am, he's Britain's richest man, so you see the strategy works... and works big.>

Taking notes from my own play book, I looked hard at the Internet industry and delighted to find that the rambunctious avarice of my competitors had created a very similar situation on the 'net to the one I'd already successfully faced with card deck publishers. The results have been the same, too: malls that have grown faster than anyone else's, faster, even, than I imagined myself when I started this quest.

Thus, what you have is the creative fusion of several different elements:

- my desire to create the largest malls in the entire world, offering superior value to the largest number of advertisers
- equally, my desire to ensure that the Internet remains accessible to the largest number of advertisers, who shall not be prevented from fully participating because of price considerations
- the advertisers' desire both to get onto the Web and to offer the maximum amount of compelling client-centered information to their prospects and pay no more than reasonable rates, and finally
- the advertisers' realization that they could best reach their objectives by joining a theme-related mall which had as its objective targeting just the right prospects... and doing everything it could, including uniting mall owner and advertisers, to bring in those prospects in the largest possible numbers.

Do you want to know just how reasonable these rates are? That's easy. All you need to do is look in the back of this book. If you're reading it within months of publication, they're probably accurate. Or use the 24 hour fax on demand (403) 425-6049, document #1 or just call us at (403) 425-2466. But I can tell you right now, you'll find they're the lowest in the industry, not just absolutely but relatively as compared to all the services we provide and the traffic we generate to help you do the only thing that matters to a business person using the Internet: making more sales faster!

Note: these days new malls are coming onto the Internet at a quick clip. As a matter of course, we visit them to check them out. And as a matter of course, we discover that their prices are higher than ours, their services elementary, their advertisers stacked helter-skelter and their marketing derisory. Bingo! Another fatality waiting to happen. Unfortunately, it's sad for the advertisers who select such malls for their poor selection leaves them with a bias against the Internet that is entirely undeserved!

Last Words

Do you know Robert Frost's celebrated poem "The Road Not Taken"? The end goes like this:

Two roads diverged in a wood, and I —
I took the one less traveled by
And that has made all the difference.

On the surface, of course, this poem is just about a man selecting one of two country lanes for a walk. More profoundly, it's about the choices that all of us have to make in life, choices which dramatically determine who we are, what happens to us. That's no less true of the choices you must make on the Internet.

If you decide to go solo, just to post a home page that's connected to nothing and nobody, you've made a life-determining choice. For the reasons I've advanced in this chapter, it's a choice I think you'll regret. As you've come to know, in that scenario you're responsible for literally everything... and you're not going to get the benefit that comes from the collective efforts of mall owner and other mall advertisers. Such collective efforts ensure that the work of all produces benefits for each.

Perhaps because Tom Sawyer is my role model, I prefer to take another route. Not only do I like having other people do things for me, but I know that that is essential for achieving maximum results. One achieves one's objective faster when one, without sacrificing one's individuality and autonomy, nonetheless can benefit from the collective actions of many. That's why I am such a tremendous advocate of participating in the right Internet mall, a mall which

- unites people around a common theme
- puts all these people — including mall owner and mall advertiser — to work to increase the traffic, thereby benefiting all, and
- is committed not just to posting information (any idiot can do that) but to working energetically with the advertisers so that they succeed in reaching their objectives... which are and must be bringing the maximum number of prospects to their home pages and ensuring that everything is done to make sure they buy as much and as quickly as possible.

These simple rules work. That is why putting your Web site in the right mall is the only sensible thing to do. To be sure, most people these days post solo Web sites. Without thinking, they condemn themselves to be responsible for everything. All too often such people are using a Web site as yet another means of ego gratification, of saying, Kilroy-like, "I was here." Really, what's the point of that? A Web site is a tool... and tools must be used in the right way to achieve maximum results. On the Web, the tool cannot be used to the maximum extent where traffic is artificially curtailed at the very outset by wrongful placement.

Of course, making a decision about which way to go is difficult, unsettling. Frost knew that.

Two roads diverged in a yellow wood,
And sorry I could not travel both
And be one traveler,
Long I stood
And looked down one as far as I could
To where it bent in the undergrowth.

That's why he comforted himself with the reflection that

Oh, I kept the first for another day!

But Frost, a hard-headed New Englander of an ancient type, didn't dwell on this comfort. Instead, he immediately went on to say,

Yet knowing how way leads on to way,
I doubted if I should ever come back.

So, it will be with you. Before deciding on the Internet road to take, think very seriously about what you're doing. Keep in mind that just by pausing and thinking, you're already in a minority, for the vast majority of people on the Web (very much including those in the most lavish executive suites) have rushed heedlessly ahead without deliberation.

Then you select the "one less traveled by," the mall option. For, ironically, this so far less traveled option certainly produces a more well visited site and thus transforms your experience on the Internet from a matter of trivial self-indulgence and predictable insignificance into one of the utmost value, one in fact that makes "all the difference."

Chapter 3

HOW TO "NETVERTISE" YOUR HOME PAGE SO YOU GET THE BUSINESS!

When was the last time this happened to you?

You're flipping through some magazine and see an ad that catches your eye. You're interested, so you fill out the response coupon and send it in. A week later, two weeks later you're still waiting for the details you were so keen about.

Or, you give the company a call. The "customer service rep" at the other end only has a dim grasp on what you want. A week later, two weeks later you're still waiting.

Or, you're ready to purchase but have just a couple of questions about the product or service you'll be getting. Problem is, it's midnight where the company is. Nobody's available to help you when you're ready to buy.

When was the last time this happened to you?

Friend, this happens to you *every* time you play the traditional advertising game. Yikes!

Let's look a little more closely at this, the occasion you have to complete a response coupon to get what you want.

You have to

- find a pencil or pen
- cut out the coupon from the magazine
- find an envelope
- address the envelope
- mail the letter.

Then you
- wait
- wait
- wait ...

... while the awesomely efficient post office does its damnedest to slow the delivery process down to the point where it sets another shocking statistic for the *Guinness Book of Records*.

At last it gets delivered to the company sending the information.

- The information gets entered in a computer
- a shipping label is generated
- an informational package assembled.

It then goes bravely into the hands of that self-same post office, ready with additional tricks of the trade for producing maximum neurosis in maximum people through minimum speed and service.

Days, weeks, even months later you get this information. And have to

- find time to rekindle your interest
- read it
- respond to it.

Get the picture!

Well, since the dawn of advertising this has been the way it is. All of us have been caught in the meshes of this excruciatingly inefficient system. True, there have been refinements over the past century: full-color printing, the 800 number, e-mail. But these have only been refinements on a system that is inherently inefficient, frustrating and irritating.

Now let me put it to you as starkly as I can: until you learn how to "netvertise" you'll be perpetuating this system, frustrating the maximum number of people, retarding the growth of your business and your own prosperity. Can this possibly be your perverse business objective?

Netvertising starts with the recognition that the Internet has changed the very nature of commercial promotion from the slow, maddeningly inefficient system which we have all grown up with to something sleek, completely client-centered, and lickety-split fast.

To succeed at netvertising, however, you've got to know precisely how it works, how, that is, to use the intrinsically superior elements of the Internet to promote the objective which ought to be closest to your heart: more profit faster.

Netvertising is not, please note, merely taking one of your existing one-dimensional space ads or classifieds and posting it on the Internet. Unfortunately, this is what a large majority of Internet advertisers do. They look at a page featuring one of their ads... and they look at a computer screen and come to the completely erroneous conclusion that one equals the other, posting their completely inappropriate one-dimensional ads accordingly. Thus they try as hard as then can to emasculate the Internet. I've set as my personal crusade stamping out that kind of Web misuse!

The Benefits of Netvertising

When you've netvertised your client-centered promotion, here's what happens:

- your prospect can indicate just what parts of your informational message are of direct interest to him
- he can get all the information he wants and needs right this minute. No waiting!
- he can get access to this information whenever he wants... 6 a.m. Sunday morning or midnight on Thursday it's equally available.
- he can become acquainted in detail with your requirements and pre-requisites. The vast majority of advertising casts as big a net as possible and relies upon later follow-up by you to qualify people. Netvertising enables you to set out every single benefit of what you're got... and every single requirement... in all necessary detail. The prospect then knows precisely where he's at and what's needed of him. He can decide to proceed... or to drop out altogether, thereby

saving you the time and money it takes to qualify people who may well be inappropriate for what you're selling.

- he can provide you with all the information you need for immediate follow-up... or can purchase your product/service directly from your site right this minute.

In other words, netvertising changes the focus of your ad from saying as little as possible (because you're paying by the word or the space) to saying as much as necessary to either finely qualify the prospect now or sell the prospect now.

You know your netvertised Web site works when people either

- send in orders with no questions
- call you to purchase your product/service knowing your requirements and what they must do to expedite matters
- contact you with very focused, intelligent questions.

Netvertising, you see, enables you to

- make money faster. In the old days of traditional advertising (wherein so many people are still stuck to their detriment), money is made slowly. You either have to spend a lot of time with people qualifying them (something I personally always detested) or sending them sales literature, waiting for their response. Boring! Time-consuming! Irritating!
- deal with more people of the better kind, that is with people who already know a good deal about what you're selling and with whom you can get down to cases (even an immediate sale) fastest. Personally, I've noticed something important since the advent of netvertising into my business life. I'm a kinder, nicer person! Why? Because the caliber of my prospects has gone up and I'm wasting a lot less time doing the irritating, albeit necessary, scut work of business — sending information packages, making follow up phone calls, answering the same questions millions of times. All that's been cut down to the bare minimum with heavenly results not only for my efficiency but for my sweet temper, too.
- constantly refine your client-centered sales message without having to junk all your advertisements. The more traditional ads you've got the more difficult your life. Every time you want to change your ad you've got to go through a series of hoops to revise it, re-do the art, ship to the publishing or advertising source, *etc.* What a bother! And expensive, too! When you're netvertised... really focused on providing your prospects and buyers what they want... you can easily make constant refinements with a minimum of fuss, aggravation and expense.
- get your information into the hands of your prospects immediately. These days, my first question to a prospect who calls is, "Do you have access to the Internet?" If so, as soon as I've taken down their name and phone number for later follow-up, I let them know that the information they require is easily available to them right this minute. I give them the specifics... then go back to whatever I was doing, leaving them free to get the details they need and turn themselves into a better informed prospect or immediate buyer... without having me drop everything to accommodate them. After all, by providing them with a fully netvertised site I have already accommodated them... all they have to do is go there to find that out for themselves.

The Structure Of Netvertising

Let me be very clear with you. These benefits don't just come about by accident. They're the result of very deliberate study and planning, of studying just how the unique Internet environment works to foster faster business... and planning to take advantage of it. It is not, I repeat, the result of brainlessly taking an existing space ad and mindlessly posting it on the Internet and then patting yourself on the back, congratulating yourself that you're on the Web. Yet this is precisely what tens of thousands of supposedly intelligent people are doing right this minute.

These non-pareils do something like this:

- get a Web site that's connected to nothing and nobody, thereby ensuring that they get minimal traffic
- post a standard space ad, the kind asking people to call them for "free details"
- sit back and await the mad rush of cash-stuffed customers.

Ridiculous! Money gets made on the Internet because you're in a high traffic mall with a fully client-centered netvertised site. Here's the basic structure of that site:

- Main Menu offering client-centered benefits
- individual client-centered pages providing the necessary detail about the benefits
- links on each page back to a page where the prospect is either asked to provide you with necessary information indicating that he is in fact a good prospect or where he can buy the product/service you're selling.

Let's look at each crucial section.

— Client-Centered Main Menu

Each netvertised Web site is actually a mini-mall of its own... even if you're only selling one product. A mall, you see, provides prospect choices. It enables the prospect to go where she wants to go when she wants to go there. It doesn't force the prospect to do things in one certain way... but rather to select just how she wants to select the business of getting the information she wants and moving towards the sale. This isn't at all how things are in the traditional advertising universe.

When people confront an ad in a magazine or newspaper, they read that ad from the headline to the response coupon or phone number. In the netvertised ad, they select the benefits they want to achieve and click on them in the order that interests them. Here, for instance, is the beginning of a full-page ad that's written by a guy claiming to be a marketing authority but who's clearly still stuck back in the dark-ages of pre-Web marketing:

"New Book Makes Marketing EASIER, FASTER, and CHEAPER than ever!

- In a Few Nights of Easy Reading, Learn the INSIDE SECRETS of DIRECT MARKETING
- Make Your Marketing 2x, 5x, 10x as Effective and yet LOWER THE COST!
- Buy this book today. Use These Low Cost Techniques By This Weekend!

A great reference tool and an unbelievable marketing guide for small businesses! Over 400 pages jam-packed with in-depth direct marketing information."

This laughably old-style ad copy continues through another 3/4 page of text.

Before netvertising this ad, let me remind you of one key point. Good advertisers don't force the customer to do things their way. Instead, they think through what the prospect/customer is going to want and then provides that to them. Believe me, when you know what the prospect wants, the prospect won't have any hesitation about grabbing for it. Your job is to position your product/service so that it's clearly based on the prospect's wants. The prospect's will provides the rest. This will is so strong that when you're speaking to what the prospect wants all you've got to do is present it... and get out of the way. Otherwise you'll be crushed by self-enthused customers rushing to acquire what you've got, what they want.

Here, then, is how this out-of-date marketing guru can really start marketing thanks to netvertising:

YES, YOU CAN REALLY MARKET YOUR PRODUCT FOR UNDER $500

Welcome to the one site where you can always get the step-by-step information you need to market your product for under $500. Yes, you find out what you can do — today — to start making more money when you have even the tiniest promotional budget. Come back every 30 days to get updated information. Bookmark this site because we're constantly adding valuable new guidelines, techniques, resources and tested success stories on how people just like you have made tens of thousands of dollars from marketing budgets of $500 — or less!

Just click on what you want and get the information now

▦	*Always* get the lowest ad rates to get more ads for less	▦	Key marketing resources from your library on the cheap
▦	write media releases that *always* get used to promote your product for free	▦	success case where $500 promo budget paid off big
▦	Tested ways to open new markets	▦	400 pages of success tips ready for you to cash in now.

What's going on here?

- We're *not* selling a book. The first problem with traditional ads — as exemplified by the tired, uninspired ad cited above — is that they're obviously selling something. Either they're asking you to identify yourself as a prospect... or they're selling direct. In either case, you're on your guard. Remember, your prospect is a cagey creature. Sure, he wants benefits, but he wants to acquire them at his own speed, not necessarily yours. He may have been burnt in the past, may have fallen victim to big claims and minimal performance, and most assuredly has limited resources (no matter how much money he has). Therefore, prospects are cautious. Netvertising is different. Netvertising is about providing the prospect with all the information he needs... and I do mean *all*... focusing principally on the benefits he gets by acting. If the benefits are substantial enough, credible enough, the prospect will act now, always assuming he has the resources to do so.

- We're building a customer relationship. Right from the start your site is about building a long-term relationship. This site starts with a clearly defined benefit in the headline "MARKET YOUR PRODUCT FOR UNDER $500." It also stresses the fact that you should "bookmark" the site and return at regular, thirty day intervals. Reason? Because people don't always act the first time they see something. No matter how client-centered and motivational you are, it may take several visits before they get around to buying the product. Thus, you've got to get them back.

This sad advertiser's standard full-page ad is a one-time and one-time-only proposition. He's betting that he can tell enough prospects all they need to know about his product in one ad to keep making the proposition profitable. To me, knowing prospects as I do, that's a very dangerous game.

Of course I want to do everything I can to motivate immediate action. Doing anything else is foolish. But you've also got to recognize that people don't always act fast. That they take action only after frequently being exposed to the benefits. That's why you want them to know the principal benefit of your site ("marketing your product for under $500") and the fact that they can get more information about doing so at least every 30 days.

Note: if you're only selling one product, take a moment and think. Almost no one makes any real money from only one product. As you get people to come back over and over again, don't just leave them with only one product to buy. Start diversifying. In other words, once you've identified prospects and trained them to return to get additional benefits, make sure you have additional things for them to buy!

What's also going on is that the prospect is being asked to select the benefits he wants in the order he wants. Remember Henry Ford's old line about the Model T: "You can have it in any color, so long as it's black"? Ford, a rigid authoritarian, knew a lot more about assembly lines than people. He figured that people would buy his cars because they were good and cheap, even if they didn't come in the colors and with the other amenities that buyers wanted. Well, he was wrong and he about busted the Ford Motor Company (completely squandering its initial competitive advantages) before the message finally got to him that people want what they want when they want it and that what each individual wants is the most important thing of all... for that person at that time. That's why netvertising relies upon client-centered benefits and choice.

Look at the "hot buttons" above

Always get the lowest ad rates to get more ads for less

write media releases that *always* get used to promote your product for free

One of your prospects is going to want information about media releases... another wants details about how to creatively cut his ad costs... either to save money or buy more ads. Well, cater to them both!

Traditional advertising is rigidly sequential. Pretty much everybody (except for that one weird guy in Peoria who always starts at the bottom and reads up) starts in the same place, reads through it the same way and in standard fashion arrives at the end.

Well, this most assuredly is not the way netvertising works.

I must stress again and again that netvertising is about catering to what people want when they want it. Your job is to think through the benefits that people want with your product/service... and then to give it to them... so that they can connect with these benefits in their own time, space, and manner.

Connecting Subsequent Pages To Main Menu Benefits

Each netvertised site has an objective: either to maximally qualify your prospect so that closing is comparably enhanced. Or to get the prospect to buy at once, no ifs, ands or buts. You already know that the Main Menu constitutes a client-centered site index; a place where you firmly indicate to the prospect what benefits you have available and ask him to dive in to get them.

Subsequent pages follow naturally from the benefits enumerated on the Main Menu.

Thus, take this benefit from the Main Menu

success case where $500 promo budget paid off big

When the prospect clicks on this benefit, she should go to a page with the same title HERE'S A SUCCESS CASE.... WHERE A $500 PROMO BUDGET PAID OFF BIG

When the prospect gets to this point, what he wants is an illustration of how a real person invested $500 or less and got a big pay-off.

Your job here is plain: give the case teeth. Make it complete, credible, exciting.

"Here's how Rebecca Smith of Saugus, Massachusetts, a 33 year old housewife and mother of two, launched her product following our tested methods."

Then follows a step-by-step Success Case, the more specific the better.

The prospect is reading this case to see whether you and your product are believable, whether you're offering a system that works... or whether you're just hyping what you've got. This moment is very important for you. That's why you've got to be as candid, forthright and detailed as possible — preferably within the confines of a single computer screen of data. Remember, the objective is not to overwhelm the prospect with facts... but to convince the prospect you know what you're talking about; that you've got what he needs; and that his next sensible step is to get what you're selling.

Because "getting what you're selling" is the whole purpose of this endeavor, the Success Case page, as all other pages, must end with a line (which is, of course, a link) like this

"Look how easy this is! Now get started making big bucks from a promotional budget of under $500 with our detailed 400-page guide."

Thus this page, like all other pages, ends by linking the benefits of this page directly with an order form for the product you're selling... or with a questionnaire that will provide you, the advertiser, with necessary prospect information so that you can sell your service. Here's sample wording linking a benefit page with a prospect questionnaire:

"Would you like to achieve results like these? Of course you would! Click here and provide us with the data we need to help you get started. We'll produce the marketing communications you need, promptly and for a price you can live with."

In this case, the link would go to a questionnaire like this:

Name

Title

Company name

Address

City/State/ZIP

day ph (   )   eve (   )   fax (   )

Marketing communication you're looking for (please check all that apply)
- ❏ two page sales letter
- ❏ four page sales letter
- ❏ standard three fold brochure
- ❏ other brochure (please specify)
- ❏ four page newsletter
- ❏ full-page ad
- ❏ 1/4 page ad   ❏ 1/8 page ad   ❏ other size (specify)
- ❏ card deck card
- ❏ Web home page (please indicate number of pages)
- ❏ other (please specify)

Your Budget
- ❏ Under $500
- ❏ $500-$999
- ❏ $1000-$2000
- ❏ $2,000-$5,000
- ❏ Over $5,000

Desired Completion Date
- ❏ within 14 days
- ❏ within thirty days
- ❏ next three months
- ❏ next six months

Any special circumstances we should be aware of?

Complete this questionnaire and e-mail to us at <address>. We'll be back to you within 24 hours!

Either way, the objective is plain: get the most highly qualified prospect possible... or make the immediate sale!

Note: If you've got 6 benefit modules on the Main Menu of your Web site, then you're going to have at least 7 subsequent pages, one detailing each benefit... and at least one for your questionnaire or actual order form.

Additional Main Menu Headings

In the example above, I've provided 6 Main Menu headings, the 6th being an order form named "400 pages of success tips ready for you to cash in now."

You must always list your leading benefits, the things your prospects and customers want, and you must always have a link to either a questionnaire (particularly useful if you're selling a service with multiple components and means of delivery) and/or order form. But there are other headings you can have, too, including

- commonly asked questions and answers. This is a very popular feature. If you're smart, you're constantly staying alert to the kinds of questions your prospects and customers are asking you. When you hear them, write them down. In your downtime, write out the best client-centered answers you can imagine, answers that are both complete and brisk. To me, one of the Web's most liberating features is that it enables you to post superb answers to every single question you're ever asked... answers that give your prospects the information they need without taking you away from your other duties. With the best will in the world, it's impossible for us in the real world to always give complete, polite, client-centered answers. Sometimes we're tired, rushed, otherwise engaged, or just downright grumpy (I know). On the Web, however, we're always the complete client-centered marketer, just as we're supposed to be!

- competitor red flags. Here's the chance to really pin your competitors by making it clear why what you're offering is better. I think, for instance, of a well-known nutritional company I've consulted to that used this technique so very well. Their competitors were always prattling on about how great their products were, making one unauthenticated assertion after another. In your "red flags" page you can list precisely what those competitors say... and your response. Obviously when you do this, you must be very accurate indeed. But when you keep letting people know that your competitors offer less value than you do... why, then, it's very difficult for those competitors to establish themselves as superior entities to you. Good for you!

- testimonials. People like to know that real people just like them are getting considerable value from your products/services. Don't just tell them they are... list the client-centered testimonials you receive. Let prospects know in no uncertain terms that you're the company, that yours is the product and the service, that generates the compliments because yours is the company that delivers the benefits.

- motivating offer. The reason businesses make offers is because people buy offers... not just products and services. Thus, on your Main Menu you can have a link that says something like this, "Act NOW and get this exciting FREE offer <specifics>." Or, "Act NOW and use this exciting FREE OFFER <specifics> to promote your product faster and make more money sooner."

I'm going to spend more time below looking at all the specific elements of profit-making cash copy. But for now, I want you to remember one significant point. Each Web site has just one purpose: producing more and more qualified prospects... or selling direct as soon as possible. Your entire Web site is a package dedicated to a single proposition.

ou are not spending your money on a Web site

- because it's the trendy thing to do (although we all know that's the reason thousands are doing so).
- or to show the flag. That's always a stupid reason for advertising. Tons of people use their advertising budgets just to say, "Hey world, we're here," or else to shore up their limited self-esteem. Neither makes any sense and neither should be finessed with your limited advertising dollars.
- or to reform the world. Reform is necessary, but don't muddle reform with the money-making objective for a business home page.
- or to educate. Egad, spare me from the closet educators who have proliferated wondrously since the inception of the Web. These people (too often distinguished by the kind of well-meaning pomposity that causes me, for one, to scream for relief) have the deadening notion that throwing more and more and still more information at people is the way to motivate them to action. Nothing could be further from the truth. But even if it were the truth, your *business* home page is not the place for such activity. Your Web site, friend, is a success if it gets you more and more qualified prospects... and more sales faster. *C'est tout.*

Your job is plain: speak to what your prospects want. Let them know you have it. Then make it easy for them to get it — now! Or, if not now, at least by conveniently and easily providing you the necessary information you need to get them what they want as fast as possible. This is what netvertising is all about... and why those who fail to use it so completely fail.

The beneficial effects of netvertising are enhanced, however, when linked to cash copy, that is the right words in the right order that expedite the movement of the prospect to where both of you, prospect and advertiser, want him to be so that the essential exchange of money for benefits can occur. Therefore no discussion of netvertising can conceivably be complete without dealing with the essential elements of cash copy.

You Get Benefit Now:
The Irreducible Essence Of Cash Copy

Just four little words lie at the heart of both cash copy and successful marketing overall: YOU GET BENEFIT NOW. When what you do is anchored in these four words, you succeed. Your copy works. Your marketing communications work. Let's look at each word to see why.

- **YOU.** All successful marketing is focused on just one person — the "you" to whom you are addressing it. Sadly, too many marketers have focused on the wrong "you," that is, on themselves. But without complete client-centered focus, what you produce is doomed from the beginning. The *only* person in marketing who matters is the prospect. Therefore, that person must be either implicit or explicit in every single marketing word you *produce*. Each word must be centered on this all-important "you", each sentence, each paragraph, each page. Once you know this you're able in an instant to see just why so much supposed marketing copy is in fact so very weak and self-defeating. If you want to move a person to act, focus exclusively on that person and make sure every marketing element never deviates.

- **GET.** The marketing process is about *acquisition*. It is about an individual moving from Point A where he's relatively disadvantaged to Point B where he's comparatively better off thanks to the acquisition of some important element. You must always remember this. This word "get" is an action verb signifying both the transfer of a benefit as well as its acquisition. This transfer is at the heart of the successful marketing transaction. The prospect must be keen that the transfer take place so that he can have, hold, enjoy, and profit from the all-important benefit.

- **BENEFIT.** Just what the prospect gets is the benefit, that is the thing that makes him relatively better off with its acquisition as compared to the state in which he previously found himself. Benefits, mind, are always comparative. With them one is comparatively richer, healthier, sexier, smarter, faster, *etc.* Benefits are always focused on the prospect's soon-to-be-superior state, never merely on the thing being transferred. Many, many marketers either forget this or just don't have a clue how to ensure that the benefit is about the prospect. Well, there's a very easy way to do that. You need to remember that each thing in the world is composed of features, that is elements. For profitable marketing each of these elements — which are by definition thing-centered — must be refocused to be about the prospect. Features involve the weight, height, size, color, position, direction, location, *etc.* of what is being sold. Benefits are about how these things benefit the user.

When you write about a feature you write things like "it has," or "it is" or "it does." However, when you write about a benefit it's *always* "you get." And, as you already know, the "you gets" are vitally important.

- **NOW.** To a marketer there's only one dimension of time: NOW! Yesterday is unimportant, tomorrow merely theoretical. Only NOW matters. That's why successful marketers do *everything* in their power to ensure that prospects act NOW... not postponing for a single instant the all-important act of prospect commitment. Thus, they ensure that when they create a marketing communication — any marketing communication — they've included a "now" element, the crucial ingredient designed to motivate the prospect to take IMMEDIATE ACTION. Without such an ingredient, they're essentially saying to the prospect, "Act whenever you like. Today. Tomorrow. Next month. It's all the same to me. Take your time." Such a sentiment, of course, is anathema to the transaction of business where NOW, NOW, NOW! means everything... and a possible sale at some vague, unspecified later date is of no value or interest whatsoever.

When you look through the microscope of these four potent little words at the "marketing" communications produced by others — some well known and regarded — you understand in an instant why so much that's produced, supposedly with the objective of selling products and services, fails so miserably; why, in fact, it could never achieve the crucial objective. Further, when you have these words at your disposal you can use them as a yardstick to gauge the probable success of your own marketing communications. Take a minute right now to see what I mean.

Before we go on, collect a couple of your current marketing communications — be it your Web site, a space ad, or your standard business brochure. Look at them carefully. Ask yourself

- Where is the "you"? Is it clear just whom you're talking to, trying to motivate? Or at you pitching your case so generally that the all-important prospect hasn't a clue you're aiming to motivate him?
- Where is the "get"? Marketing, remember, is about acquisition. Your job is to put the prospect's mind to work for you. Your job is to seize his will. The way to do that is to make the prospect feel that he already has your product/service, make him imagine its benefits, put him mentally in that superior place where he'll be with your product/service and remind him of what life will be like without it; (the sadder, the better).
- Where is the "benefit"? If you ever want to see for yourself just how most of what's produced supposedly for marketing is in fact a tragic waste of resources, leaf through magazine ads and Web sites and all the company brochures you find. You'll see in an instant that the vast majority of them focus on the sender... on the advertiser. They're about what the advertiser has... where the advertiser is... the advertiser's state. In short, there's no client-centered benefit at all. Yet only by piling one benefit on another are prospects motivated to take action.
- Where is the "NOW"? Where is the stimulus, in short, that makes the prospect sit up, take notice, and commit RIGHT THIS MINUTE? Tragically, wastefully, absolutely avoidably, in all too many marketing communications there's no now, now as Gertrude Stein might have said. However in marketing if you haven't motivated NOW, you've failed! This is why the focus must be and always remain on getting the prospect to take action IMMEDIATELY!

Critical Elements Of Cash Copy

I've now given you a magic wand, an immensely valuable wand enabling you to determine whether any marketing communication you're looking at is promising, holding the prospect of profit, a wand to help you create your own client-centered cash copy, be it for your netvertised Web site or your next two-page sales letter. Now let's look at the essential elements of cash copy.

Cash copy is built, not merely written. Like all architecture of substance, it's composed of absolutely necessary building blocks, which I like to call modules. When you use these, the likelihood of success — that is, generating more and better qualified prospects and selling more of your product/service faster — is enhanced. Leave them out, and you're pulling away the necessary elements that keep the building up and strong. Is this really what you want to do?

Here are those essential elements

- the offer
- benefit blocks
- client-centered testimonials
- all prospect questions answered
- maximum prospect response possibilities.

Let's look at each.

— hooking with the motivating offer

Last night the vital importance of the motivating offer was again born home to me. It was Friday night. I was tired. I'd just put in an extremely long and busy day and looked forward to retreating into a vegetative state. Then the damned fax arrived saying, "I'm going to pass up the next card deck." My first reaction was, "It's Friday. I'll live." My second, more characteristic, was Sherlock Holmes-like, "The game's afoot!" I called the guy who just moments before had issued a flat "No way."

The first thing I said was, "You're about to make a mistake. And after you hear my offer, I predict you're not going to make it." I then presented not reasons why he should participate but the "offer you're not going to refuse."

Within 10 minutes of the original fax being received, we'd worked through the several developmental steps from my "I don't feel like doing it" to the prospect's "I'll think about it" to the prospect's enthusiastic "I'll do it!"

What was going on here anyway?

We live in a world where people with means are surfeited on things. We don't have enough. We have too much. It's a world where in many cases it really doesn't matter if we take action today… we could probably wait just as well until tomorrow. For a marketer, this is like living on a planet made of quick sand. At any moment, our marketing messages can easily get swallowed up.

WELL, WE JUST CAN'T LET THAT HAPPEN!!!

That's where The Offer comes in.

The offer is designed to pull, tug, compel, and absolutely motivate that sluggish prospect to take IMMEDIATE ACTION. With the offer, we marketers recognize that it is important to us whether the prospect acts now or later. We don't want later. We must motivate action NOW! Thus, we lay down a proposition that goes something like this: "Act now, get this EXTRA MEANINGFUL THING. Don't act now, lose it. Your call, buddy."

No matter how elegantly phrased, there's always something confrontational, "in your face", about an offer. It starts from the proposition that the human animal can be a sluggish beast… but that our success as marketers depends on motivating that beast to take faster actions than he may really want to take. The offer is a prod, candy-coated to be sure, but a prod nonetheless. Offers, therefore, are no places for the weak-willed or those who don't want to "bother" anybody.

Offers are designed to "bother." They're designed to push. They're designed, in short, to get IMMEDIATE ACTION.

As such, here are some offer types to consider:

- act now and get special price
- act now and get extra amount of whatever you're selling
- act now and get free shipping
- act now and get related benefit to what you're selling (*e.g.* vase for flowers)
- act now and get something others who act later won't get.

Get the drift? We're motivating here!

To work, offers must be limited and must have deadlines. They must force the pace. Personally, I like to make offers that dwindle down as a stated deadline approaches. With my card deck, I use this kind of offer a lot. Day 1 "Just 7 more people can get this benefit." Day 2 "Just 5 more people can get this benefit." Day 3, "Just 3 more people can get this benefit." And "absolutely last call for this benefit."

On your home page, as in any good marketing communication, the real job is to sell the offer. Thus, you should state your offer on the Main Menu of your Web site. In other words, let people know — right now — how they can get the offer; don't force the prospect to read through your entire message. Offers motivate. So, let your offer motivate the prospect NOW, instead of forcing him to read through all your verbiage.

Also, restate the offer on other pages in your Web site... and reinforce it at the conclusion of your home page, in a sort of client-centered post-script. In short, think well and carefully about the offer; make sure that it really does offer benefit... and then sell the hell out of it! Remember, "the offer sells; your message tells."

— heaping benefits on prospect-centered benefits

The next module you should work on is the Benefit Module. Begin by listing every single benefit you've got for the prospect and, once you've got them, make sure that every single page in your Web site bristles with them. Remember, your job is *not* to provide information; it's to provide client-centered benefits that unrelentingly carry home the point that what you've got will improve the prospect's situation.

In other words, first you brainstorm every single benefit you can think of for purchasing your product/service... then you arrange these benefits in the most motivating way for each group you wish to take faster action. Mind, this may well mean reshuffling the benefits, changing their order depending on just who you're trying to motivate on any given page!

Many people misunderstand the concept of benefits. But if you don't get it, you're severely weakening your marketing copy. Besides, benefits aren't so very hard to understand — so long as you're willing to take yourself out of the proposition and concentrate completely, unswervingly on the prospect!

You see, there are really only two kinds of marketing: "marketing" that concentrates on the advertiser and marketing that concentrates on the prospect/customer.

The first is composed of features... that is, copy that talks about what you're selling.

The second concentrates on benefits... that is, what the prospect is really buying.

Now tell me which would you rather have...

> *"100,000 two color cards that cost $1449", or*

> *"get the lowest prices in the entire card-deck industry... just about 1.4 cents a card. Nobody in the entire industry can offer you lower prices... and your second color is free!"*

It's obvious, isn't it? The first line is nothing but facts, features, and as such egotistically focuses on what it being sold. WRONG! The second takes the facts and refashions them so that they're about the purchaser. As such they are designed for prompt action and commitment.

To make sure you've considered all the features of what you're selling and transformed every single one into a client-centered benefit, create a little chart for yourself:

feature ("it is") benefit of feature ("you get")

Hint: benefits are always comparative. Implicitly or explicitly they compare what you're offering to what your competitors are offering. Note that in the example above, I use the comparative words "lowest" and "lower." These words are both factually accurate (always important) and motivating.

When you're in business, you're always competing with someone for scarce dollars. Your job is to think why you are comparatively better than the people you're competing against and to tell your prospects just why you're better. Not, note, by throwing around a lot of hyperbole either, like "world-class," "top of the line," "best," *etc.* These are just egotistical assertions.

Meaningful benefits are always based on facts. Your job is to take these facts (features) and put them into a client-centered context so that their full meaning is impressed upon the prospect, and he is motivated to act as quickly as possible. Throwing a lot of hype at the prospect is most decidedly not the objective. Because so many advertisers have done just that, prospects are justly skeptical about what they see and hear. Thus, if you want to truly motivate people, tell the truth... but make sure you've positioned it for maximum motivational impact.

How many benefits should you have? Well, the correct answer, the delphic answer is, "As many as it takes to persuade the qualified prospect to buy." Unfortunately, like many other inscrutable responses from the Oracle, this answer isn't very helpful. How many should you have? My rule of thumb is to present at least three benefits per page of your Web site where you discuss just what the prospect gets by using your product/service.

Note: benefits must always be prioritized on each page. Always lead with your most motivating benefit. Then follow with the next most motivating, the next, then the next, etc.

— reassuring with client-centered testimonials

As I said above, as you know yourself from the way you purchase products/services, prospects nowadays are rightly skeptical. We live in a world of very limited resources and more and more people who will do anything to get their hands on them. Never have the words "caveat emptor" been truer than today, and they'll be truer still tomorrow and the day after.

Since this is the often poisonous environment in which we all operate, we as Internet and other marketers must do everything we can to understand the unavoidable incredulity of our prospects... and do everything we can to overcome it.

Rock-solid benefits based on fact, not hype, go a long way to establishing advertiser credibility. So do client-centered testimonials.

We're all familiar with testimonials. My dictionary defines a testimonial as "an acknowledgment of services or worth." While true, these words are inadequate. A testimonial to be effective must make clear precisely what the buyer got by using the product or service in question. In other words, the basis for a testimonial goes like this, "I acquired the product/service. I used the product/service. I achieved these <specific> results with the product/service. As a result, I am not only happy with the product/service myself and intend to keep on using it, but I am enthusiastic about recommending it to other people who have the same kind of problem I had and wish to receive results as good or better than mine." Or as a marketing Caesar might put it, "I suffered. I used. I improved."

Do you see how different this is from the run of testimonials you may see on the Web and in other places? These generally say, "I loved product X. I'd recommend it to you." That's just not good enough.

Keep in mind that prospects are not only rightly skeptical; they also rightly want to know just what they can expect to achieve if they invest in the product/service and use it properly. In short, they want the data which will enable them to make an intelligent investment decision. All good testimonials give them what they need… and thus help motivate faster purchase.

Now that you know what a testimonial must contain, you're probably asking yourself how you can get them. Well, to begin with, as with all these modules, you need to open a computer file where you can store all these data. Set as your objective not just getting a few testimonials, but getting a client-centered testimonial from *every* single person who purchases and uses your product/service. You can do this by asking every single customer to provide such a testimonial. Give each customer a form requesting a testimonial. If it takes some time for your product/service to produce optimum results, let the customer know you'll be requesting a testimonial later; then follow up at an appropriate time.

Note: if you can, provide a small gift for people who provide testimonials. (Information-packed special reports are always appropriate, especially when they relate to improving the results of what you're selling.) This is a polite acknowledgment that customers took the time to do you a good turn. This also ensures a steady stream of testimonials of the quality you need as marketing motivators.

Make sure each testimonial comes with name, address and phone number. While you won't use complete address or phone number as part of your Web site, you will want this information on file in case you are ever questioned about what you've published. Keep in mind that in our rightly skeptical age, a testimonial without complete validating information is suspect.

Over time you will gather dozens, if not hundreds, of testimonials and can select from among the best. Just as you should!

— *answering all prospect questions so there's no reason for further "thought" or procrastination*

If the Internet is used properly, your Web site will quickly become not only fully client-centered but painstakingly complete in the information you provide to your prospects.

Remember your objective: if you're smart, you want your prospects to be as highly qualified as possible… and/or to get all the information they need from you about what you're selling so that they need as little of your time as possible. This means considering just what questions your prospects have and going out of your way to provide the client-centered detail they need.

To begin this process, consider the way you spend your time nowadays. I bet if you're like most business people you're constantly in client meetings or on the telephone providing prospects with the same information, answering the same questions over and over again.

Now consider what this is like. It's boring to keep answering the same questions constantly, isn't it? Admit it, the fortieth time you've answered a question, you're probably not going to be as enthusiastic and complete about doing so as the first time, right? In short, the more often you answer a question, the worse you probably do it.

That's where your Web site comes in.

When you've got a home page on the Internet, the answers you give are always complete, they're always client-centered, they're never rushed, and they're always up-to-date. In short, a home page enables you to be at your best — all the time!

To achieve this objective, start by writing down every single question your prospects ask you, the important ones and the ones which seem unbelievably trivial. Every time a prospect asks you a question, put it on the list. The first week or two you do this, you'll probably be adding questions to your list daily, even hourly.

Questions may include any or all of the following:

- how long have you been in business?
- what professional credentials do you have?
- do you have references?
- where are you located?
- what are your hours of business?
- are you open after 5 p.m. any days?
- are you open on the week-end?
- who should I contact for <particular product/service>?
- who should I contact for <technical assistance for particular product service>?
- who can I call after standard business hours?
- what are your payment terms?
- what credit cards do you take?
- do you deliver?
- what is the cost for delivery?
- do you send COD?

Get the drift?

You must list every single question your prospects ask about you, your product and service.

As time allows, start answering these questions in a client-centered manner. Put yourself in the prospects' shoes. This is your opportunity to shine by considering the question not as an impertinence but as a matter of prospect concern. Remember, prospects will evaluate you not only by what you say, but by how you say it. They want to get not only a technically proficient response, but one which validates them as a valuable individual.

Make sure that every answer is centered on the "you," that is your prospect. Overindulgence using "you" is far better than saying, "we, we, we."

Call this section "Frequently asked questions about <name of your business, or product, or service.>" Never let a prospect question go by without adding it to your list and working to perfect your answer. MAKE SURE THESE ANSWERS ARE KEPT UP-TO-DATE. It completely defeats the purpose if you're disseminating out-of-date information. Remember, one of the best things about the Internet is the ease with which information can be updated, literally minute by minute if necessary!

Personal note: just how necessary this kind of client-centered question/answer section is for every business is born home to me every single day. On any given day, I find myself tussling with my office supplies store, printer or fax machine repair shop, or with a foreign auction house to get basic information. When I call, several minutes are always spend getting the run-around from receptionists and other company personnel who ought to know answers to commonly asked questions — who ought to consider it their job to know — but who most assuredly do not know.

We're always hearing about how we live in the Information Age. Well, try telling that to the average shop assistant, who persists in remaining in the Age of Determined Ignorance. There isn't a business in the world which wouldn't benefit from having a list of commonly asked questions and precise client-centered answers posted on the Internet and updated regularly, the more so since more and more company personnel regard the acquisition and proper use of information about their company as *infra dig*. If you don't believe me, try impersonating a customer one day and calling your own business asking for perfectly legitimate information. I think you'll be appalled that your money is going to support such wanton ignorance. Do this once, and you won't hesitate to create a client-centered "frequently asked questions" section in your Web site as quick as a bunny.

— providing a number of ways the prospect can respond NOW.

Different strokes for different folks. We all know the line, but when it comes to marketing, we don't apply the message. Different people like to respond to advertisements in different ways. You've got to be prepared for them.

Here are the ways people can respond to home pages on the Internet:

- e-mail
- phone
- fax
- mail.

Use them all!

Make sure that your home page provides all four response tools so that prospects can contact you when they want and in the way they want.

Gathering The Cash Copy Information You Need, Storing It, Getting Ready To Use It

As you can see, when you build your marketing communications from cash copy modules, you can and must do the bulk of the work before you ever start to write your document, be it Web site or space ad. This means thinking about the information you need, gathering it and storing it in a place that's easy to retrieve. Thus

- open a computer file for your offers, benefits, testimonials, prospect questions and your answers, competitor red flags, *etc.*
- as you find useful information don't write it down on scraps of paper or just cut it out of magazines, ready to get lost. Store it in the appropriate file at *once*.
- as time permits go through this information and tweak it, making it as client-centered as you can. Remember, each bit of information that you're even thinking of using must be reformulated using the YOU GET BENEFIT NOW yard-stick.

Tips For Profitably Laying Out Each Page In Your Web Site

Remember, your Web site can only do one of two things (or both), generate more highly qualified prospects or sell direct. Thus, each page in your Web site must assist in achieving the site's overall objective. Keeping this in mind, let's look at each page that's part of a fully netvertised Web site:

- Main Menu
- specific client-centered benefit pages
- question and answer page
- red flags page
- complete product/service description page
- prospect questionnaire
- order form.

— Your Main Menu

The Main Menu is where your prospects start. It's also where they may finish if you don't make it clear to them that you've got benefits. Thus, on your Main Menu make sure to do the following:

- list the benefits of visiting every subsequent page in your Web site. Don't focus on the features of these pages, give the leading reason why your prospects should visit. Base these benefit headings on the key "you get benefit now" principle. Thus, don't say, "information for our product." Say instead, "Lose 30 pounds in the next thirty days. Find out how."
- make sure that there's an offer link on this Main Menu, too. In other words, make it clear that you've got a dynamite reason why prospects should respond today, such as "Act today. Save $50 cleaning your oriental rugs."

Remember, your Main Menu must be packed with client-centered benefits and motivating devices. Do not make the common mistake made by so many on the Internet, that is treating your Main Menu like it's a library index. It's not. It's your first and arguably most important opportunity to snag the attention of your prospect; thus make it abundantly clear to that prospect that you've got benefits, in spades, and offers he just can't refuse. If the offers convince, if the benefits persuade, why, by jingo, he's going to have to buy your product or service to get them, right?

— specific client-centered benefit pages

Again, remember those four key words: YOU GET BENEFIT NOW! They provide the structure for each subsequent page in your Web site. Thus, each subsequent page must begin, as I've already said, by repeating the client-centered benefit heading that appears on the Main Menu. This Main Menu essentially is the "tell 'em what you're going to tell 'em" section. Each benefit page is the "tell 'em" section.

Thus, if your Main Menu heading is "lose 30 pounds in 30 days," the page connecting to this heading must start

YES, YOU CAN LOSE 30 POUNDS IN 30 DAYS!

Then tell them how!

Please note: do not start by saying "Buy my product." That's no good. Instead, make it clear that by doing a series of specific steps they can, thirty days from now, be up to 30 pounds lighter. Obviously, one of these steps is buying your product. That's why at the bottom of each page crammed with benefits, you say, "Ready to get started losing those 30 pounds? Good. Click here." In other words, if the benefits are persuasive... believe me, you won't be able to stop the enthusiastic prospect from clicking on that link to acquire the product. Benefits, you see, seize the prospect mind, and once that mind has been seized, get out of the way so you won't get trampled by the horde of truly motivated prospects!!!

— question and answer page

You already know what to do with this, don't you? Everything your prospects want to know about your product, service, how you work, *etc.* gets listed and answered here. Remember, just because your prospects are enthused by your benefits doesn't mean they won't have a hundred niggling questions; in fact, the more enthusiastic they are, the more you can be assured they're going to have questions to ask. Prepare yourself accordingly... and use the Web to save yourself a ton of time and trouble.

— red flags page

Whether you know it or not, you're in a race with your competitors to absorb as many as possible of the relatively limited resources being spent to acquire what you're selling. That doesn't mean, however, that you necessarily need a red flags page. Many businesses don't need to tussle with their competitors in this way. Instead, they can evaluate the Web sites and other advertising tools being used by their competitors and answer their leading points in their own marketing communications without referring to their competitors by name. However, the larger the company, the more fierce the competition, the more you're probably going to need a red flags page.

Here you point out what your competitors are saying and make it absolutely clear that what you're offering is superior. In this case

- list what your competitor said
- provide the source (very important)

- point out why either what was said is inaccurate or why what you're offering is superior.

A red flags page enables you to emerge as the conscience of your industry, as a place where people can go to get seemingly objective information; (it's only "seemingly objective" because you're only going to post things that are in your interest, although you need never tell that to anyone). You'll emerge as the most significant company in your industry, the one that's rigorously client-centered and insistent that only the truth be told (however painful that may be to your competitors).

The tone of a red flag page is "above the fray", dedicated to the highest professional standards, but clearly positioning yourself all the while as the only company that makes any sense to deal with. It's a wonderful page and highly useful competitively when you need to score off those companies trying to score off you.

Note: I hope I don't need to say that the red flags page, like every other page in your Web site, links back to your prospect questionnaire and/or order form. After you've demolished your competitors, that's precisely the moment to ask for prospect commitment to you.

— complete product/service description

Here's your chance to make it very clear just what the customer is getting in terms of your product/service. Up until now I have stressed benefits, benefits, benefits — and rightly so. But in this portion of your Web site, you need to be crystal-clear on precisely what your buyers get from you. Thus

- describe your product fully. Remember, the more complete you can be about what it is and how it works, the fewer questions you're going to have to answer.
- ditto, your service. What do you do first, second, third, with the service in question? Don't assume your prospect knows anything. The Web is so useful a marketing tool because it enables you to be complete, to inform your prospects just what kind of service they're getting, who does what, when, and so fully put them in the picture in ways standard marketing communications either don't do or haven't done.

— prospect questionnaire

Your prospect questionnaire must be complete. It must get all the information you need to be able to close the sale as fast as possible. Thus, review your prospect contacts, by telephone, in person, *etc.* What do you find yourself needing to know? If you need it, make sure you ask the prospect to provide it... and get it back to you immediately via

- e-mail
- fax
- phone and
- (oh, yes) regular mail.

Note: if getting your product/service requires certain prerequisites, be sure to say what they are — right here. Be clear about what you require. That way, when the prospect responds, having completed your questionnaire, you can be reasonably sure you're getting a qualified prospect.

— order form

The same goes for your order form. This form must include
- customer name
- address
- business phone
- home phone
- fax
- e-mail
- credit cards accepted
- card number
- expiration dates (don't forget!)
- kind of shipping the customer wants, such as
    - ❏ next day air   ❏ two-day air   ❏ three day ground   ❏ regular ground, *etc.*
- if customer would like shipping charged to a shipping account like Federal Express, in which case you need account name, account number, kind of shipment desired
- whatever guarantees you offer.

Get the drift? It's not enough just to ask for a name, address, credit card number and phone. You've got to think through all the order questions your customers will ask... and make sure they're fully answered on your order form.

Using Testimonials

There are a couple of ways of using testimonials:
> 1) use them to punctuate your benefits. That is, every time you cite a benefit, provide a client-centered testimonial that reinforces that benefit.
> 2) have a page or two of fully attributed testimonials.

You'll probably want to start with (1). But the larger your Web site grows, the more people who use your products and services successfully, the more you'll find yourself just adding those dandy testimonials to their own page. In this case your Main Menu heading would be "Find out what people like you are saying about <name of product/service>," or "Discover the results real people like you get from <name of product/service>."

Use Visuals

The Web is a visual medium. Therefore you must get the prospect's eye working for you. You do this by dishing up interesting and relevant visuals, visuals that reinforce the message of what you're selling. Your visuals should be linked to the benefits of what you're selling. Do you have or can you get a visual that simply and enticingly presents your primary benefit? Your second benefit? *Etc.*

Don't hesitate to use captions with your visuals... or to use connecting devices to make it clear which aspects of the text connect to the visual. In other words, know the point you're trying to make... then make sure both text and graphic make it and emphasize it.

Use a marquee to enhance a line of text. This works by having a line of text scroll across the screen when someone visits a page. You can also hyperlink a marquee to another important page or sound clip or video. Marquees can scroll indefinitely or bounce from side to side or enter from the left or right and then stay on the screen.

Use Audio

It's now possible for even the smallest business to use audio clips as part of their Web site. That's right, now you can have a talking home page, a home page that not only delivers your client-centered message in printed words but in voice, too. Here are some tips.

First, you've got to think of what you're trying to achieve with audio. In my view, the best thing you can stress with your audio message is the chief benefit of your home page. In other words, why should people keep coming back to check out your site? Think of your audio message as your opportunity to tell your prospects the most important things about your Web site/store.

Keep in mind that currently you're only going to have 15-20 seconds to deliver this message. So it's got to be pungent and right on the money.

You've got to know

- who you're trying to attract
- what they're looking for
- what you've got to meet their wants.

Here's an example.

If you're an investment advisor specializing in pension planning for Baby Boomers, your 20 seconds should go something like this,

"Welcome to 'The Good Life After 60' a Web site dedicated to helping you have the money you need for the good life you want to lead after retirement. Come back on the first of every month to find new information on

- current investments paying high returns with low risk
- investments to avoid
- how to get maximum tax deductions
- how to provide for your spouse and children, and
- other important information about what's happening right *now* on the investment scene.

Be sure to complete the visitor questionnaire before you leave so we can provide the information you need to enjoy THE GOOD LIFE AFTER 60."

Here are some key points about your message. It must

- be timeless. You don't always want to be taping a new audio clip unless you've got an up-to-date computer with audio capability or your brother-in-law happens to run an audio studio and is willing to help you keep your message current.
- indicate that new information is being put up at regular intervals. Remember, the objective is to develop a clientele, just as with any other retail store. Your visitor may not take any action the first time she visits. That's life. But if she knows that every 30 days you post new information on current investments, she may

bookmark your site to pop back again and again. Remember, it may take several visits before she acts. However if you keep the message on something she wants — in this case "The Good Life After 60" — and provide the information she needs to achieve it, believe me, she'll be back — as a customer, not a browser!

- hit the key things your designated prospect wants. Don't talk about yourself or waste time in a long folksy greeting. Focus rigorously on the prospect... on what the prospect wants... and on what the prospect gets from you to achieve what he wants. Remember, in marketing the most important person is always the prospect; nothing happens until this person says, "Here's something for me. Here's something I want. Here's something I have to take action to get or else I'll lose the benefits I desire." Unless your audio message moves to this beat, it fails.

To achieve the result you want means planning your audio clip carefully. Or, should I say clips? Since you're probably going to have to go to a recording studio anyway to do your clip (unless your computer is 1996 state-of-the-art), brainstorm a half dozen or more 20 second commercials (for what else are these anyway?) so you can do them all at the same time. Let's go back to "The Good Life After 60". Brainstorm various audio alternatives, including messages that focus on

- getting the highest current yield from investments
- starting an investment program
- taking care of your spouse and family.

All these themes are part of the big theme of "The Good Life After 60" but accentuate different aspects of it. Since it's not very expensive to change your audio message (at Worldprofit we charge $10-$15), you might want to have one message for, say, 90 days... then change to another. But you should tape them all at the same time for maximum efficiency, convenience and savings.

A Few Technical Tips

Here are some technical things to keep in mind about your audio clip:

- it has to be short, right now not more than 20 seconds (250 Kbytes). This amount of time will increase, of course, as technology improves, but I'd be wary if I were you about just how long I made my announcement. People get impatient. No matter how good the technology gets, I'd never suggest an audio message of more than a minute; 30 seconds preferably!

- if you've got a newer computer (since 1996), you will be able to use it for the recording since all new computers now come with sound cards and a microphone; (ask before you buy). Of course, you can use a recorder at home, too, but this is not recommended because of poor sound quality. If you do decide to go to a studio, you'll probably be paying about $50 for a 20 second recording. You may record in .wav, .mid, and in .au. As yet there is no standard for sound recording on the Internet.

- If you've got a computer, you can download free software off the Internet that will allow you to make recordings onto the Internet. To find free software, simply go to any search engine and type in the subject related to the software you wish to find. The search engine will allow you to select "software" as an option.

This means all returns from the search will be software related. In addition, many new computers come with this software already installed. You simply turn on the microphone and start talking. The file can then be posted to the Internet by any content provider such as Worldprofit.

- once you've got your audio clip you can send it either by e-mail or on diskette. At Worldprofit, it usually takes about a day to post your new audio message and to use it to accentuate your home page's visual presentation.

A Note On Video

You can, of course, also have video on your site to accentuate the message and presentation of your key points. However, right now, the cost of providing such video is prohibitive for all but the most well-heeled. Does this mean you can't use video at all? By no means. On the Internet there are stock graphic video images — like a spinning globe of the Earth or steaming coffee cup. They are called .avi files. You can find them all over the Internet. A good place to start is by going to any search engine and typing in "video" at the search prompt. Here are some other ways to get video clips:

- Corel Draw 6.0 for Windows 95. This program comes with about 100 short videos that can be posted to the Internet. They can take between 65 Kilobytes-5 Megabytes. The larger they are, the slower to view (especially at 9600 baud), so try to use under 200K.

- Java also makes objects move. Java is a program language that George Kosch tells me is destined to become one of the main programming languages used on the Internet. Right now Java allows you to make images move, lines wiggle, text move or dance about, text scroll across the screen and many other small effects. For instance, you can use Java to create an effect where data screens continually change. Use it to feature three aspects of your company like "benefits," "key questions & answers," and "order form," or, if you're in MLM, "products," "pay plan," and "sign-up information", or "good," "better," and "best" reasons for buying what you're selling. Each screen would be set up to automatically cycle into the next. Although Java is still in development, some companies have already released programming interfaces that allow you to put together a Java applet; (an applet is a short program with a specific purpose, like moving text). Symantec, for instance, has a very good one that sells on the Internet for about $100.

- Look for Microsoft's VB Scripting. It's another programming language with similarities to Java. Another Microsoft innovation is Jakarta. It's still in its infancy but promises to be an easier Internet-based programming language. You can always drop in at http://www.microsoft.com for up-to-date details on these developments.

Too, read the *Worldgram*. George Kosch's "TechAdvance" column includes video programming developments.

If you do decide on video, here's how you should handle things:

- Make sure you have an idea of what a working video actually looks like. Review some already on the Internet. Go to http://www.microsoft.com and select the Explorer option. You'll get an idea of what some stock .avi files look like.

- Consider having an audio clip run along with the video in the background.
- Tell your media people your plan. See if it makes sense to them. If so, go ahead with your recording time.

Video on the Internet is very much in its infancy just now and will stay that way so long as the average connect speed is only 9600 baud, making large video files impractical. We're all awaiting video development impatiently. By the next edition of this book, Internet video will be much further along. In the meantime, if you want video, stick to a stock .avi file. At Worldprofit, we'll load it onto your home page for $65 and can make suggestions about stock video images that can enhance your Web site.

Tips For Writing Profit-Making Prospect-Centered Netvertising Copy

Once you've done everything else in this chapter, you'll be ready to finalize your netvertised Web site by giving it a final review using these profit-making cash copy tips.

- Keep all verbs in the active sense. Passive voice doesn't work on the 'net — or anywhere else.
- Ensure your sentences are short, shorter, shortest. Everybody knows that the general attention span is more abbreviated every year. Don't fight it. Keep your sentences short and active.
- Ditto paragraphs. Long paragraphs on the 'net — or anywhere else in marketing — are death to readership, death to buyership.
- Use lots of punctuating devices to draw attention to key words. The Internet is great for this. Use
  - audio clips to point out the chief benefits of what you've got, the chief reason for immediate action
  - flashing text. Again, put the really important words in text that just keeps flashing and flashing and flashing.
  - marquees. Scroll your crucial client-centered messages across the page to increase the likelihood that the person you've trying to motivate really sees what you've got.
  - video clips. Again, focus on the key buyer-motivating ideas and words.
  - color graphics (including image maps) and color text. The Internet is not a bland medium. It's fast-moving and visually exciting. Keep asking yourself, is what I'm using the best thing I can use to get the prospect to stop in his tracks, pay attention to what I'm saying and get him to act **RIGHT THIS MINUTE**?

Also use
  - bullets (notice I use them a lot. Why? They work!)
  - indentations (from the left)
  - indentations (from the right)
  - CAPITAL LETTERS
  - ellipses...
  - ... exclamation points!!!

Remember, you're not writing a formal paper for some obscure scientific society. You're writing copy designed to do just this: capture a prospect, interest that prospect, get that prospect to respond *AS FAST AS POSSIBLE!!!*

Keeping Your Web Site Store Up-To-Date

You know now how to build a dynamic, compelling, client-centered and fully netvertised Web site, one that looks and sounds full of benefits. Congratulations. You're way ahead in this game. If you've done any 'net surfing lately, you already know there's a ton of garbage out there, information that doesn't begin to meet the criteria I've laid down in this chapter for a profit-making home page. That's because too many people are selfish beasts who haven't a clue what it takes to motivate the other creatures who inhabit Mega-Mall Earth.

You get ahead in this life by figuring out as fast as possible what it takes to motivate other people... applying what you've learned... and committing yourself to learning even more about this vital game... and applying that, too, as quickly as possible.

This means not only delivering an initial client-centered Web site... but always keeping that site excitingly client-centered.

Remember, you're running a store; that's what your Web site really is. If you were running a traditional physical emporium, you wouldn't just dump everything anywhere and hope for the best. Remember your *Gone With The Wind*. That's what Frank Kennedy did in his Atlanta store after the Civil War. Result? He didn't make much money. However when the very entrepreneurial Scarlett took over after she married him, the store's sales shot up because she focused on attractive presentation of the goods and sales, sales, sales. (She also made sure people paid their long overdue bills. This embarrassed Frank, but was very sound business.) Compelling client-centered presentation, in short, is crucial.

That's why you've got to keep scrutinizing your home page, keep asking yourself a series of questions designed to make it even more client-centered and profitable, questions like:

- Is my offer as client-centered and motivating as it can be? Can I strengthen it?
- Am I clear, crystal clear, on just who I'm trying to attract?
- Have I done everything possible to make the benefits as motivating as possible?
- Do I understand that prospects are necessarily skeptical these days, and have I done everything possible to get and post client-centered testimonials that talk about real results received by real people?
- Have I answered the questions my prospects have as clearly and fully as possible?
- Have I examined what my competitors are doing and answered what they think their strong points are, either by incorporating my rebuttal in my overall presentation or by specifically addressing each of their claims and insertions on my "red flag" page?
- Have I presented my message in words (both written and audio) and in pictures (video) that are as client-centered as possible? If I saw this message, these pictures, would I get excited about the presentation and want to take action to acquire the benefits?

Last Words

As you finish this chapter, you'll know why so many people on the Web complain about poor results. There are, of course, lots of reasons why people fail on the Web. Trying to go solo with your Web site or trying to make money in a mall that's not adequately promoted and organized are, of course, important reasons. But so is trying to ram an uninteresting, boring home page down a prospect's throat.

You can't bore people into buying! You can't self-righteous them into buying; "this is good for you, good for you, so do it, do it, DO IT I TELL YOU!" You can't obscure them into buying! You can't "I'm so great I don't have to motivate you" into buying! You can't condescend them into buying! You can't talk over their heads them into buying!

Yet I bet that every single home page advertiser on the Web who fails because they used these — and other selfish — gambits, blames the Web! Amazing!!!

As I have constantly stressed in this resource and my articles, the Web isn't some kind of magic elixir where you can drop in marketing junk and pull out a sale. The Web is a tool. A fabulous tool! Indeed, the most exciting marketing tool in the entire world, or as a friend of mine told me when he began really understanding and using the Web, "It's a cash hose!"

Indeed it is!

A CASH HOSE.

Remember these words, for that is precisely what the Web is. Your Web site is the hose itself, directing the message at the prospect... and the money at you!

I close this chapter by reminding you that no hose works unless you turn on the spigot. Your Web spigot is making sure that your home page is rigorously client-centered to begin with... and that you take the time and trouble to make sure that its content remains client-centered and up-to-date at all time...

... as well as doing everything you can to promote this unceasingly client-centered entity as unrelentingly as you can. See the next page. It's time to get serious about promotion!

Chapter 4

WHAT YOU HAVE TO DO TO PROMOTE YOUR HOME PAGE WITHIN THE INTERNET

The three biggest elements of Internet success are

- position
- presentation, and
- promotion.

The Three Ps.

By now you know about POSITION, *where* you should be...

... you also know *what* you should say and *how* you should PRESENT it.

It's time, therefore, to discuss the third all-important P: PROMOTION!

I cannot remind you sufficiently often just how crucial this is for your Web success.

A Penny-Pinching Scotman's Guide To Successful Promotion

We Scots (I'm of the Clan MacMillan, you know) have a justly deserved reputation for being tight with a penny. If you've ever been to Scotland, you know why. Much of it is a poor land with poor soil. The existence is generally rugged and hard. Money's always been scarce and people have always been challenged to live by their wits — which is why many of the world's most successful people proudly claim Scottish heritage.

On the Web, the challenge is getting maximum exposure for minimum expense. To succeed at this game, I rely on my hereditary instincts to accomplish more for less. So that you can do this, too, I herewith make you an honorary Scot (should you not have the inestimable advantage of already being one) and wish to share with you my canny Scotman's tricks of the trade for penny-pinching promotion of your home page. In this chapter we'll deal with promoting your home page on the Web itself. In the next, we'll take up promotion outside the Web.

— Determine Who's Responsible for Promotion

In too many businesses, Web promotion is an afterthought. It's something someone gets around to when there's not something more important (like planning an office birthday party) to do. This is ridiculous.

The first rule of successful intra-Internet promotion is to determine just who's responsible for handling it. If you operate a home-based micro business with one employee, this isn't so difficult. The responsible individual is YOU. The key to this situation is actually *appointing* yourself director of Web site promotion. Does this sound unnecessary?

Well, I believe in making things crystal clear; the way to do this is not just to *think* that you're responsible… but to *assign* yourself an explicit commission of responsibility. In other words, to hire yourself.

In larger companies, the same rule applies. Don't just casually say, "Oh, by the way, Marty, you're in charge of promoting our Web site." That's no good. Make an explicit appointment.

— Make It Clear What You Expect

When appointing, make your expectations clear. Do you want monthly promotion? Weekly? Daily?

I know what my objectives are: unrelenting Web site promotion through all available means with daily gambits on and off the Web.

Remember, intra-Internet promotion is crucial for the success of your Web site. In this connection, there isn't a day that goes by that I'm not at work at promoting my malls and the Web sites in them. What about you? Will you be happy with monthly promotion? Or will you do what's necessary to get weekly promotion at the very least? Ask yourself if you really can live with less. But in any case, make your expectations clear.

— Brainstorm Promotional Angles

The key to successful promotion is developing a promotional mind, learning to think like a promoter… then doing what's necessary to execute the ideas you've come up with.

I've written an entire book about these two things. It's called THE UNABASHED SELF-PROMOTER'S GUIDE, and I recommend it to you. Remember, just saying "We're here. We're great," isn't going to get you much attention. You've got to provide *reasons* why people should visit your Web site.

Keep in mind that the entire idea of "promotion" on the Internet is viewed by many with the utmost suspicion. The Web, of course, was designed for the prompt communication of succinct information. Many people wanted — and still want — to keep it only this way. They view the entire promotional process with distaste and alarm. Moreover, extremists do *everything* they can to sabotage this process.

This conduct, of course, is both short-sighted and reprehensible. Without promotion, which is a necessary part of successful commercial development, the Web would have remained an underdeveloped backwater, the plaything of a few nerds with social problems. That these nerds do not quite see things this way is understandable. More importantly, since they can make difficulties it is, however unfortunately, necessary to take their entirely fatuous feelings into account.

Thus, you've got to develop promotional angles which are acceptable in the Web context. Here are the four major angles on which your promotion should be based:

– *something free*

– *something new*

– something newsworthy

– something improved.

The best thing to do is to brainstorm just what you've got in every category and to record your ideas. This means opening up an "idea" file divided into these four parts.

— What have you got that's free?

- a catalog
- information kit
- audio cassette
- video cassette
- newsletter
- consultation
- situation review
- special report
- booklet.

List everything in the "free" file. It's true that people on the Internet are freebie mad. It's equally true that a certain percentage of people on the Internet are not very responsible about their requests for freebies. This bothers a lot of people. It is, however, part of the Web environment, and you've got to be aware of it. The key to the freebies you dish out is that

- They shouldn't cost you a lot.
- They should be presented as strongly and in as benefit-anchored, prospect-centered manner as possible.
- Furthermore, you should request the necessary qualifying information from the prospect before sending anything. (In other words, if you ask for a phone number and don't get it... why, then, you should strongly consider not sending anything. After all, you're not in the freebie distribution business, you're in the business of using any given freebie to get real prospects to present themselves and provide the information you need to take intelligent action. If you don't feel some of the people who have presented themselves are in fact sufficiently good prospects for you — for whatever reason — dump them without a second thought.)

— What have you got that's new?

Every time you introduce something into your business... something that makes the lives of your prospects better, that's the time to do intra-Internet promotion. Here are some new things to get your creative juices flowing:

- product
- service
- enhanced product feature of existing product
- enhanced service feature of existing service
- personnel
- location

- operating hours
- improved shipping, *etc.*

Get it? Never do *anything* new without considering its promotional advantage. To introduce a new product… or even a new color for an older product… without considering the intra-Web promotional advantages and determining to squeeze the utmost advantage from them is crazy. Everything new, properly handled, is grist for the promotional mill.

— What have you got that's newsworthy?

Developing a promotional brain means seeing how things can be positioned to be of interest to others while handing you the marketing benefit. This means being able to judge when something's newsworthy. Think about

- expanded operations
- scientific surveys and results
- personnel accomplishments
- patents
- copyrights
- prizes and awards (both received and given)
- educational achievements.

You get the idea.

— What have you got that's improved?

Don't just improve. Promote the improvements. One without the other just doesn't make sense. You want your prospects to know that, at your shop, things are better and better every day… that you're using your time, money and other resources to improve things so that your customers get more benefit. So, what have you got that's improved?

- hours of business
- sites (size, location and customer-centered amenities)
- personnel with better skills
- more personnel
- product features that do more, provide more benefits
- ditto service features.

Note: THESE LISTS ARE NOT EXHAUSTIVE. They're simply designed to get you thinking about promotional angles. What's important is that you

- learn to see everything you do in your business not just as a task to be completed or as an objective accomplished but as a promotional lever to be used to increase Web traffic,
- that you do nothing without brainstorming the promotional possibilities, and
- that you do not see the business task finished unless and until you have done all you can to squeeze the utmost promotional benefit from it.

Keep A "Promotional Module" File In Your Computer: Actual Language

Once you see how many categories lead to promotional advantage (there's scarcely anything in a business that cannot be promoted and cannot be used as the basis for promotional modules), it's time to start writing the actual promotional modules. These are of two kinds: timely and timeless. Some things that are happening in your business need to be promoted right this minute — like the introduction of a new technology that leaves your competitors in the dust. You want to promote that just as quick you can. Other things are timeless... meaning that if they don't get promoted today there's no great loss. They have a promotional advantage, to be sure, but can be used as necessary to meet your promotional quota and round out a slow day at the ranch.

Either way, the promotional modules must be written in a certain way, a way guaranteed not just to impart information ... but to get people to take action, including visiting your Web site to get complete details. To show you what I mean, here's a module that a company with a new product line could use:

MILLIONS ARE OVERPAYING EVERY TIME THEY GET GAS FOR THEIR VEHICLES. DON'T BE ONE OF THEM! SAVE UP TO 15 CENTS PER GALLON IMMEDIATELY!!

Every time you fill up your family car or truck you're probably overpaying for gas, says Gas Pump, Inc. Gas prices have increased over 25% in the last 120 days with no end in sight. Can you live with this? Or would you like to do something about it besides waiting for prices to come down... if they ever do! Gas Pump, Inc. has introduced its new nationwide gas price-cutting coupons. Take these to any participating station — there are thousands nationwide — and you save 15 cents per gallon. Get all the details — and three free coupons worth $5 — just by visiting http://www.worldprofit.com/lowgas.

What's going on here?

- First, the module is short. Remember, all the details are posted at the advertiser's Web site. The purpose of this module is to whet peoples' appetites. Don't try to stuff a complete meal in a paragraph.
- Make sure your headline is either pain- or gain-centered. The headline above is about pain, about people paying too much and being able to avoid it

Note: in this illustration, I've lead with pain and followed up with gain "save up to 15 cents per gallon." This is perfectly acceptable and hits both bases. You may, of course, always start with a gain headline like:

SAVE 15 CENTS ON EVERY GALLON OF GAS YOU BUY WITH "GAS SAVE" COUPONS! VISIT http://www.worldprofit.com/low gas STOP OVERPAYING FOR THE GAS YOU BUY!

- Make sure there are no dates. Unless you're absolutely sure your promotional module will be used immediately (as we are, for instance, when we publish an issue of the *Worldgram*) and/or you're certain the information will be removed by a certain time, don't use dates. Dates age material, and you've got to be sure that an old date doesn't undermine the impact of your message.
- since everyone who reads an intra-Internet promotion is on the Internet, always direct people to your Web site for complete details.

- make an offer whenever possible. Offers are levers designed to get people to move faster. Remember, in the Internet environment you're constantly competing against other site owners who want to capture traffic. Your job is to strike first, strike most often, and promote the necessary motivating devices that ensure faster action. This means having an offer — in this case "three free coupons worth $5." The dollar value is crucial. The assigned value is the tangible benefit. Coupons themselves are merely features. Always stress the maximum benefit of visiting your site to provide maximum prospect motivation.

Note: if you're smart you'll keep reusing modules you've already written. Take the example above. Gas prices are always going to fluctuate. So long as you have "gas save" coupons whenever the price of gas starts going up, you take out your module, make any necessary revisions, and send it out. How often could you do this? Well, friend, you could use this module as the basis for future promotion for as long as gas prices escalate and as long as you're in business. In other words, for a very long time.

Hint: whenever possible link your promotions to what's happening in the news. As I write, for instance, gas prices really are escalating at a very rapid rate. That's good news for people like my fictional Gas Pump, Inc. Each time a news story comes out about the problem that their product addresses, they can piggyback on this development to stimulate greater site traffic. Nor should they be hesitate about incorporating hard news and editorial opinion from the standard news media to beef up their module.

Thus, as facts are reported about higher prices, the promoters should put such information into their module, with complete attribution of course. "The New York Times has reported that pump prices have jumped 25% in just the last three months alone." Or, "nationally syndicated columnist Pete Smith reports that 'future anticipated price rises will take gasoline prices at least 65 cents higher per gallon.'" Get the drift?

Your objective, always your objective, is to get people to visit your Web site. All's fair in love and war and in marketing. Thus, take the useful bits of articles you read and reports you hear on electronic media and incorporate them into your promotional modules. Remember, you want the pain to be as painful (and therefore as motivating) as possible… and the gain to be as substantial as possible!

A personal note. Does writing these modules seem like a lot of work? It isn't really. Modules emanate from a state of mind and from the mastery of technique. I work on my modules as I walk to the post office every morning and back again. I decide what I want to write about today and what the angle should be. I make it a point to write at least one module a day, often more. I also make it a point not to take very long, about 15 minutes, to do so; after all, like you, I have a lot to accomplish today.

— Your Signature File

Someone has to "deliver" the module to its actual destination, the place where you want prospects to find it. This person has what's called a signature file, language which identifies the person. This signature file is and should be a promotional module in its own right. Let's take a look at George Kosch's.

George Kosch M.Sc.
Worldprofit, Inc.
9010-106 Ave., Suite 208
Edmonton, Alberta T5H 4K3 (403) 425-2466
Check out our 10 Malls at http://www.worldprofit.com
Information on advertising by fax on demand (403) 425-6049 doc #1
or http://www.worldprofit.com

What's going on here?

- First, remember that a signature file is separate from any promotional module that may, from time to time, be coupled to it.
- it should contain standard follow-up information, like name, company name, address, phone number.
- it should contain information about what you're selling, what you want to promote, in this case "our 10 malls".
- this information should be timeless
- it should also include whenever possible information on your fax-on-demand and URL address.

In other words, the signature file should not just tell people who you are but what you've got and how to get it. It's like mobile office stationery, if you will. The promotional module follows naturally and should, of course, be regularly changed.

— Keeping Lists of Search Engines and How To Use Them

There are two key ways you must use to promote your Web site and what you're marketing on the Internet: search engines and newsgroups. Here are my comments about the first.

A search engine is like a library card catalog or subject index, although of course it's far superior to the indexes we all used in high school! A search engine is a place people go to find what's available on the Internet so that they can go get it.

As I write there are about 400 such search engines on the Internet and the number goes up each day. Why? Because the cost to establish a search engine is moderate (about $20,000 right now) and because search engines get a lot of traffic at zero cost. People with home pages come to the search engine to get listed and while they're there they can check out the search engine's advertisers. People looking for specific information go to search engines to find out where it might be, and while they're there are also exposed to the advertising messages.

However, before you rush out and establish your own search engines, I'd think twice if I were you. There are a number of very well-known sites already established, like Lycos, Yahoo, Excite (which gives away its own search engine software for free), InfoSeek, Alta Vista, Open Text, Webcrawler, and others. These sites are used by millions daily and advertising on them can be very costly, like $5,000 a month or more!

To get started listing your home page with a search engine, go to these three sources:

- http://www.lycos.com
- http://www.yahoo.com
- http://www.infoseek.com

Although there doesn't seem to be a single list of every Internet search computer (please tell me if you find one), each of these search engines lists alternatives just in case you can't find what you're looking for with them. So, bit by bit you'll be able to develop a more complete list.

Getting Your URL Listed

Getting your own URL address listed with these search computers can be tricky to say the least. Basically, you can select from the home page of any search computer an option to "list url" or "add url." This will take you to a form-based page with information to fill in such as URL address, name of home page, descriptive paragraph, what is the subject (they usually provide a list to choose from), and information about yourself. After typing in this information, you click on a submit button. Your information will either be accepted by the computer or it will display what you've typed and ask you to confirm that it is in fact correct. If the information has an error, you can make the change and then resubmit. This service is free, but it can be time-consuming.

Some search computers (or search engines, as they are also called) accept the registration and add you to their database immediately, or that same day. Most, however, take up to 3 weeks — or even longer — to post information. This is because they are back-logged with requests. Keep in mind that there are no limits to the number of listings you have or any additional costs, so everyone with a Web site flocks to get listed, only lengthening the waiting period. As a result, lately some search engines are charging a $5 "rush fee" for people who want to jump the queue and get listed immediately. It's another little straw in the wind that the early "free for all" days on the Internet aren't going to last forever.

What You Should List

Just what you should list depends on what you've got available and the kinds of people you want to attract to your Web site. Make what you post both as detailed and as enticing as possible. Your listing should be not more than 25 words and should be thought out before you arrive at the search computer. It's clear that most people write their listings off the tops of their heads; this is stupid. Your listing is a free 25-word ad and should be treated accordingly. Let me give you an illustration:

Bad listing: We sell business books and seminars. You'll find listings of lots of the best in business books, most subject areas. Drop by anytime. Always open!

Better listing: 100's of money-making books, business development materials & workshops! Free marketing newsletter just for stopping by! Materials for every business size/ type!

See the difference? Don't (listlessly) *tell* in your listing, (aggressively) *sell*!

If, after you've slept on it, you decide the URL you've registered is just too dull to do you any good, rewrite and go back to re-register it. Your new listing will overwrite the old one. If you terminate your URL, good manners suggests that you go back to the search computer and terminate your listing. This is precisely what most people don't do and leads to lots of junk staying on the Internet. If you ever leave the Internet, cancel your search computer listings by selecting "remove url."

About The Worldprofit Search Computer

Not surprisingly, our resident information genius George Kosch has created a fabulous search computer at Worldprofit that automatically lists each of our hundreds and hundreds of advertisers. When visitors arrive at the Worldprofit search computer, they can type in as many key words as they like to locate a particular Web site or subject matter. They then click on the submit button.

The search engine then checks the listings on a special search source page and presents the result of the search. The result may list as many as 100 possibilities from which searchers can then narrow their options. When the searchers have determined where they'd like to go, they simply click to go there.

How current are the listings? Well, at Worldprofit we update our search computer up to 3 times *every day*! Would you like to check out the Worldprofit search computer now? Go to http://www.worldprofit.com/search.htm

Keeping Records Of The Search Engines You're Registered At

Obviously, as long as you stay on the Internet you're going to be involved with search computers. Each time you update your site and add new products/services, you'll want to update your search computer entry accordingly. Thus, you need to keep good records of the search engines you've found. That's easy to do: you simply "bookmark" them when you visit, and you'll automatically save them for easy reference.

In the notes you keep, make sure to record

- search engine name
- how to access
- what information they want from you
- how you need to provide it.

Special Search Computer Registration Service

If you're just too busy to register your Web site and its key aspects with search computers or want to make sure its done right with all the crucial ones, use the registration service offered by Incor Enterprises, Inc. They'll be happy to register your Web site with the 20 major search computers for a one-time fee of $49.95. Either call (403) 425-2466 or use fax-on-demand (403) 425-6049, document #8. Note: don't wait to do this. Registering your site with search computers automatically increases your traffic substantially!

— Keeping Lists of Newsgroups and How to Use Them

The second key element of Internet promotion is the newsgroups.

A newsgroup is a body of people with related interests. Groups range from the very arcane where just a few people drop by to swap recherché stories... to places where tens of thousands regularly visit. The important thing is that a newsgroup brings together people who are interested in the same kinds of things. If these people would be interested in what you've got, you need to drop by regularly, too. Here's how to profitably use these groups.

- review all available newsgroup sources. When using Netscape 3.0 or Microsoft Explorer 3.0, you simply click on "newsgroups" on the menu at the top of the program. This instantly accesses all available newsgroups that the service provider has decided to list. This is usually at least 15,000 groups!

The newsgroup window shows the newsgroups in alphabetical order with the first level being the main subjects and then each type of group following under those subjects. Example: the alt.groups stand for "alternative" and currently contain about 5,000 different groups, including alt.multi-level and alt.business, *etc.*

- record those that look most germane to what you're selling. To do this, you simply click on a box beside the group(s) you're interested in and the browser will remember to bring up the latest posting the next time you open the newsgroup window. This is called subscribing to the newsgroup. There is no limit to the number of newsgroups you can subscribe to.
- pop by to take a look at them. If they're appealing to the kinds of people you want to appeal to, note that information.
- peruse the kinds of messages people are leaving to get a sense of what's permissible in any given newsgroup. Remember, not all newsgroups are the same in their standards and what's allowable. You definitely want to promote to the limit of what that group regards as acceptable!

The most acceptable form of posting to most groups is free information and NO ADS. As soon as you post any form of ad you will be "flamed." There are nit-pickers in every group just waiting to announce their moral outrage that there is advertising present. It's stupid, but, for the moment, we have to live with these silly restrictions. Here's what you may post acceptably:

- an announcement
- place a small ad in your signature file as discussed above (should not exceed 4 lines of text)
- an article with a resource box
- places to visit for information on a subject. Note: postings recognize html links so that if you include a URL address, the link will actually work when someone reads the posting. All they have to do is click on the URL to get there. Thus, it's very important to include a link in your signature file.
- offer a free subscription.

Keep in mind that some newsgroups are moderated, meaning that a person reviews all postings before allowing them to be viewed by everyone else. This avoids flaming and ads. Such groups, unsurprisingly, tend to be far more sedate than the unmoderated ones where Internet limits are constantly being tested and where the war between uncommercial geeks and unrestrained capitalists is being fought out.

Suggestion: whenever possible tailor your announcement to any given newsgroup by putting the group's name either in the body of the announcement or above the headline, as "Special for <name of newsgroup>."

Remember, newsgroups are constantly changing. New ones pop up, old ones lose their appeal. The important thing is that you stay abreast of developments. I'll give you a hint that should help. No matter whose newsgroup you've visiting, your job is to squeeze the promotional possibilities from it. You want to be in touch with all the relevant people from that group and motivate them to visit your Web site and take the appropriate actions when they're there.

Promotion is not a business for the faint-hearted. In a sense, each newsgroup that you visit is actually your group. You've got to start with the idea that this group exists for you, to promote what you've got. Thus make it your business to understand each group and to exploit each group regularly. A systematic client-centered approach is the key to promotional success on the Internet.

You'll find that most of the people who drop by the newsgroups are, by comparison, rank amateurs, people without a mission, an objective, a system, or a client-centered message. In such a situation you, armed as you are with so many advantages, must succeed. There may well be grumbling comments about all the promotional advantages you get; losers can hardly be expected to be gracious. But so long as you keep the focus on the benefits the prospects get, these prospects will be grateful and take the action they need to take to benefit you. And that, in the final analysis, is really all that matters.

— Thanking People

One way you can distinguish yourself is to post a thank-you note whenever possible. If losers are distinguished by their alkaline grumbling, winners are forever gracious. To be gracious in victory is one true mark of a champion. This means regularly thanking people. Thank them for trifling services, like allowing you to post notices, thank them for anything more important they do. Thanking people is a critical part of promotion. Chances are that when you express your appreciation, not just with an offhand thanks, but with a gracious note posted for all to see, that you'll be one of the few, perhaps the only one, doing so. This distinguishes you as a person of breeding and consequence and is in itself yet another form of promotion.

Last Words

This chapter has dealt with intra-Internet promotion. As long as you have a Web site, you'll be doing this. Or at least *should* be doing this, because the plain fact is that the vast majority of people with home pages do little or none of this promotion at all.

Why not? I think it's for several reasons including

- lack of understanding of how the Internet works. Day after day I talk to people who think the Web is some kind of self-promoting machine; that all you have to do is post a message and that that message somehow gets magically brought to the attention of just the right people or that, even more magically, these people will drop by on their own initiative. Just writing down this prevalent belief should show you how absurd it is.

- lack of knowledge about the available promotional tools, such as search engines and newsgroups. If you don't know what tools are available, how can you possibly use them to your advantage?

- failure to conceptualize each thing done by your business or organization in terms of its promotional angles. Have you ever watched a bird's head move. It moves in a rapid, angular fashion allowing the creature's eyes to take in a situation from many, many different angles before making up its mind what to do. Across the courtyard from where I write there's a small but determined colony of starlings who live here all year round. I've learned a lot about thinking and planning by watching these methodical creatures contemplate their options before deciding just what to do. Unsurprisingly, when they do take action, they do so unhesitatingly and with an extraordinarily high success rate. A good metaphor for all of us. Your job is to keep reviewing any given aspect of your business to find the maximum number of promotional angles and then to create the necessary modules based on these angles.

- no systematic promotional plan. There are probably only a handful of days of the year when I allow myself the luxury of not doing something promotional. The rest of the time, I am systematically reviewing promotional possibilities and implementing them, both on the Internet and off. You must do the same. Promotion is not something you do when you feel like it or when you "have the time" or when there is nothing better to do. Systematic, continuous promotion is at the heart of business success. In the intra-Internet context this means keeping the search engines up-to-date as things develop... not two weeks later, not two months later, but when you're ready to welcome new visitors. Similarly, it means dropping by all newsgroups on a regular, predictable schedule, not 10 days late, not 60 days late, but systematically, certainly.

If you're the kind of person to whom system is anathema, who thinks that it somehow curbs your creativity and (in some strange way) constrains and diminishes you, all this is going to sound like very weary work. Well, friend, it can be wearying, to be sure. There are days, believe me, when I most assuredly do *not* feel like creating yet another promotional module (I've written so many in my life) or arranging for it to be posted... or, God forgive me, sending a thank-you note to someone who has helped me (if only a little). Champions, however, always extend themselves just that little bit extra, which is, when you consider it, the very reason they are champions. That's why, since you're champion material, too, you'll extract the greatest possible advantage from your Web site by implementing the most organized and aggressive promotional program, too, including using all the suggestions in this chapter... and the next!

Chapter 5

WHAT YOU HAVE TO DO TO PROMOTE YOUR HOME PAGE OFF THE INTERNET

Very well, now you've seen how to promote your home page *within* the Web. Those vital exercises must continue so long as you've got a home page that you want visited — which means so long as you're on the Web at all!

Now it's time for Part II of my Canny Scotman's Parsimonious Hints For Promotional Success: promoting your home page *off* the Web.

Position Is Promotion

The first — and arguably most important — thing you must do to promote your Home Page in the Real World is select the proper mall. I've already stressed the vital importance of this choice, but this decision is so important I'm going to reinforce it here.

Consider this.

Look what I, as mall proprietor, do to promote my malls and increase their traffic:

- at least 75 cards in each of my 100,000 quarterly circulation Sales & Marketing Success card decks are published with a Worldprofit URL/Web address. Because 100,000 copies of each card are dispersed, that means that every 90 days at least 7,500,000 cards go out with Worldprofit URL addresses in my deck alone. Here's a sample of some of the cards I run personally:

You're just one fax away from reaching 30,000,000+ people worldwide through

Dr. Jeffrey Lant's 10 Internet Malls

Look at all the advantages of having your own Home Page in our Malls:

- LOWEST PRICES in the Internet industry. Monthly charges lower than $17 — you're never going to beat that!
- Advertise *everything* your prospects need to know about what you're selling.
- THERE IS NO LIMIT TO THE AMOUNT OF MATERIAL YOU CAN ADVERTISE!
- You're never closed. People can buy what you're selling 24 hours a day, *every single day!*
- We aggressively promote the Malls to get you traffic. A Home Page without promotion is crazy.
- Change your ad as often as you want!

Use our Fax-on-Demand service!

Let your prospects get your information 24 hours a day! And we can get you a position on our Main Menu so prospects see you first!

Fax Today to see how you can get a FREE 60 character line on the InternetConnect card (circ 100,000)

Side 1 shown

- This result is significantly enhanced when you consider the *many* other decks in which I run cards *and* in which our mall advertisers run cards. There is scarcely a deck in the industry now that doesn't publish our mall address in every single issue one way or another.

Note: obviously when advertisers run these cards they are directing traffic right to their individual home page, but once prospects have perused that site they don't just leave the mall. They carry on, reviewing many other home pages during their visit.

- I also run up to four InternetConnect cards in every issue of my Sales & Marketing Success Card Deck. This card, as you can see, is composed of Web classifieds. Each card promotes 30-40 advertiser Web sites. New one-year advertisers in any of my malls get their first listing for free; thereafter the cost is $90 for each insertion. Either way, it's a very inexpensive way to bring traffic to your individual Web site... and improve the general mall traffic at the same time!

- I run ads in hundreds of opportunity, mail order, entrepreneurial and other "get ahead" publications. These ads have a dual purpose, to get new advertisers into the malls and to increase the overall traffic of the malls. Literally millions of people are exposed to ads like this on a regular basis:

- I run a "Resource Box" at the conclusion of every single article that's published as part of my "Sure-Fire Business Success" and "Qwik-Smarts w/Dr. Jeffrey Lant" columns. You already know that over 200 publications — both print and electronic — around the world publish these articles on a regular basis. At least 1.5 million people monthly get access to my ultra-practical, high energy "get ahead" guidelines. And *every* article ends with a box that looks like this one which happens to conclude my article entitled "The Astonishingly Profitable Combination — Card Decks and the World Wide Web: What You've Got To Do To Use Them To Maximum Advantage."

Resource Box

Harvard-educated Dr. Jeffrey Lant is proprietor of the world's largest and least expensive card-deck, the quarterly 100,000 circulation Sales & Marketing Success Deck. His many malls on the Internet feature the lowest prices in the World Wide Web industry for both home pages and fax-on-demand. To get a card in the next issue of his deck, call (617) 547-6372. For 24 hour fax on demand details about his card-deck and malls, fax (403) 425-6049 (document #1) or call (403) 425-2466. Access the Worldprofit malls at http://www.worldprofit.com Malls include THE MONEY MALL, THE BETTER HEALTH MALL, THE TOTAL HOME & GARDEN MALL, THE NETWORK MARKETING MALL, THE GIFTS MALL, THE CHRISTIAN MALL and THE HOME-BASED BUSINESS MALL, THE BUSINESS TO BUSINESS MALL, THE MAIL ORDER MALL, and many others. To get a free year's subscription to his quarterly 32-page Sure-Fire Business Success Catalog, call (617) 547-6372. E-mail webmaster@worldprofit.com to get a free subscription to Jeffrey's twice-monthly marketing and business development *Worldgram* newsletter!

- I run many mall-related items in my quarterly Sure-Fire Business Success Catalog which goes out to at least 140,000 people per issue. These items include the promotion of specific aspects of the malls (like the *Worldprofit On-line Magazine*) as well as how to advertise in the malls and, of course, all the reports I've written on different aspects of how to build a profit-making home page.

- the malls are promoted in my twice-monthly *Worldgram* newsletter, a very popular Worldprofit feature. This potent promotional source draws its "mailing" list from many sources, including ads and card decks but also from many other publications and entrepreneurs who use a free *Worldgram* subscription as an offer to sell their own products and services.

- Information about the malls is included in all my books and all the packages in which these books — and my many other products — are mailed. (If you got this book in a package from me, check out the shipping labels to see what I mean. It's a small thing, but in the interests of developing maximum Worldprofit traffic, nothing can be overlooked! Here's a sample label.)

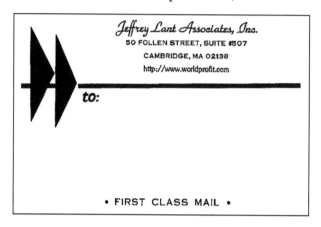

- Information on the malls appears in my many video cassettes as part of an end-of-video "resource box."

Importantly, I'm also in charge of marshaling the resources of all the advertisers in the malls to whom I regularly supply marketing tips and guidelines about how to build individual home pages to maximum extent. These step-by-step guidelines go out, first, in the welcome letter I send to all new advertisers. This letter makes it clear that each advertiser can do his/her bit to improve the overall traffic... and just what can be done for minimum cost and maximum results. This promotional development message is continually reinforced in my *Worldgram* newsletter. The editorial thrust of this newsletter is distinctly activist in nature. I believe that every single advertiser should do his/her part — every single day! — to increase his/her own traffic and thus, by extension, increase the overall traffic of the mall.

Active Promotion: A Secret of Web Success

To my horror and continuing astonishment, too many people on the Web have the absolutely ridiculous idea that the Web is a sort of closet in which you stack information. Once you've posted this information in your own black hole, you never make adjustments and never do what's necessary to get people to visit. This is, of course, a prescription for disaster!

My concept is different — very, very different.

I believe in Web eco-thinking. I believe the only place to be on the Web is in an aggressively promoted mall. I believe that each person in such a mall (not just the management) has a responsibility to do everything to promote that Web site. And I believe that if each person in that mall does everything he can to promote his home page, the mall overall — and each advertiser within it — will prosper accordingly.

That's what this chapter is really about: prospering to the max by doing everything you can to help yourself... knowing that everything you're doing is being matched — in the well-organized malls — by hundreds, perhaps thousands of other advertisers. These people, by working strenuously on their own behalf, are working equally strenuously for the good of all. Yes, the realization of this concept makes me feel very socially responsible indeed. Doing well by doing good. I like it!

Taking An Inventory Of Where/How You Can Promote Your Home Page In The Real World

To be in business is to be in promotion. To the extent that you market, so shall you thrive. That, of course, is generally true. It is also specifically true about your home page. But the trick isn't just promoting; it's integrating your promotion into your regular business life so that you are neither overburdening yourself nor your budget. That's just not smart. Your job is to make what you do now do double duty as a promotional engine for your home page and, by extension, for your profit.

You do this, first, by taking an inventory of the things in your office that can assist your Web marketing, including

- business stationery
- envelopes
- shipping labels
- checks
- any items used as advertising specialties (including pens, calendars, t-shirts, *etc.*)
- flyers
- cover letters
- brochures
- business cards
- card deck cards
- space ads
- workshop handouts
- article/report "resource boxes"
- company newsletters
- labels on audio/video cassettes
- package stuffers
- catalogs
- books, *etc.*

What should be a part of this inventory?

- Every single thing you already use to market your product/service.
- Every single thing you use to connect with prospects and customers as part of the normal way you do business.

Note: it may take you a while 1) to complete this inventory and 2) to retool your thinking about these items. First, you've got to get over the notion that a home page promotes itself. Just as the items in your closet do not promote themselves... so home pages on the Web don't promote themselves either. If you want maximum traffic, you've got to do everything you can to achieve it!

Second, you've got to think about how you run your business, all the items you use as part of your marketing... all the items that touch your prospects and customers... and all the things you use that could carry information about your home page if you consider them in a new light as promotional tools (like your checks, for instance, both business and personal.)

What Message Should They Carry

For some odd reason, most people with home pages think that just providing their URL address is enough to get everyone and his brother to visit. More nonsense.

Marketing is the art and science of getting people to stop doing what they're doing... to change direction... and to do what you want them to do by being motivated to get something they want.

Now I ask you. If I say to you "visit us at http://www.myhomepage", are you going to drop everything to visit? Probably not. With URL addresses everywhere these days, what's the incentive to visit when I just give you an *address*?

A URL address is, after all, nothing more than a kind of telephone number. Merely providing a prospect with a phone number isn't nearly good enough to motivate that person to take prompt action. Thus, just because you say, "I've got a home page, visit me," you're not doing much to motivate that visit, are you? That's why you've got to consider very carefully just what you say as part of your home page promotion.

Just like a classified ad, any promotion you do of your URL address must be divided into two parts — benefit + address.

The address is easily disposed of: "http://www.<your unique identifier>". Obviously this must be a part of any promotion you do of your home page. This information is vital... but it is not motivating.

Thus, you must make sure that *everything* you use contains both a motivator and an actual address.

The real question is, what kind of motivator should you use?

General vs. Specific Motivators

Broadly speaking, there are only two kinds of motivators that should be used in conjunction with your URL address: general motivators and specific motivators. Here's the difference.

General motivators are timeless. They provide an overall description of the purp
your home page and they are based on very broad themes, such as

- love
- money
- autonomy
- better health
- longer life
- salvation
- social advantage
- excitement
- beauty
- personal improvement, *etc.*

Whether you know it or not, your home page always fits into at least one such general theme.

- If you're selling a business opportunity, you're really selling money and autonomy.
- If you're selling some health product, you're actually selling feeling better and a longer or better life.
- If you're selling a trip to England, you're really selling excitement, education, or social superiority.

Remember, what you're selling is always a feature. What people are buying is always a benefit.

Thus, you've got to be clear about the overall broad theme of your home page... so you can use that to motivate people to visit.

Thus, "Lose weight now. http://www.thinneryou."

Or, "Make $100,000+ a year in a home-based business of your own. http://www.greatjob."

Or, "Travel the world at discount prices. http://www.getaround."

Or, "Clean your colon. Live longer. http://www.longlife."

Several things are going on here in just a few words:

- you're letting your prospects know, with great economy of language, the kind of benefit they get when they visit your home page;
- you're presenting this benefit generally. For example, when they get to "thinneryou", you might well have dozens of different weight loss products/services — not just one.
- you've factored your URL address into the general theme. Most people continue the egotistical self-destructiveness of their marketing by giving themselves a URL address that is highly self-centered. What's the point of that? As I have continually stressed, marketing is always about motivating prospects and getting them to act fastest. If you're interested in traveling, what's more motivational: "http.//www.smithco." or "http.//www.getaround"? "Smithco" does you no good whatsoever; "getaround" reinforces your general theme. And that's all to the good.

The great benefit of general themes is that once you've got your theme right and added it to all your marketing communications and anything that prospects/clients see, it becomes as automatic to use as your phone number or fax. I like that. Remember, marketing is always to a significant extent a numbers game. Your objective is to be clear on

- your home page theme
- who you want to attract
- the benefit these people want
- making sure they know they can get this benefit from you by visiting your home page, and by
- ensuring that this benefit (connected to your URL address) is part of everything leaving your office that a prospect/customer could possibly see.

Do you do this now?

I doubt it!

But you will, dear reader, or your home page traffic *will* suffer... and that would be a pity, no?

Specific Motivators

Most people, given all the things we have to do in our generally maddening and trivia-infested existences, will rest perfectly happy doing what I've just suggested, creating what amounts to a mini-classified ad consisting of prospect-centered benefit + URL address and doing their damnedness to ensure that it becomes a part of everything sent out from the office. While that is not playing the game at the very top, it would, I admit, be a vast improvement from the way the home page promotion game is currently being played in 99% of the offices currently sporting a Web site.

When you want to get slick, however, you'll start using specific motivators. These provide more exactness for the prospect. These kinds of motivators are

- specific
- time limited
- highly motivating
- tied in with specific copy, a specific offer at your home page.

Thus, "Free Hawaii vacation. Visit http://www.getaround by April 1."

Or, "Free weight loss clinic ($75 value) Thursday June 30th. http://www.thinneryou."

Or, "Limited municipal bond offering paying 8% p.a. http://www.yourmoney".

See what's happening? Every single one of these messages is a sub-set of a larger home page theme.

These messages are all specific, time limited, highly motivating (if you're in the targeted prospect group), and must be linked to specific copy on your home page.

Remember, a home page is not and never will be a static place, a place to dump information, and let it get dark and moldy. That will never, never do. A home page is a store. As with traditional stores we're all familiar with, you've got to act the part of the creative, client-centered, motivating P.T. Barnum. It is your job, and must always be your objective, to do everything you possibly can to get people to visit... and to do what you want them to do (including buying what you're selling as fast as possible.)

The truth is, many people in business, many people with home pages, hate this aspect of affairs. Ironically, many people on the Internet are very poor communicators and very bad with people in the flesh. When I say that they must do everything they can to motivate real people to take the fastest action in pursuit of temptingly presented benefits, something in them cringes. In short, lots of people are hiding behind their computers hoping against hope that they won't have to use the motivating activities they have to use in the real world to succeed in cyberspace. Of course, such a sentiment dooms them to failure from the very start.

The sooner you bite the bullet and accept the undeniable fact that success on the Internet entails constant promotion, the better. And constant promotion means constantly upgrading and improving the marketing message and the marketing offers you make on your home page.

Your job, therefore, is to brainstorm as many specific offers as possible… and to promote these offers through your regular marketing activities.

Now let me be very clear with you. I am most assuredly NOT advocating that you go out and place a lot of ads just to promote your Web site. That's daft. What I am suggesting is that you use all appropriate marketing means to increase home page traffic.

I know a woman for instance who does workshops on network marketing nationally. She spends a ton of money on advertising them. But she never derives maximum advantage from this expenditure because she just won't factor the Internet into her marketing mix.

You know, people who attend workshops have predictable questions about them:

- what's the benefit of attending
- what will I learn
- what written hand-outs and materials will I get
- what have others who have taken this workshop said about it
- where is the workshop being given
- how do I get there
- what's the price
- how can I pay (check? credit cards?).

In short, they have lots and lots of perfectly reasonable questions.

Now the big benefit of the Web, as you already know, is that these perfectly legitimate questions can all be answered by posting perfectly detailed answers in a home page — a home page that's always up-to-date and complete.

My daft acquaintance says she understands this… but never takes the appropriate action — the action that will benefit both her and her prospects.

Instead of integrating the Web into her marketing, she merely runs old-fashioned space ads. These ads require every single person to call her office. Then this happens:

- someone has to answer the phone
- someone has to spend time listening to the prospect's query
- someone has to take the appropriate action in response (providing information on the phone… sending an information package)

However you slice it, this is an old-fashioned, backwards way of handling a business on the cusp of the 21st century.

Indeed I'll go farther: it's a downright infuriating way of handling business because

- the seminar provider (being often on the road) isn't available to answer questions;
- staff people aren't always well-briefed (the sins of inadequate and unprepared office help are legion);
- in a busy office (like that of someone doing a national workshop tour) it isn't always possible to devote enough time to prospects, to make each and every one of them feel you "care", that you're client-centered;
- it takes time and money to fax and mail responses and necessary materials.

Who's kidding whom here? If this is the "system" you use, it's severely flawed.

Yet this woman brags in her ads that the system she's offering in her workshops is "cutting edge"… the very quintessence of success. Egad! The very way she does business herself belies her self-praising promotion. What credence should we have in a person who claims that she's "cutting edge" in her business ideas when the very way she runs her business is so antique?

Of course, she should have a home page on the Web. Equally, she should be promoting it like this: "Complete workshop details all cities. http://www.MLMsuccess." Or, "Get complete Baltimore workshop details, ditto."

Now she's positioned to make everyone's life easier — hers, her office staff's, and, yes, those all-important prospects! Every ad she runs enables interested people to go directly to a place where they can get relevant detail on relevant detail, a place which is always client-centered and never out of date! And if they still need more information, or require personal attention, they can call her office, just as they do now.

A Look At Specific Promotional Formats

Before concluding this chapter, I'm going to romp through some specific promotional formats that will help you increase the traffic of your home page. I'm not going to deal with every single means available; what I say for one, you'll understand, can be used in many ways. Be creative! Remember, the objective is to bring maximum traffic to your home page, provide these people with what they need to know to become better, faster customers, and, simultaneously, to cut your own work load so you can spin another promotional, profit-making plate in the air.

— Business Stationery

Do you have a home page? Do you have business stationery? Is your URL address listed on your business stationery? Is there a benefit listed for visiting it?

If you've answered "No" four times, you should have been born in Neolithic times. You're a caveperson (see how strange that sounds), baby.

Of course, the correct sequence of answers is

Yes!

Yes!!

Yes!!!

Yes!!!!

A piece of letterhead (and, by extension, business envelopes… shipping labels… business cards, *etc.*) is not merely what it seems to be. It is a mini-billboard designed to carry your client-centered message to people you want to motivate and profit from.

How many pieces of stationery do you use in a year? Just a thousand? Or, like me, tens of thousands of pieces? However you slice it, when that item goes out without a focused client-centered classified ad and URL number, you're wasting some fraction of your money. That's just plain stupid.

If you use printed stationery, your message needs to be timeless. It should focus on the biggest potential benefit your home page offers. If you use specific benefits, you're in the business of constantly changing them whenever you go back to reprint. That's a hassle.

Instead, keep to the big, cosmic themes, like "Today's highest yielding investments. http://www.bigreturn."

Or, "Free health improvement information." Or, "Make $100,000+ every year with your own home-based business."

Get it?

Touch the prospect's nerve. Get her interested. Make her say, "I want that. So I'll do what's necessary to get it."

Just providing a URL address, necessary though that is in the entire equation, won't ever achieve prospect motivation. If you don't believe me, try walking into a room someday, looking a prospect in the eye, and giving that number! The prospect is going to look at you oddly, at best. But when you start talking about benefits, the prospect will say, "I want that. How do I get it?" That's when your URL address comes into its own.

Note: I haven't used printed stationery for years. I print all my letters from my computer onto regular laser printer paper. This is smart and enables me to change my benefit message minute by minute, if I like. If you do this, make your messages as specific as possible.

— any items used as advertising specialties (including pens, calendars, t-shirts, *etc.*)

For reasons unknown, business people persist in thinking that advertising specialties are sensible, that spending money on plastic cups with their logo is an intelligent way to spend money. I don't agree, but that, as they say, is another subject. If you're one of those critters who likes emptying your pockets on

- t-shirts with logos (yes, I know I said I have my own, but just as nifty — and cheap — presents)
- imprinted umbrellas and
- disposable pens with your company name and phone number (to say nothing of the thousands of other things that supposedly bright business people spend their money on to "promote" their business) then listen up!

In future, make sure all these items include your URL address + motivating benefit not just a cute four-color logo or address and phone number. That's just not marketing!

— space ads

Check out your daily newspaper... publications you receive... card decks you get in the mail. More and more you're seeing smart advertisers include a URL address. Unfortunately, they ordinarily *only* include a URL address — not a benefit for responding to that URL. That's like trying to ride half a horse.

Now look at the space ads you're running. Have you even got a URL in them? If not, you're not using your noodle, and you're certainly not deriving full benefit from all the money you spend on your ads.

Ads are designed either to generate the most qualified prospect or to sell directly. Either way your URL — and the benefit for visiting your Web site — should be included.

— if you're eliciting a qualified prospect

Want a qualified prospect? In this case, stuff your ad with prospect-centered benefits. Tell prospects all they can get simply by responding to this ad:

Benefit #1

Benefit #2

Benefit #3

Then tell them what to do

• Call now!

• Fax now!

• e-mail now!

• Mail in coupon now!

AND

• get even more prospect-centered information, including product/service specifications, answers to frequently asked questions, and order coupon by visiting http://www.homepage.

In other words, you've got to do *everything* you can to move prospects to the next step, the purchase step. By directing them to your home page — where you've got more useful information — you assist in this process.

— if you're selling direct

All too often people will put off to tomorrow the purchase decision you want them to make today. Don't allow your Web home page to assist them in this debilitating procrastination ... which is so bad for your pocketbook.

In this case, you can do one of two things:

• Tell the prospect about other, related benefits you have available in your home page. Thus, "To get free information about how to build your home-based business with all the money-making resources we've got, see http://www.moneybooks." Here what you're doing is building the sale. Your ad snags the attention of people who are, in this case, running a home-based business and want to make theirs more profitable. Once snagged by Product 1 which you're trying to sell them NOW... you let them know that there's even more good stuff available just a few keystrokes away. Thus, you use the ad to close... and simultaneously use the ad to build faster additional sales. Smart.

- Let the prospect know that if he has questions, your home page can help. Thus, "To get more information on this and our complete line of money-making books for the home-based business, see http://www.moneybooks." You'll notice that even here the emphasis is on "our complete line of money-making books", not just getting additional information. You see, at all times you should be attempting to build the largest possible sale... not just providing "more information." Lots of people on the Web make the classic error of disseminating "information." Instead, you should be pounding home all the valuable BENEFITS you have. Remember, benefits sell. Leave information dissemination to public libraries.

A Special Note On Business Card Decks

I run America's single largest card-deck, the Sales & Marketing Success Deck. It's been a success for any number of reasons:

- lowest prices in the industry. When I set up this deck years ago, I purposefully set the prices low to confound the competition. It's worked.
- free second-color. Other decks charge you for a second color. I never have. It's part of the basic price.
- four-color process printing at cost. If you want four-color with your card, I charge you what I'm charged. Unsurprisingly, a lot of people think this is a real good deal. Result? More four-color cards in my deck than in any other.
- card-deck responsive names. Good names are at the heart of success in the card-deck business. Without them, you're doomed. My sources have provided me for many years with the most responsive names possible, people who have responded to card deck offers in the last 90 days. That's what you want!
- always on-time mailing. Other decks often delay their mailings until they've got a certain number of cards. I push hard to make sure my quota is filled early so I can mail on time.

All this is good. But now what's better is that I've linked my deck to the many malls at worldprofit.com to increase advertiser benefits.

Up until I created my malls, you could really only use card-decks to generate leads; selling direct from cards generally doesn't work well. Card decks are for generating qualified leads, and lots of them. Once you got the lead you had to spend your time/money qualifying it to make sure that any investment in this person made sense.

Add a Web home page to the mix and the game changes significantly.

Now you can use your card to really stress the benefits of what you're selling and, while of course providing more traditional means of response (phone, fax, mail-in address and now e-mail, *etc.*), you can also direct prospects to your home page. There you should include

- a motivating offer that gets prospects to buy NOW
- complete benefits of what you're selling

- client-centered testimonials. The words of people who have used what you're selling successfully.... and are happy to inform the world that they're better off as a result.
- answers to frequently asked questions, and
- an order form so that your prospect can buy NOW!

In other words, you use the card and its client-centered message to stress (in the most emphatic way possible) all the benefits of what you've got... and you use your home page to finalize the deal.

Note: once you've started advertising this way, don't stop! There are those who use a start-stop approach to card decks. They run in one issue... then disappear for months... only to reappear to start the process again. This is madness. Smart card-deck advertisers work to refine their deck advertising procedures so that their supply of prospect leads never stops... while simultaneously working hard to ensure that their home pages are always prospect-centered and designed to provide all the information any prospect needs... while motivating them to ACT NOW!

— company newsletters and other publications

Company newsletters and other publications try to cram as much information as possible in the space available. An admirable objective, but not always a smart one.

Remember, when you're in business, you've got just two objectives: increasing sales and decreasing expenses. Net result: more profit all around. Everything you do must do one or the other of these things. Everything. Including any newsletters or publications you produce.

The people who run such publications often have a Walter Mitty fantasy that they should be running *The New York Times*. Nice for daydreaming, but lousy for identifying new prospects and closing them as fast as possible.

Say you're selling remodeled kitchens and baths and produce a quarterly four-page newsletter for your business. You should be clear that the purpose of this newsletter is *not* to produce this newsletter; it's to identify new prospects, get them all hot and bothered about the fabulous kitchens and baths you can produce for the money, and get them to take action now to connect with you and get started.

Thus, all articles should be geared to specific questions people have... and using the answers to these questions to motivate prospects to act. For instance, an article on "how to save 25% on new kitchen appliances," should be concluded with a Resource Box saying, "Contact us now to get information on how to save up to 25% on all new kitchen appliances and see the appliances now available. Contact Bob at <your company, your phone.> Also check out the dozens of detailed listings with specific recommendations on which products it makes sense to buy now by visiting http://www.betterhouse."

Of course, you want the prospect to call you. But do you *really* have time to go through every single oven type with every single prospect who calls to inquire? Doesn't it make more sense to let prospects know as much as you can about saving money on ovens in a newsletter article... and then direct them to a more complete listing in your home page?

Thus, start with a section on your high-end appliances. Obviously, you want to sell these first. Provide client-centered detail about why these appliances are so good and the benefits the customer derives from them. Face it. You know as well as I do that in "real life" you cannot spend the kind of time with every customer that enables you to provide this kind of detailed customer-centered information. All too often we take short-cuts, short-changing prospects on the kinds and amount of information we provide them… and therefore not using all this information to motivate a faster sale. This is crazy all around!

On the Web things are different. You can provide all the client-centered information about every single product that customers need… whether they're purchasing low-, middle- or high-end merchandise. Moreover, you can keep stressing — as you must also stress when you connect with them personally or on the phone — why it makes sense for them to purchase better quality merchandise.

Thus, the prospect-centered sequence goes something like this:

- in your newsletter, publish an article on a subject of real interest to your prospects. "How-to" articles are excellent. "How you can save $35 every week on your grocery bill." "How to fly from New York to London and back for just $200." "How to build a client-centered home page for under $100." Get the idea? Articles should be client-centered, specific and packed with useful information.

- End each article with a "Resource Box," a block of text that invites the prospect to take action now, first, to acquire the benefit discussed in the article; second, to get even more information on what you've been discussing by accessing your home page.

- Just as you get the prospect's name, address and phone number when he calls you, make sure that you include a means in your home page so prospects can leave you the same information after they've visited your site for further details. These are very good prospects and should be followed up immediately.

— Catalogs

We're all familiar with catalogs… at least the old style catalogs where advertisers present merchandise which we either buy or do not buy. In the Age of Internet catalogs can — and should — be different.

Remember, when you've got a home page you've got a store, and when you're sending a catalog from a store you should be presenting things a bit differently.

Of course you want to sell directly, immediately, and as much as possible from the catalog. That's only sensible. Thus, you must continue to

- make offers stimulating immediate action
- present benefits making it clear what the prospect gets from the product/service you're promoting.

That'll never change.

However, the high cost of paper and postage (two variables which hang like the sword of Damocles over all of us in the catalog business) presents us with difficult choices.

- We can keep the amount of merchandise the same… just cut the amount of presentation space for each, or
- we can keep the presentations the same… and expand the catalog, eating greater paper and postage costs.

Which is it to be?

Well, instead of dancing on the edge of this knife (which is sure to cut one way or another), do this:

- Provide all the information the prospect needs to make a purchase decision for as many items — particularly higher priced items — as you can. In other words, focus on what will bring in the most money.
- Make it clear in your catalog that the catalog only constitutes the advance brigade of your stronger army, that the prospects need to be aware of your home page and visit for more products, more services, more information altogether. When you've got a home page on the Web, higher paper and postage prices will not force you to cut merchandise; because of the far lower costs of advertising on the Web, you can actually add new items!
- Develop a system whereby prospects know which products/services are further presented in your home page. Just a ** will do. ** means, "Get to our home page ASAP for lots more useful information about this item." Then make sure that you give it to them!

In short, your catalog is simultaneously a tool enabling you to sell direct and a hook gathering in prospects who either a) need more information about selected products/services or b) want to review other, related products/services. In this role, the catalog is your client-centered carnival barker!

Note: fax-on-demand works well here, too. When you use fax-on-demand technology as part of your Web site, when you send your catalog you can let people know that by accessing your fax-on-demand number they can get more detailed information about a number of items of particular interest to them. To use this tool, you simply include a box in your catalog saying, in effect, "For more information about these items (give a few details), call 24-hour fax on demand (403) 425-6049, get document #68." The people who are interested will get this more detailed information. You've expanded your catalog at minimal cost and enabled yourself to get information into the hands of just the people who want it — on their dime! Smart, huh?

Last Words

One way and another, every business spends a ton of money on promoting itself. For many, marketing costs are right under personnel costs as the most significant business expenditures. Unfortunately, much of what's spent is pointless, failing to bring in sufficient prospects and customers to pay for itself. That's why you've got to adopt a different, cannier means of promoting your home page. You'have noticed, for instance, that I have not advocated running ads that promote your home page alone. And I won't. That's like taking an ad to promote an ad. Where will that kind of marketing madness end?

No, things must be done differently.

- You must remember that position is promotion… that where you decide to put your home page will go far towards determining your volume of traffic. If you place your home page in isolation or put it into a mall with minimum traffic, you're effectively sabotaging your stay on the Web and any results you expect to get.
- Having made the right decision on where to place your home page, make sure that you don't just promote the fact that you have a URL address. Lead with the major client-centered benefit of visiting your home page, follow with URL. Thus, benefit + URL = increased traffic.
- review all the means you're using in your office to generate prospects and connect with customers. There may well be dozens. Every single one of them must be integrated into your promotional efforts.

Every envelope you mail… every space ad you run… every brochure you distribute… every article you publish… every handout you pass out at a workshop… must feature both benefit and URL address. And they must do so day in, day out.

If you've got a home page, do you do this now? I doubt it. It's easy to get a home page on the Web; it's easier to get bored promoting it. See for yourself. If you've already got a home page, what percentage of the items you use to connect with prospects and clients actually help promote your home page? Yet, every time you market without stressing the *benefit* of visiting your home page + its URL address, you're wasting a percentage of your marketing budget and damaging your home page traffic and the results you could reasonably expect from that page. Stupid.

Fortunately, you're not going to make that mistake now, *are you*? You're going to approach the business of promoting your home page — both inside and outside the Web — with the kind of focused deliberateness, passion and intensity it deserves. Why? BECAUSE YOU WANT MAXIMUM TRAFFIC ALL THE TIME!!!

Now you know just what it takes to get it!!!

Chapter 6

WHY YOU NEED TO ADD FAX-ON-DEMAND (FOD) CAPABILITY TO YOUR HOME PAGE

Is this familiar?

You're working away on a deadline... something important that's got to be done TO-DAY. The phone rings and an insistent prospect (is there any other kind?) says, "I want your information and I want it NOW!"

The last mail pick up of the day leaves in 15 minutes, so you've got to drop everything to

- take down all the prospect's follow-up information
- print your personalized sales letter
- assemble your sales package, then
- rush out to meet the postman before he gets away!

Does this sound familiar?

In tens of thousands of offices around the world, this is how business gets done. But think of the price!

- you lose your train of thought
- get frustrated and irritated (while trying to stay prospect-centered, mind)
- build up a good head of stress, and
- come home to spend another jolly night with the family, who are all advised by your Significant Other to tread warily for fear of the consequences.

Isn't this just about the size of it?

Well, now when you get a home page in the right mall, you can go far towards solving this problem. If you get a fax-on-demand (FOD).

What Is FOD Anyway?

Most business people (but, to my astonishment, by no means all) are familiar with the traditional fax. In this scenario, if you want to transmit a letter or other fairly standard-sized communication to someone fast, you ask if they've got a fax machine, get their fax number and transmit the document. If their machine's not broken... or if they've got a free line (lots of people still don't have a dedicated line)... or if they're not out of fax paper (another frequent irritant), they get your communication at once. And because it's come by fax, they are much more likely to read it right away.

Fax-on-demand extends this process. In this scenario, your objective is to discover whether callers seeking information about you, your company, your products, services, special offers, *etc.* has a fax. If they do, they can access the information you want them to have on their fax machine — and, let it be emphasized on *their* phone bill — and get it immediately. All they do is dial your FOD number and, once connected, punch in a document number on their telephone key pad. Thus, "To be information on our church organ repair service, touch 3." The information the prospect wants is faxed back to him immediately.

Now reconsider the scene that opened this chapter. You're working away on a deadline. You've got something INCREDIBLY IMPORTANT to do. The phone is also ringing off the hook because your latest client-centered ad's just hit; (I mean, you do use the tips in my book **Cash Copy**, right?) Now when a prospect calls, you say

- "May I have your name, address, phone and fax number?" (You need this information, of course, so you can add this prospect to your mailing list and engage in more traditional follow-up later, when it's more convenient for you.)
- When the prospect provides her fax, you say, "Great! You can get the information you want on how to repair your church organ by dialing this 24-hour fax-on-demand number, <number>. When the machine picks up, follow the directions. You'll touch #3 on the number pad for Document #3. You'll get the information immediately."

Now, you've got what you need to follow up... and the prospect has what she needs to get immediate service. You can go on with your important work, saving yourself some time and stress. And the prospect can get the information she needs when she wants it. Which may be now... or may be at midnight. (Unsurprisingly, people who have become familiar with fax-on-demand technology often make their information-seeking calls at times when phone rates are lower. Smart.)

Does this sound great, or what?

There is hardly a business in the world that wouldn't be improved by having fax-on-demand capability... which is why you need to look upon it as an essential feature of your successful home page.

Making Sure Your Mall Has Fax-On-Demand Capability... Making Sure You Don't Overpay For It

Since a home-page must have FOD capability, you'd better be sure any mall you're assessing can provide it. Astonishingly, there are actually malls on the Internet that cannot give you FOD. That's just plain dumb. Thus, make sure to inquire of any mall owner/manager, "Do you have fax-on-demand capability?" And, importantly, "What does it cost?"

As I write, you should be able to get FOD capability for about 25-35 CENTS per day! Many malls predictably sock you for a great deal more. But now you know to scoff at such information highway robbery.

What You Should Put In Your Fax-On-Demand Communication

Once you're sure your mall has FOD and that its price is fair, it's time to consider just what you should put in your document. Most FOD marketing communications range between 1-3 pages.

Before writing the transmission document, you've got to answer one important question: "Do I want the prospect receiving this to call me back to order my product/service... or do I want the prospect receiving this to complete an order coupon that is part of this transmission and either fax or mail it back to me already completed?

In other words, are you trying to upgrade the quality of your prospect... or are you trying to make an immediate sale? That, it seems to me, is largely a function of price.

In the example above, I used a consulting/technical service provided by a craftsman who contracts with churches nationwide to rehabilitate their organs. Given that this man is based in Massachusetts and that his clients are virtually anywhere, also given that the typical assignment may well involve several days on site, not just reviewing the situation but making often intricate repairs to the instrument, this service demands a fairly considerable investment on the part of the church.

In a case like this, it takes time for the organization to make a decision. Many people have to be consulted. Comparative shopping may take place, *etc.* Thus, it's extremely unlikely that anyone receiving this information is going to say after a brief reading of a fax-on-demand document, "We're ready to sign on the dotted line." Extremely unlikely.

That's why a document for a business in this situation needs to be different from one that sells a $99 instructional course on how to get a college scholarship. In the first instance, much discussion and client tailoring need to occur. In the second, it's quite possible — and entirely desirable — to present all the information the prospect needs so he can make a prompt purchase decision and return order form and payment as soon as possible.

Let's look more closely at both kinds of fax-on-demand communications.

— Where You Want To Inform Your Prospects And Further Qualify Them

Remember, the ultimate objective of a fax-on-demand is to assist in getting you a faster sale. You must never forget that. The objective is never just to transmit information. You are not, after all, in the "information business." Instead, you're a church organ consultant... or a seller of instructional videos... or an auction house wanting to build a larger client base... or someone who sells discount cruises on short notice. The objective for all these people — and the millions of other business people for whom FOD is appropriate — is the same: faster, more efficient sales.

If you need to upgrade your prospects, here's what your FOD document should include:

Page 1

Lead with your best possible offer. What is the single best thing you've got to motivate faster decision making from the prospect?

"Call within 3 days and receive — absolutely free — your choice of either of these 10-page Special Reports. Select from either '10 Things You Can Do To Save Thousands of

Dollars On Your Next Organ Purchase,' or 'How To Renovate Your Church Organ For A Fraction Of What A New Organ Costs'."

Remember, you provide an offer to motivate faster response. Make sure that your offer is motivating and that the prospect gets something of real value by responding!

Start the main body of text by showing that you are empathetic with the prospect's situation and that you can help.

"We're pleased to provide you with this information on our church organ rehabilitation service. You're probably getting it either because your organ isn't working as well as it used to... because its external or internal condition has deteriorated and you're concerned that further deterioration may result in your instrument losing all value... and/or because you want to see whether the instrument you've got can be repaired so that your church won't have to lay out the substantial sum necessary to purchase an new organ.

I'm pleased to say, we can help you."

Right away, you've indicated that you are familiar with what brings the prospect to your door. You've opened with a clear understanding of why the prospect has come to you... and you've indicated that you can help. In other words, you've been prospect-centered!

Now, let the prospect know something about the services you provide and how long you've provided them.

"For 8 years now, we've been helping churches just like yours to have an organ they can be proud of. We do this in many ways, including

- helping churches select an organ
- getting them the best possible price
- advising them on fund-raising strategies to help pay for the organ
- making condition reports on your existing organ
- making suggestions on what needs to be done to improve performance for reasonable price
- undertaking to do the necessary restorations and repairs, and (where possible)
- finding local craftsmen to assist in the restoration process.

We'd like to help you, too.

Note: Sprinkle this presentation with testimonials. My rule of thumb is that you should have two prospect-centered testimonials per page of text. Thus,

> "Our church organ was gradually deteriorating in both appearance and sound. We were alarmed because we both needed a proper organ and feared it would be difficult to raise the cost of a new one with so many other church expenses needing attention. ABC Organ Consultation knew just what to do. They reviewed the situation, came up with a feasible and reasonably priced restoration plan and did the work expertly. We are certainly glad to recommend them to other churches which want to renew their organ!"
>
> P.J. Jenkins, Pastor, First Baptist Church, Little Rock, AR

Page 2

On page 2 provide a list of frequently asked questions and their answers. Here's your opportunity to inform the prospect about crucial things he needs to know about what you do and how you work, things like

- How long have you been in business?
- What professional qualifications do you have?
- Are references available?
- How do you determine what work needs to be done?
- How long does the work take?
- How much does the work cost?
- What kinds of credit and financing terms are available?

All these questions are designed to let the prospect know you know what you're doing and you understand the kinds of information he needs. In writing this page of questions and answers, you need to think like a prospect. That is, put yourself in the prospect's place and brainstorm the kinds of questions he'll have about what you do... and what information he needs to make the best possible decision.

End this series of questions and answers with this very important query:

- What do we need to do first?

Your answer will go something like this: To get started, complete the questionnaire on page 3 telling us as much as you can about what you want, your budget, time-table, *etc.* Don't forget to let us know which free special report you want, too.

Page 3

Here it's the prospect's turn to show you just how good a prospect he is. These are the kinds of things you need to know:

- prospect name
- prospect title
- organization name
- address
- telephone (make sure to request area code; you can't imagine how many people don't provide it!)
- fax
- e-mail
- brand of current organ
- age of current organ
- when last rehabilitated
- who rehabilitated by
- brief description of problem (please feel free to provide as long a description as you think helpful to our understanding)

- brief description of objective (if you can do this in the form of prospect choices, do. Thus, *please check all that apply*:
- I/we am/are interested in:
  - ❏ rehabilitating our existing organ   ❏ getting a new organ   ❏ fund raising assistance.
- when you'd like to get started. (Again, provide options.)
  - ❏ ASAP   ❏ 1 month   ❏ 3 months   ❏ six months   ❏ not sure.
- budget   ❏ under $5,000   ❏ $5,000-$10,000   ❏ $10,000+
- Which free 10-page special report you'd like
  - ❏ "10 Things You Can Do To Save Thousands of Dollars On Your Next Organ Purchase"
  - ❏ "How To Renovate Your Church Organ For A Fraction Of What A New Organ Costs."

Now provide details on how they can get this information to you:
- fax this page to <number>
- e-mail this page to <number>
- mail this page to <name, address>

Want to speak to someone faster? Call <name, phone number>.

Also, for further details on how to rehabilitate your existing organ or purchase a new organ for the best possible price, see http://www.organs.

Note: don't hesitate to include a good prospect-centered testimonial on the top of page 3. Remember, at all times the objective is to let the prospect know just how good you are (without having to say so yourself) and to foster the motivational process that gets the prospect to contact you as fast as possible with all the useful information you need.

A Few Words About Prospect Assessment

There are good prospects, mediocre prospects, and people who say they're prospects but are clearly delusional. It's your job to see which animal you're dealing with.

Let me be very direct with you. You're not in the business of sending out free reports and information packets. You're in the business of selling as many of your products/services as promptly as you can. That means learning how to qualify prospects, spending time only with those who deserve it.

People who provide detail are people who want a solution to their problem. Thus, look for specifics. Has the person provided what you need to evaluate her situation? Or does she do things like fail to provide a means of contacting you? Is what he provides legible, or like an insistent fax I received today from Botswana so messy that there's just no way I can possibly read it? In other words, has this person acted like a good, responsible prospect (which means doing his part to expedite his business)... or is he just demanding attention without being very helpful in return?

I feel very strongly about this kind of situation and will share a few thoughts on what you should do. You are under no obligation to respond to every prospect information form or request that comes in. In other words, just because someone has dashed off an incomplete response and insisted on your sending your free report doesn't mean you have to send it. Your job is to do what's necessary to help responsible people tell you they're responsible... and to give you evidence that they're responsible. You need only help those who are willing to help you. The circular file was invented for the rest!

— When You Want To Sell Direct

If the job of the first fax-on-demand document package is to generate the best qualified prospect, the job of this one is to sell as quickly as possible. This may or may not take three pages. Remember, if you can comfortably handle your sales presentation in less space, do so. Getting the sale's the objective, providing a certain length sales presentation is not.

Thus,

Page 1

Again, open with your best prospect-centered offer. What will you do to stimulate fastest possible action?

> *Order within 72 hours and receive — absolutely free —*
> *our exclusive 55 minute audio cassette on 'How to double your*
> *sales in the next 365 days!' ($15 value!)*

Open with gain. Or open with pain.

That is, start off by painting in the brightest possible colors the gain that your product can deliver. Or the pain that the prospect is in, the pain that he can get rid of with the assistance of what you're selling.

Don't be afraid to lay it on thick in either instance. And be sure to speak directly to the prospect. "Prospect, here's what you want." Or, "Prospect, here's the pain you're in (or could be in, if you fail to take prompt action)."

Be direct with the prospect. Say, "If you really want those benefits, we can help." Or "Of course, you want to avoid that pain, or get rid of that pain. We can help!"

Then hit the prospect with the benefits of what you're selling, always leading with the most important, then the next most important, *etc.* Your job is to stack benefits on top of each other, the most important always preceding the less important.

Reinforce the benefits with prospect-centered testimonials. If you've said that one of your benefits is speed, provide a testimonial emphasizing how fast your product does its work. If one of your product's benefits is its price, again underscore that price benefit with a satisfied customer quote on price. In short, don't just provide benefits in your fax-on-demand; reinforce them with prospect-centered testimonials!

Page 2

Your prospect-centered presentation may well take two pages. No problem. Just make sure that your strongly motivational argument doesn't wane just because you've gone onto a second page.

On page 2 you may also include a list of the features of what you're selling, including

- size
- weight
- color
- length
- anything that gives the prospect an exact sense of what he's receiving from you. The more you can put what you're selling in the prospect's mind, making him see it, hear it, feel it, taste it, even smell it, the better off you are. Remember, the prospect must "own" the product in his mind before he acts to get it in fact.

Make sure to end with a post script. Everyone in the mail order business knows the importance of a good prospect-centered post script. It's your last opportunity to motivate the not-yet-persuaded prospect. In your post script hit the major benefit of what you're selling… and emphasize the value of your offer. Remind prospects they can get both benefit and offer just by taking immediate action. Advise them to complete your order form on page 3.

Page 3

Here's where you ask the prospects for commitment. Make sure that you get them to commit to the benefit you're providing, not just spending money on a product. Remember, nobody likes to spend money. Everybody likes to get benefits… and we've come to know, through long experience, that the only way to get the benefit is to spend the money. You need to make this as easy on the prospects as possible; get them to commit to the benefit they want, and the money will follow. Thus,

❑ Yes, I want to get <benefit you're offering.> Send me ASAP <product>. Send it to
- prospect name
- title
- organization name
- street address (for UPS shipping)
- city, state, zipcode

If sending outside Continental U.S.A. indicate
    ❑ surface   ❑ air shipping
Check made payable to <your company>
Credit cards accepted (list)
Credit card number/expiration date
signature for credit card orders
Where to
- fax order
- phone order
- e-mail order
- mail order

Also inform the customer how quickly orders are shipped/when customer can expect to receive.

Note: if you sell related products to the one you're promoting on this particular fax-on-demand, don't hesitate to add them to your order form. Also, do not hesitate to make a package offer that upgrades the sale. In other words, "buy A and B for lower price than you can get A and B for individually."

Remember, the objective of this fax-on-demand is NOT to disseminate information; it's to build the greatest sale possible.

How Often Should You Change Your FOD message?

The quick answer is, as often as it takes to keep it up-to-date and client-centered. But let's see if we can do better than that.

To begin with, try to develop your FOD message so that it's simultaneously client-centered, focused on the major items you're selling, and timeless. Take my example of the church organ consultant mentioned above.

He has two major aspects to his business, rehabilitating church organs and advising churches on how to acquire new organs that suit their needs at prices they can afford. These elements are not going to change.

His offer involves providing one of two special reports that he's developed, one for each of his major services. Note that the special reports (which should be available on computer and be personalized with the prospect's name when printed) can be updated. Thus, this savvy marketer has created a timeless, prospect-centered FOD with motivating offer. This is smart.

You see, you don't always want to be fiddling around with your FOD, making changes. Changes cost money, although at Worldprofit we only charge about $25 to update your materials.

To achieve what you want:

- review your FOD to make sure that there's nothing in it that will be outmoded within the next 90 days. If you're selling things whose pricing you do not control, check with the distributor to get price quotes that are good for at least the next three months.

- whenever possible create offers that last a while. Thus, "This special offer is good for the first 250 people who respond," or "Act now and get your free copy of our handy 16-page booklet 'How to save thousands of dollars on this year's property taxes' ($10 value)."

- keep the items needing changes to a single page of your FOD (like your order form). It's cheaper to change a single page than two or three pages.

How Many FODs Do You Need?

As your business grows and you're offering more products and services you'll find, as I have, that one FOD just isn't going to meet your needs. Here are some growth steps:

- start by seeing if a single FOD makes sense. It will if all your services are thematically linked and can be promoted within the confines of a single three-page document or if you can provide sufficient detail about your products so that customers have what they need to make an immediate purchase decision.

- before making your FOD available to prospects, read it over as a prospect. Are you providing all the information a reasonable prospect needs either to a) identify himself as a qualified prospect or b) purchase what you're selling? Or do you have the uneasy feeling that because of space limitations you're leaving out vital information that the prospect really needs? As soon as that queasiness sets in, you definitely need another FOD.

- if you're promoting a variety of different, unconnected products and services, you're going to need multiple FODs right away. For instance, our Mall Reseller Program could not comfortably be marketed along with information on participating in my quarterly Sales & Marketing Success Card Deck. Both are, however, high ticket items where prospects have many questions. Deduction? Each one needs its own FOD. (Do, however, cross-reference your FODs. At the bottom of each FOD document, say "Here are other helpful products/services you can access through our fax-on-demand system. Then write what amounts to a classified ad on each, ending with the phone and individual document number. In other words, use each FOD document to market all the others.)

Helpful Hint: One good way to determine how many FODs you need is to look at the way you or your reps spend their telephone time. Look at what prospects are calling in to request assistance with. During the course of my day, for example, these are just some of the things people are likely to call about:

- How do I get a home page on one of your Malls?
- I don't know anything about card decks. Can you give me some information?
- I'm looking for a lucrative business opportunity? Have you got any information that will help me?
- I need copywriting assistance for my marketing communications. How do you assist in providing them?
- I've heard about your Worldprofit Dealer program. Can you get me the details?

Get the drift? Lots of questions on lots of different kinds of things.

In the dear old days of yore (now thankfully as dead as a doornail), I had to

- take down all the prospect's information, including name, address, phone, fax, *etc.*
- spend my money not only developing but printing information packages
- spend time putting all the necessary prospect packages together
- spend more money mailing them out
- wait until the good old U.S. Post Office got around to delivering the prospect packages (or pay more so other carriers could do the work the Post Office couldn't efficiently take care of), then
- call the prospect, too often to be told "I haven't gotten around to reading that yet. Call back later."

Not a pretty picture!

Now I do things differently. I figure out just what FODs I'm going to need and assign each of them unique item numbers. Thus, (403) 425-6049 Document #1 is always about how to get a Web site in my malls; document #6 is always about how to hire me as a consultant and get cash copy and netvertising consulting assistance; document #5 is always about how to become a Mall Reseller; document #7 is always about becoming a Worldprofit dealer *etc.*

Thus, when a prospect calls nowadays and says, "I don't know much about card-decks. What is a card-deck? How do they work?," I ask for his name, address, phone and (crucial detail) fax. As soon as I know he's got a fax machine, I say, "you can dial (403) 425-6049, select document #3 on your fax machine and the information you want will be faxed back to you immediately." I then add his name to my prospect list and follow up later, when I have the time. He's gotten the information immediately, at his expense, and I can process many more people, much more efficiently. What's more, I know that if this prospect can't be bothered to get the FOD information, he's not a very good prospect at all, and I can downgrade his significance and treat him accordingly. In other words, whether a prospect will get the FOD or not is a good qualifying device.

Now, think how this could be done at your company. Think of all the time you're handling telephone calls or about how your switchboard handles information calls.

Try calling your company some day and asking for information about one of your products and services. You'll be astonished at just how ineptly these calls are generally handled. The fact is, in our sophisticated "Information Age" the vital flow of information from your company is very often stymied by the very people you're paying to efficiently handle your affairs.

> Prospect: "Can I get information on this service?"
>
> Secretary: "Maryann is out to lunch. I don't know when she'll be back."
>
> Prospect: "Could you send me information on Product A?"
>
> Secretary: "I'm kinda new around here. I don't know how to do that. Mr. Jones is out right now. I'll see what I can do."
>
> Prospect: "I'm really interested in your Service B. Can you get me information about it right away?"
>
> Secretary: "It's not my department. I don't think you can get the information for at least a couple of weeks. I'm sorry I can't help you. Have a nice day."

Multiply these by hundreds of thousands of similarly grotesque instances every single day, and you see why I'm so keen on FOD.

> Prospect: "Can I get information on this service?"
>
> Secretary: "May I take your name, address, phone and fax number?" If there is no fax number, the secretary knows, because of the specific instructions you've provided, just what to do, who to give this message to. However, if the prospect provides a fax number, the secretary is equally prepared.
>
> "You can get the information you need by dialing this 24-hour fax on demand number, (403) 425-6049. When the telephone picks up, listen to the message and touch number 14 on the number pad. The information will be faxed back to you immediately!"

By the way, don't expect secretaries or other helpers to remember this wording. Write it down for them and post it where they can clearly see it. Just the other day I did a television program where the host's remarks were scripted right down to her name. If major studios don't expect their on-air people to remember even their own names, I think it a very good idea to write down precisely what you want secretaries to say so that prospects get the FOD information they need for immediate *action*.

Promoting FOD Availability

Amazingly people with FODs don't promote them. Instead, they wait until people call them and then, one by one, provide the information, as in my illustration above. There's nothing wrong, of course, with providing this information to people this way — so long as it's only one of the ways you use to let people know you've got FODs that'll help them.

Just yesterday a fellow who runs in my card deck called me to discuss his camera-ready art work for the next issue. During the course of the conversation I pointedly reminded him to use his FOD number on the card. Amazingly, he told me that he wasn't going to use his FOD number on the card because he "didn't have the space." 100,000 people were going to be sent his message, but he couldn't find, what, a line or two to promote the availability of his FOD and the benefit to the prospect of calling it? I thought, "It's your funeral" and (uncharacteristically) held my peace. As a result, this marketing genius lost the opportunity to have up to 100,000 prospects nationwide download his information at their expense!

Do you have an FOD? Do you have office stationery? Brochures? Ads? Cover letters? Reports? Do you publish articles? Give workshops and talk programs where you disseminate hand-outs and other information? Is your FOD listed on any of these? Bingo!

As with your URL, so with your FOD. You've got to offer benefit + FOD number. It's not enough to just say, "24-hour fax on demand number." You've got to say, "Get complete details on how to rehabilitate your existing church organ. Call 24 hour fax on demand <phone & document numbers>."

See the difference?

People need to know what they're going to get when they make the call. They want to be assured that the price of the call is a good investment compared to what they'll get when they make it. Thus, saying "Here's my FOD number," isn't nearly good enough. An FOD number is a *feature*... and features don't motivate, don't persuade, don't sell. Benefits do.

Again, as with your URL, you want to promote your FOD in such a way that you're not constantly changing your stationery... unless, like me, you print your stationery from your computer so that it could literally be changed with every letter you ever send. (I haven't had printed stationery now for well over 10 years, maybe more; I like the freedom that comes from being able to continually change my messages, letter by letter if necessary.)

Thus, do the following:

- make sure that your FOD is listed on both all your marketing communications and on the tools you're using to connect with prospects and customers.
- write down the benefit that people get when they access that FOD. Thus, "Senior citizen discount travel program," or "lose 10 pounds in the next 30 days," or "Complete year's auction schedule." Get the picture?
- list benefit + FOD. "Free details on 100K+ annual home-based business opportunity. <FOD number>"
- start using them!

Note: where you've got multiple FODs like I do, you'll quickly move to a mini bingo card format where you'll list as many FOD benefits and numbers as you've got space for. The objective, after all, is to let your prospects know what they'll get when they call... and to stimulate immediate action. I do this particularly through my Sure-Fire Business Success Catalog where I promote both my own FODs in a large spread and also those of selected card-deck and Worldprofit Mall clients. Want to be one? Call me!

Following Up

When you start putting a benefit plus FOD number on your letterhead... brochures... workshop pass-outs... in your newsletters... as part of the Resource Box in your articles, *etc.*, you're not always going to know just who's accessing your information. This makes some people nervous because you're not always going to have the information you need (name, address, phone, fax, e-mail, *etc.*) to follow-up. Such people moan that some of their prospects are "getting away."

I don't feel this way at all.

You see, marketing is a numbers game. You throw your net into a school of fish and haul up today's catch. Some of those fish are going to get away. That's life. Sure, it would be nice to know where every single one of those fish went so that we could spend every waking minute of our lives trying to capture them. Such obsessions, fortunately, are for the pages of literature. Remember Captain Ahab and his Great White Whale?

Face it. When you're not just using your FOD but *promoting* your FOD you're not going to get everyone's follow-up information. You can only get that when the prospects call you and you direct them to the FOD yourself. So, first, don't worry about lost prospects. In my experience, the people who access your FOD and who are really interested in what you've got will contact you. They may not do it today; they may not do it tomorrow. Indeed, one of the interesting (if occasionally infuriating) things about the FOD phenomenon is just how long people hold on to the information they've received. Weeks or even months may go by. When you ask the prospect what took so long, their answer is likely to be something like, "I'm ready now." And that's that. Different strokes (or response periods) for different folks.

However, rather than get bent out of shape getting irritated about something you can-not control, do the best you can with what you *can* control, namely what you do with the prospects who call you and whom you direct to your FOD. Here are some helpful guide-lines for dealing with them.

— Get the follow-up information you need

One of the dumbest things you can do before directing a prospect to your FOD is failing to get the follow-up information you need. The correct way to handle this situation is to get this information first. "May I have your name, company, address, phone, fax and e-mail, please?" Then, once you've got this information, you can say, "Since you've got a fax number you can immediately get information on how to lose weight now by using this 24-hour fax-on-demand number <number>. When the machine picks up, touch one on your touch-tone phone and the information will be faxed to you immediately."

If at all possible, try to assess your prospect at this stage, too. It's helpful later. Let's say the person who called was interested in my quarterly card deck and I'm within 30 days of my deadline. I might say, "Are you considering purchasing advertising space with us in the next thirty days, for our April issue?" The answers might range from

"Yes, that's a definite possibility," to "Well, I read an article you'd written about card decks and I'd just like to see what they look like."

What the prospect says at this point, based on the assessing questions you've asked, will help determine what you do next.

— Follow up promptly

If what you've heard is positive ("yes, advertising in the next 30 days is a possibility") then determine your response strategy accordingly. Just how long should you wait? That depends on both how anxious you are to make the sale... and how long the prospect needs to really consider your offer. If you're selling something with a finite number or a definite publication date (like cards in a card deck) where there's a built-in urgency, you might call within 8 hours, certainly within 24. If the prospect needs more time, give them, say, 48-72 hours to access the material and peruse it.

— When you follow up, make sure they've accessed the FOD

The first thing to do when you follow up is ask if the prospect has in fact accessed the FOD number. "Hi, this is Joe Follow-Up from ABC. You called our office yesterday to request information on <benefit you offer.> I'm calling to see if you've accessed the fax-on-demand number to receive the information and whether you're ready to get started."

Responses will range from

- "I haven't had a chance to do it yet. But I'm going to do it right away!"
- "I couldn't figure out how to operate the fax-on-demand. Can you help me?"
- "I got the information but really haven't had a chance to review it yet," to
- "Yes, I found the information very helpful. I've got a few questions," or even
- "Yes, I'm ready to get started. I'll be faxing in the order form later today." (Yes, folks, just as smooth as that!)

— What to do when your prospect hasn't bothered to get the FOD information

What's important is how you handle those prospects who haven't bothered to access the FOD. You've got to discover whether they're real prospects or just time-wasters who don't deserve another follow-up call. Remember, you want to spend your time with the real prospects; other people can always get your FOD and mull things over in their own time. Most of them will not go anywhere, but at least you haven't had to spend your time and money sending them materials which they weren't going to act on anyway.

Ask the prospect just when he/she will be accessing the information. The response you get is going to tell you a lot about the kind of prospect you're dealing with.

- "I'm not sure when I'll get around to it. But when I do, if I'm interested, I'll call you."
- "I'm pretty busy right now, but I'm hoping to do it within a day or two."
- "I'm going to do it today."
- "I promise I'll do it the very minute we disconnect."

In every case, provide the prospect with motivating encouragement for faster accessing. "I'd love to give you our current 30% discount, so do get the information just as fast as you can, so you can benefit from it. When should I call you back to answer your questions? Would tomorrow afternoon be good for you?"

Remember, real prospects want specificity. They are willing to tell you precisely when they are going to do something and precisely when they can talk to you. They respect the fact that you're busy and have lots of other things to do; they want you to respect that fact with them, too. They may not have the money to purchase your product/service now, but if they say, "call me in four weeks since I'll be ready to make a decision then," you'll know just what to do and there's clarity all around. Note: in this case, send a note either by post, fax or e-mail (e-mail as faster and cheaper is better) thanking the prospect for his time and indicating just when you intend to get back to him and just what you're hoping to accomplish when you do. "I'm looking forward to speaking with you on <date> at <time>. I want you to get <benefit you offer>."

By the same token, people who are not prospects want to keep everything vague and are quick to turn the tables on you, accusing you of being pushy, or worse, when you try to exercise good follow-up skills. "Gosh, I'm not really sure when I'll get around to getting the information. And I don't really know when a good time for you to call would be. I'll let you know." Assuredly, this is not a good prospect, and you should proceed (or not) accordingly.

— Don't hesitate to discard unpromising prospects

Once of the great things about having an FOD, an FOD which is properly promoted, mind, is that new prospects are popping up all the time. I know. I get a *daily* report on how many people access my various FOD numbers. Some days the totals are truly staggering with FODs going out virtually every minute. In fact, I've now got two dedicated lines pumping out FODs all day, all night. Under these circumstances, you may well imagine that I'm looking for real prospects only. The rest can mull over the information in their own time, but they're very unlikely to hear personally from me or my reps.

Remember, FODs enable you to get out reams of information without paying to disseminate it. Lots of people who access this information may not either be truly interested or, more likely, may not have the money to proceed just now. That's life. Your job, therefore, is in all circumstances to assess prospects as promptly as you can. When you've decided someone is not a prospect right now, by all means end any conversation with them, but not before planting a seed for the future. "Well, as soon as you're ready, we'd love to talk with you more about how to lose 10 pounds in the next 30 days. Here's our phone number." Remember, benefits motivate. Use them.

Note: in our discussion of what should be in a fax-on-demand document, you'll remember I discussed the benefits of including a prospect-centered questionnaire. This questionnaire enables the prospect to tell you what he's interested in and important matters like what his budget is and just when he wants to accomplish his objective. Including this kind of questionnaire on your FOD enables you to handle your follow-up with professional aplomb. For instance, when a prospect faxes back a questionnaire that tells you he's got $3,000 and would like to accomplish his objective within 90 days, you can fax back a response saying, in effect, "We'll be back in touch with you at <particular time> so that you can reach your objective in the time you wish."

You should have this response available in a computer-generated template. As the questionnaire responses come in by mail, fax or e-mail, you simply fill in the prospect's name and respond accordingly, mailed questionnaires getting mailed responses, those coming in by fax being responded to the same way, *etc*. I can tell you this, in our infuriatingly selfish and inefficient age prospects are genuinely astonished and grateful for prompt response. They like the feeling that they're dealing with the consummate professional who knows what they want and gives it to them. Thus, people often comment on the fact that within minutes of their faxing a document to me, I've faxed back a detailed response. But let's be clear about something. I'd thought through that response previously, had created the necessary document as a template. I only have to insert the prospect's name, address, fax, *etc.* (information which simultaneously goes into a data base for later follow-up) and any particular comments made necessary by prospect questions and, voilà, the response communication is on its way to aid and abet my not-so-secret campaign of taking over the world, one client-centered transmission at a time.

Last Words

The benefits of fax-on-demand were born home to me again just last night. It was Friday. It was late. I was in my usual catatonic state after the usual too-long workday. I was indulging myself in my own personal escape, pouring over Christie's and Sotheby's sale catalogs. The phone rang. It was a fellow from Australia who wanted information on how to participate in both card deck and malls. I wasn't in the mood to be client-centered; I wanted to be Jeffrey-centered! But I dutifully took down his information and then gave him the information on how he could get all the information he wanted within just the next few minutes. The conversation took only a minute or two, just enough time to find out what he wanted, when he wanted it (important, remember, for follow-up), and provide the details he needed so he could take action — immediately if he wanted — to get the information he wanted. I'd been client-centered. I'd been astonishingly efficient. The prospect got the information he needed... if he was serious about doing what he said he'd do.

With dispatch, I was able to get back to the essential business at hand: determining which luxurious object to add next to my burgeoning collections, while knowing I had done what was necessary to continue the process of producing the revenues I need to sustain this obsessive self-indulgence.

Smart person that you are, I'm sure it takes no prophet to tell you that fax-on-demand capability is in your near future. And I scarcely need to say that when you dial my FOD at (403) 425-6049 and touch 1 on the number pad, you'll get precisely what you need to add it to the tools making you richer. And, yes, you should do it now.

Chapter 7

HOW TO GROW YOUR LOCAL SERVICE BUSINESS THROUGH THE INTERNET

If you're running a business, you're going to be on the Web. Yet some people — particularly people running service businesses catering primarily to a locate clientele — have definitely not gotten the message. They shrug off the Web saying things like

- "The Web's international, my client's are local. I don't need the Internet."
- "We mail out information about our business. That's the way we've always done it... and that's the way we're going to keep on doing it."
- "I don't even have a computer. Why would I need the Internet?"
- "My marketing works. I don't need anything else."

Well, I'm especially dedicating this chapter to such obstinate and short-sighted curmudgeons running service businesses. King Canute-like, they order the future not to progress another inch, and are incredulous that their ukase is not obeyed! Listen up! You can either turn the trends that determine the future to your advantage... or you can fight them every step of the way, exhausting yourself and losing the chance to profit from them. The silliest thing of all is to hang on for dear life to ideas and procedures that just don't work anymore. Ask your Studebaker dealer.

The Web's For You, Service Business Owner

If any of the following conditions apply, the Web's for you, no matter what kind of service business you run, no matter where and how you run it:

- You run ads of any kind.
- People call and ask for sales information to be sent them.
- People call and ask questions like "what services do you provide?", "how long does it take to schedule an appointment?", "how long does it take to get results?", "what are your payment and credit terms?"
- you aren't open 24 hours a day, 7 days a week, 365 days a year
- you don't always have time to provide the most complete answers possible when people call for information
- you don't always feel like talking to prospects to provide the information they need
- you can't seem to return all the phone calls made to your company seeking answers to specific questions

- dealing with prospects is difficult because you spend most of your time providing the service and it's not always convenient to call prospects back
- you make regular alternations in your sales literature that render what you've previously used outmoded... or you don't make the kinds of changes you should be making in your sales literature because you know it will make what you're using outmoded and you've still got a lot of it left
- you feel your sales literature, because of space limitations, does not adequately explain all your services, thus prompting questions you feel might be handled more efficiently in other ways
- you're not as prompt about mailing your sales information as you'd like to be. Requests for information aren't handled immediately; prospects wait. You often get calls saying, "Where's the information I requested two weeks ago?"
- you find yourself irritated about the amount of time marketing takes as opposed to actually providing your service.

If you've nodded your head to even a single one of these utterly characteristic problems in your service business, a home page with fax-on-demand is in your future.

A Few General Remarks

Just because the Web is international, doesn't mean that it isn't local. There are, as you know, many reasons for going on the Web. One is certainly to encourage new business to buy from you. Both intra- and off-the-Web promotion assists in achieving this objective. If you're in the right mall, you'll benefit from this aspect of the Web, too, even if you're running a small local service business. But that aspect won't necessarily be the primary reason for you to use the Web. No, for you, business efficiency and prompt client-centered behavior constitute the prime reasons.

You'll use the Web to run your business more efficiency, to process prospects more expeditiously, and handle delivery of your money-making service so that you do in fact make more money. Thus, the idea that you'll forego the Web because you run a local service business and most people on the Web cannot buy that service ceases to have any validity whatsoever when you consider just how stream-lined and efficient it's sure to make your business and, thus, how useful it must be for building your profit.

Taking An Inventory Of How You Spend Your Time

When you decide to use the Web, you decide to run your business in the most efficient, profitable way possible. Sadly, that's not how many service business owners run their businesses. Instead, they just "go with the flow", equal weighting all activities, not making any deliberate attempt to maximize efficiency and profit and minimize the administrivia that's constantly threatening to overwhelm all of us. Your road to enhanced efficiency and profit starts with an inventory of how you spend your time... so that you can do what's necessary to increase profit-making tasks and minimize the rest.

For one week do the following. Record this information in a computer file or if, Heaven forbid, you're still not computerized, keep a notebook handy to jot down the information.

- Note precisely how much time you actually spend providing your service and how much money you actually make from doing so.

- write down every business question that is asked of you on the telephone, by fax, and in person. These questions will run the gamut from "Are you open on Saturday?" to "Do you take American Express?" to "Do you provide <name of service>?"
- Record what you do in response to these questions. You may
  — answer the question on the telephone
  — respond by fax
  — have to take a message because you're busy and must call back later
  — mail information
  — not know the answer to the question and may have to spend time getting it.
- Note how long it takes you to respond and grade yourself on how completely and courteously you provide the necessary information. Write down candid comments like these:
  — kept caller on hold for five minutes while I dealt with another caller. Prospect sounded irritated when I got back to her. Didn't spend more than 2 minutes with caller because of lack of time. Didn't feel I gave the fullest response possible.
  — took prospect's name and address. Sent information out in next day's mail.
  — Didn't have precise information the prospect wanted. Took 5 days until I was able to send personalized response by mail.

You get the idea.

It's very important that you not only note how long it takes you to respond, but whether you're providing — completely and courteously — the information the prospect wants.

Reviewing The Situation

As Fagin sings in "Oliver!", "I'm reviewing the situation." When his first conclusions don't look so good he decides to "think it out again." Well, do you like what you see? Or is it time to "think it out again"? I suspect that as a result of reviewing your business situation for just one average week you're going to discover a number of interesting, and alarming, things:

- it's taking you too long to respond to prospects
- your answers, when provided, are incomplete
- you're constantly rushed, never really able to focus on a prospect, always pulled away to give your attention to other prospects or other problems
- courtesy has just about evaporated from your responses. You find yourself, in an attempt to be efficient, forgetting that people don't just buy because of efficiency. They buy because they've been treated well, too. They want efficiency, yes, but they want courteous, client-centered treatment, too.
- you're being pulled away from providing the actual service, which, remember, is what actually produces the money, to running an information bureau about what services are available, *etc.*
- you can't seem to *think* anymore... it's all react, react, react. And you feel you're not in control.

Well, friend, it's time to change all that. Immediately.

Crafting Your Home Page, Crafting Your Fax-on-Demand

Just having a home page with FOD capability isn't the solution to your problems. But thinking about what you want to achieve with them and then crafting them to achieve this objective can certainly be. That's why you need, first, to look at your current situation and then consider how a home page with FOD can make things better for you, for expediting your business and making it more profitable faster. That's the objective.

The easiest place to begin is by creating a "Commonly Asked Questions & Answers" page, even though this won't actually be the first thing your prospects see in your home page. Here list the questions people constantly ask you... and provide your most complete, client-centered answers:

- where are you located? (provide a map)
- what are your hours of business?
- how long have you been in business?
- what professional qualifications do you have?
- can you provide us with testimonials and references?
- what are your payment/credit terms?
- who handles what in your business? (Names, extension numbers, *etc.* of the right people who do various things.)

Note: while it's true that making changes to your home page costs money and you should be as complete as possible right from the start, if you do not think of every prospect question and answer it the first time you put your information up, don't worry. Keep a list in your computer of things that need to be added. Then update your home page monthly.

On another page, provide a list of your services. Just exactly what you do and how you work. Remember to keep the copy prospect-centered and fast moving. List things like

- service name
- what people get when they purchase this service from you
- dimensions of service
- whether prospect must come to you... or whether you go to prospect
- how far ahead service must be booked/how long it takes to get service
- price of service (if not exact price, then a price range).

On another page, provide a prospect questionnaire so that the prospects can tell you what they want, when they want it, how much their budget is, *etc.* Remember, good business relationships are a two-way street. Good prospects know they need certain things from you, the service provider, but they also know they must provide you with the information you need to get the service they want. Here's where they have the opportunity to provide that information.

Make sure your questionnaire is designed to elicit all the information you're going to need to provide superior service. Here are the kinds of information you may well want to know:

- prospect name
- address
- day phone, evening phone
- fax
- e-mail
- service prospect is looking for
- when prospect wants service
- prospect's budget for service
- any special conditions that apply, *etc.*

Make it clear that providing this information will help you provide the best possible service and provide various ways the prospect can get it to you, including

- e-mail
- fax
- mail.

Let the prospect know just when you'll be following up the information he/she provides. "Within 8 hours of receiving your information, you can expect to hear from us to discuss your situation in more detail."

Note: even if you cannot get back to a prospect with a complete response, you can always send an acknowledgment within 8 hours indicating just when you'll be contacting the prospect, or you can call the prospect to schedule an introductory consultation. In short, you can be both efficient and client-centered, even if you don't have the time to provide all the answers right away.

Document Order

Ordinarily, these documents will be in this sequence:

- service description
- commonly asked questions and answers
- prospect-centered questionnaire.

People want to know what you can do for them... then they want their questions answered.. and finally, they want to tell you just what they need. Then it's up to you to consider what they've told you and get back to them with a prompt, sensible response.

The Cherry on the Cake: Your Offer

As you are well aware, the object of all this is to get a qualified prospect and to enhance your revenues. Here's where the offer comes in.

As you know, an offer is designed to motivate faster prospect action. Your offer must say in effect, "Act now, get this special benefit which you are not going to get if you wait."

This offer should go at the top of your first page. In other words, it should be the first thing the prospect sees.

Just what you should offer depends on the kind of service you provide:

- a copywriter can provide a free copy review of a prospect's existing brochure or sales letter
- a day care center can provide a free child's game or book
- a veterinarian can give a free special report on pet vaccinations.

The idea is to provide something of real value to the prospect that doesn't cost you, the service provider, very much but that motivates faster action.

Two things:

1) bad at coming up with these offers yourself? Just check out the daily newspaper, publications you read and advertising materials you review from competitors and others. Look at the offers they make and craft yours accordingly. If an offer motivates you, it'll probably motivate others.

2) don't just make an offer. Make sure that your offer is given a value. What would you rather have, 1) a free copy review or 2) a free copy review worth $75? Obvious, isn't it? Your job is to build the *value* of the offer, so that the prospect feels its worth and does what's necessary to take action to acquire it — fast!

Note: one of the great things about the Internet is how you can emphasize key text. You can use color, underlining, flashing text, a moving marquee to get your message across. Do this with your offer. In other words, sell the offer. *When you do, it forces the prospect to take action to acquire it.*

Other Useful Materials To Include In Your Home Page

You can bolster the prospect-centered effectiveness of your home page by including some or all of the following:

- testimonials
- media excerpts
- information about your service providers
- a service outline indicating what happens when.

Let's look at these.

— Testimonials

Prospects like to know that you've done good work for others. Let them know by including testimonials in your home page. There are several ways to do this. 1) You can emphasize a benefit by including a testimonial along with it. 2) You can also include a section of your home page that lists all the good things that customers say about you. As you get dozens

of testimonials, of course, you'll be using the second approach more and more, jus[t]
I can assure you, a prospect finds it both impressive and reassuring to discover j[ust]
many people are willing to testify to the effectiveness of your work.

Note: never do a job without saying to the customer, "When I'm finished with ᴛʜɪs job
to your satisfaction I'd like to get a testimonial from you about what I've done, the results
you've gotten." Say this *before* you've done any work and then when you've finished with
your customary efficiency and technical expertise, ask for that testimonial. Then use it as
part of your home page to generate future business.

— Media Excerpts

Pick up your local newspaper today, and you're sure to find at least a sprinkling of
stories about people running service businesses. Why shouldn't you be featured in these
pages or in the thousands of other media sources that rely on service providers for at least
part of their editorial content? If you're not being featured regularly in the media, grab a
copy of my well-known book **The Unabashed Self-Promoter's Guide: What Every Man,
Woman, Child And Organization In America Needs To Know About Getting Ahead By
Exploiting The Media**. In these perky pages you'll find hundreds of suggestions about
how to promote your business, product, service, cause or organization through every kind
of free media.

Once you start appearing in print, don't just share the clippings with your mother. Put
them on the Web! Do not hesitate to include in your home page entire articles or pertinent
excerpts that deal with what you do. What's great about the Web is that you can blow up
these sections... use call-outs to differentiate and draw attention to them... use flashing
arrows to move prospects' eyes to what you want them to see. In other words, you can
accentuate the positive.

— Information about your service providers

Prospects like to know who'll be doing their job. Tell them. But don't just include
random biographical details; include pertinent information designed principally to reassure the prospect that the service provider knows what he's doing. Thus, instead of saying
"Joe has been in this business for 13 years," say "During the 13 years Joe has worked for
us, he's delivered <prime benefit> to literally thousands of people in this area. They know
him as one of the area's top craftspeople, truly a client-centered master." Get the drift?
Facts about Joe are just features. These features need to be turned into client-centered
benefits that make the prospect feel secure about entrusting his important business to your
company and specifically to this person.

To create this section of your home page

- list every single person who has a hand in providing the service(s) you sell
- have these people jot down 5-10 things about what they do to assist the customer
- then take these facts and reposition them as client-centered benefits.

Let's take the receptionist, for instance, who answers the phone.

Facts: Nancy Brown, 2 years at our company, picks up the phone, finds out what the
prospect wants, provides prompt, courteous, accurate information on how the prospect's
going to get what he wants.

Now these facts rewritten as prospect-centered benefit copy suitable for your highly focused, motivating home page: When you call <name of company> our crackerjack secretary Nancy Brown's likely to answer. For the last two years, Nancy's been helping prospects by promptly, courteously and accurately processing their calls. Just tell friendly Nancy exactly what you're looking for, and she'll put you in touch with the people you need to speak to get <benefit you want.>

After reading copy like this, when the prospect calls, he'll be saying things like, "Oh, you're Nancy Brown. I read about you. Here's what I want. Can you help me?" And Nancy will know just what to do:

- take down prospect's name, address, phone, fax, e-mail, *etc.*
- take down an indication of why the prospect is calling (in other words, start the prospect assessment process)
- direct prospect to your fax-on-demand
- transfer the prospect to the proper person within your company.

When you've got modules about service providers as part of your home page, you humanize your operation and start familiarizing the prospect with people he's likely to deal with. This helps the prospect develop necessary confidence in your operation and expedites business. Which is precisely what you want!

— Service outline indicating what happens when

Every single day you as a service provider are immersed in the details of your job. Nobody knows better than you do just what you do, what benefits you provide, and how you work. As such, it's easy to be condescending and brusque with prospects who don't know 1% of what you know about your operation. Whoa! Remember, these people pay your bills! It's important that you do not let your superior knowledge about what you do stand in the way of both making them feel comfortable and getting their business.

One thing that helps is providing prospects with a service outline indicating how you handle their business. Such an outline walks the prospect through all stages of his relationship with you and demonstrates just what you do and when you do it from the moment the prospect contacts you.

- You, the prospect, read necessary information that's part of our home page.
- You complete the prospect questionnaire that's part of this home page and fax, e-mail, or mail to us so we can better assist you.
- Within 24 hours of receipt, you hear from <name of designated customer service representative). Or, you hear from one of our customer service representatives. Note: I prefer, whenever possible to use the names of real people. That personalizes the information. If you have one, two or three customer service reps, you can say, "You will hear from either Suzanne Martin, Joe Peterson or Wally Archer, our customer service reps." If there are more, using names becomes cumbersome. If there is only one customer service rep whose name you use and this person leaves, remember you can change your home page within the day!
- You provide the customer service representative with a clear understanding of what you want, when you want it, your budget, *etc.*

- The representative will let you know how we can best help and will provide, whenever possible, various service alternatives which meet your objectives. Please keep in mind that it may take a little time for the representative to analyze your situation and provide you with the helpful information you need. The representative will make it clear to you just how long he needs and will get back to you when he says he will. The representative may at this time schedule a convenient appointment for you. Such an appointment will enable us to gather more information about your situation and to provide you with more useful information.

Note: Here's what's going on in this outline. You are letting the prospect know, in advance, just what he'll find and what you'll need and do to assist him. When people have knowledge, they feel empowered. They know what's going to happen and they're prepared for it. Your job is to let people know that you are interested in your prospect feeling comfortable and being clear at all times just what you intend to do and how you intend to do it. This kind of clarity is enormously important in making the prospect feel at home with you and in expediting the business.

Your job, therefore, is to make this outline as clear and detailed as possible without overcommitting yourself. Remember, this outline presents a commitment from you about how you treat prospects and what you do to satisfactorily handle their business. Don't blow it! Never promise more than you deliver. Instead, aim for steady credibility. When you do that you get testimonials that say, "They delivered far more than they promised!"

Your Fax-On-Demand Document

You should now be as knowledgeable as I am about what goes into your service business FOD. However, let's hit the high spots again to make sure.

Your FOD should

- open with an offer. What will you provide your prospect to reward faster action? More of your service? A special price? A service-related special report, audio or video cassette? A free consultation? Whatever you offer, remember to include its *value*. People don't just want free stuff; they want stuff that's free but which has real worth.

- highlight your key services. Tell prospects just what you do.

- follow with a page of frequently asked questions and client-centered answers.

- conclude with a questionnaire designed to elicit important information from the prospect so that you'll be able to present options that make sense given her budget, schedule and deadline, location, *etc.*

Remember, an FOD must be sleek, fast-moving, client-centered, featuring short sentences beginning with those crucial words "you get". Don't burden the reader with dense text and lengthy paragraphs. Remember, in this case the objective of the FOD is to impart enough information so that the prospect takes the next step to connect with you.

How To Integrate Service Business Home Page Promotion Into The Advertising Your Currently Do

As you already know, I'm not a big advocate of spending extra money to promote your home page. That's not smart. But I am a very big advocate of making sure that all the advertising and promotion you do features your URL address AND the crucial benefit people get when they visit your Web site.

Service businesses do a lot of marketing, including

- yellow pages and other space ads
- business cards
- brochures
- flyers
- advertising specialties.

They also use

- cover letters
- shipping labels
- envelopes, and
- other items that are not commonly considered marketing vehicles but which should most assuredly become so (like checks and invoices).

Remember, these things work only to the extent that they increase your business. And they'll increase your business only to the extent that they're clearly focused on the prospect and on the benefit he gets by taking action to connect with you.

Thus, make sure that

1) you include your URL address in every single thing that is either explicitly designed or is likely to connect with a prospect or customer
2) you never run this URL address alone, but always with a major client-centered benefit, the principal thing the prospect gets by connecting with you.

Remember, a URL address doesn't sell anyone on anything. It's no more evocative and motivating than a phone number. It's critical, of course, as part of the connecting process, but it's the *benefit* you promote that makes the prospect want to visit your home page.

Proper Prospect Processing

When you have an FOD and a home page, the objective is to use them to decrease your work, increase the number of prospects you can deal with, while simultaneously providing prospects with the information they need so that they can access it at their leisure and better inform themselves about what you do, the benefits you provide, and how they can best work with you to achieve the results they want.

Consider the way you work now.

The phone rings, you're clearly busy doing something else which must be put aside. The prospect wants you to handle his situation promptly, accurately, completely. But you're busy, busy, busy!!! You've got to drop one thing, refocus on another, irritated to be drawn away from what you were doing while understanding the "the customer is always right." Under these circumstances, it's doubtful that you give that prospect your full attention and it's doubtful that today's ultra demanding customer goes away feeling that you've done him full justice. Long before he became the Mahatma, Mohandas K Ghandi, while practicing law in South Africa, faced this all-too-common situation and made a stab at solving it by posting a very large sign that reminded his employees that the customer was the most important part of their business. That's the way we all ought to feel... and act... but all too often we don't.

Now enter the fax-on-demand and the home page into the life of the harried service seller.

The Mise-En-Scène

You working away as always on many projects. Then, THE PHONE RINGS!

"How can I help you?"

"I'm responding to your ad in the yellow pages and would like to get information on your school tutoring services."

"Certainly. I'll be glad to help you get the information you need. Can you please give me your name, address, phone, e-mail and fax?"

As soon as you have recorded this information, you say

"You can get the school tutoring information immediately by dialing our 24 hour fax-on-demand number. Dial <number> and touch 1 on your number pad for document number 1."

Note: if you intend to follow up in the next day or two, say so. Thus, "After reading the material, you may either call back, or we'll call you within 24 hours. Would that be convenient for you?"

The idea, of course, is that you're both in control and prospect-centered. You want to process this lead as fast as possible but you also want to have the information you'll need to follow up and you want the prospect to have the information he needs both to access the details about your service and to do it when he has the time or inclination.

Note: before ringing off with this prospect, you might inquire if he has access to the Web. If so, do not hesitate to provide your URL address and to explain that detailed information about your service is there available. If the prospect is responding to one of your ads, brochures, flyers, etc., of course, then he should have your URL at his fingertips. If he doesn't, you need to make sure to provide the printer with a new version of the marketing communication in question, one that provides this crucial information.

Scenario II: The prospect only has access to the Web

If the prospect has no fax... but does have access to the Web, get the necessary follow-up details and direct the prospect to your home page. Indicate that all the information you'd otherwise mail is conveniently available on-line. Again, in this case make it clear just when and how you'll follow up. If the prospect indicates that he'll access your on-line information immediately, you may wish to schedule a precise time now for follow-up. Remember, you want to do everything possible to move this prospect to a sale... and that may well mean the necessity for a follow-up phone or in-person appointment.

Scenario III: No fax, no Internet access

Ever watch a science fiction film about The Future? In it, all technology is the same, nothing's old, everything's new. Well, that's not just fiction, it's fantasy. In reality, reality doesn't work that way. At any given time, the world is littered both with the remains of old technologies which many people still use and with people who fight a stubborn rearguard action against whatever technology makes them feel uncomfortable and necessitates changes in their lives. It is only in fiction where everyone always has, understands, and uses the most advanced technology and feels perfectly at home with it.

In my life, scarcely a day goes by that people don't call and say (as one fellow did just today), "I know I ought to have a fax... I know I ought to be on the Internet... but I'm afraid of technology." There are plenty of such people. For whatever reason... sloth, laziness, procrastination, lack of interest, lack of money, lack of training, fear of the future, detestation of change, such people mean that those of us in business will never be as efficient as existing technology enables us to be. The technologically lame, halt and challenged will always retard us. So be it.

For them, we must continue to use the old ways, taking down the prospect's name, dropping everything to do a tailored letter, assembling an information package, rushing out to get it into the post, *etc.* WAIT! Before doing this, make sure you have done absolutely everything you can to assess this prospect and his potential. Technology is creating a new kind of class structure. People who understand and use technology are the new élite and should be treated as such. People who, for whatever reason, either cannot be bothered about technology or do not have the means to integrate it into their lives must be regarded with suspicion. Before you spend your resources catering to them, do what you can to see if any expenditure on them makes sense.

When you direct prospects to an FOD, they're spending their time and money to get your information. That's smart for you... and is both a wonderful way of promptly disseminating information and qualifying prospects simultaneously. If the prospect cannot be bothered to make a phone call that will immediately provide him with information about something he says he's interested in, I have no hesitation in saying he's not much of a prospect and doesn't deserve much consideration.

By the same token, if an individual doesn't have access to the Internet when access nowadays is so reasonably priced, he has, to my mind, made a statement about who he is and how he stands relative to today's advanced technology and the benefits it confers on both private citizens and businesses. Those of us who have yoked technology to our success chariots have a right to be suspicious of those who have, for whatever reason, decided to forego this mighty benefit.

Thus carefully assess and scrutinize.

Before dropping everything, before spending your money to assemble information and mail it, ask this "prospect" the questions you need to have answered, questions like

- What are you looking for?
- When do want to have it?
- What is your budget?
- Have you looked at other alternatives?
- What kinds of prices have you been coming up with?
- Are you near a decision?
- What will help you make it, *etc.*?

In short, take charge of this situation. Good prospects understand that you need information to do your job. Bad prospects get all huffy and bent out of shape, shrieking about the invasiveness and impropriety of your perfectly logical and legitimate questions. Such people, friend, are not prospects at all but merely time wasters and must be treated accordingly.

One major reason why I like the technological advances of the FOD and the Internet so much is that they have enabled me to deal with such people as they ought to be dealt with; by remaining at all times single mindedly client- centered, by providing them with the details on how they can get all the information they need, and, once having provided these details, by going back to whatever important work I have in hand... even if that work is snuggling on the couch with a good book.

The good prospects, the motivated prospects will do what's necessary to acquire your client-centered information. The rest... well, the rest will do what they always do: nothing, and with maximum fuss. However, at least they will have eaten away less of your valuable time and money than they do nowadays. And I say Hallelujah to that. Hallelujah! Hallelujah!

A Home Page, A Fax-On-Demand Is Not An Archive, Or Keeping Your Prospect-Centered Materials Up-To-Date

Ever gone to a home page that promotes some long-expired offer? That looks old? Pointless? Cruelly out of date? It happens all the time on the Web where nit-wits forget that if patina is important on old silver, it does nothing whatsoever to sell prospects looking for the best in current products and services. Prospects on the Web rightly discard anything that comes with the taint of the passé. That's why you've got to do what's necessary to keep both your home page and fax-on-demand documents fresh and timely.

- Stay abreast of technical enhancements on the Web. The technology is constantly changing, improving, both incrementally and absolutely. You're busy, of course, and may not be technically inclined (I'm certainly not). Keeping up on the technology is difficult in those circumstances. That's why we e-mail easy-to-understand tech notes to all our mall participants. Edited by cyber-guru George Kosch, whose delight in and mastery of technology are always wondrous to behold, these notes tell you what's new, what's in, what's not, how best to acquire and how to use what's happening in Web technology. When you sign up at Worldprofit, be sure to leave us an e-mail address so you get these notes every two weeks. Warning: If you're in another mall or have a free-standing home page, you have to stay abreast of all these developments yourself!

- Use offers with dates and other restrictions. We live in a world of endless consumer possibilities. There will always be too few dollars chasing too many options for spending them. That's why you've got to be smart about motivating your prospects. Use these motivators:
  - special price expiring at certain date
  - special (extra) portion expiring at certain date
  - limited supply of product/service available
  - special bonus/benefit/gift for first <number of> people responding.

The great thing about these kinds of motivating offers is, you don't have to invent them all yourself. As you leaf through your daily newspaper, trade publications or watch television, listen to the offers. Put the good ones in a hard copy "offer file" or list them on your computer. Don't hesitate for an instant to swipe offers that look good to you and that you can conveniently adapt to the product/service you're selling.

People with no business sense suffer from the completely ridiculous notion that prospects will somehow magically find their way to your good stuff without all the gymnastics that distinguish successful business people. That's nonsense. Without doubt, mastering the art of the offer is one of the most important things you will do for the success of your business.

The important thing when you're dealing with both FOD and Web, however, is that you must simultaneously create motivating offers while always remembering that when you wish to change these offers you're going to pay a surcharge to the mall of which you're a part for the work they must do to incorporate your changes. Hence this advice:

- If you use an expiration date, keep it to not more than 60 days after you post the offer. Dates are powerful motivators, but you don't want it to be either so close you have to keep making changes that add up in expense or so far off as to be meaningless.
- Use a number that implies an expiration date but doesn't actually state it, such as "Just 7 Specials Remaining." Note: this message should go at the top of your first FOD page or home page.
- Stimulate action by indicating the offer is limited, but phrase it in such a way it doesn't have to be continually changed, such as "<Special offer> if you're one of the first 25 responding!"

Hint: I run all aspects of my life using management by objectives techniques. I set my objectives, give them a reality test to make sure they're do-able, write them down, then arrange my resources to bring home the bacon. While my overall goals are cosmic, my objectives are always rigidly numerical. I want <quantifiable thing> by <specific date.> I've been doing this for a long, long time now; (in high school, for instance, I was notorious for posting my objectives on a big piece of poster board on the back of the door to my clothes closet along with a list of the things I'd succeeded in doing and those, humblingly, I had not. So impressed was one of my grandmothers by this system that, unbeknownst to me, she copied it down during one of her visits. Her notes were found in her purse, years later, when she died.

Venture a guess at how many products, how many units of your service you want to sell through your FOD, your home page. Then calculate your offer accordingly. If you want to sell 25, make your special offer for the first 25 only. If you want to sell 50 units of your service, make the offer correspondingly motivating so that 50 people will want to purchase what you've got in the designated time period. THEN DO EVERYTHING YOU CAN TO MAKE THAT HAPPEN!

The business of sales is never static. It's never automatic. And a sale can never be taken for granted. I've become, dare I admit, notorious over the years for never taking no for an answer. Indeed, when a prospect says no it only intrigues me the more; it becomes at once an intellectual game and a matter of personal respect for me to formulate an offer and to present it in such a way that even the most recalcitrant prospect must accept it. Indeed, the quest for the Perfect Offer has become a sort of corporate Holy Grail for me and while I think each new offer meritorious, I am ruthless about purging an offer from the repertoire either 1) because it has done all the good it can, or 2) because it has demonstrably failed to do so.

Your job is clear. Don't just post a home page or an FOD. Post an objective, like I used to do on the back of a closet door, where I was forced to see it every living day, grinding it into my brain and informing my behavior so as to reach the noted objective and avoid any future failures — which were, remember, prominently posted, too. Post your objective and then turn your documents into tools that help you achieve them.

Keep a list of all the offers that work. You'll want to use them again.

Keep a list of all the offers that don't work. These you can avoid.

From time to time someone with an FOD will call me... or an Internet advertiser, or, Heaven forbid, an advertiser in one of my own malls and say, "Nothing's working. I get no traffic. The Internet doesn't work. I'm going to drop off the Internet and never, never, never use it again."

I'd like to tell you that I'm nice to these people, patient, understanding, comfortable as an old shoe, providing the solace of Motherdear and the unconditional affection of Fido. I'd like to tell you this... but it would be a big, fat lie.

In fact, I'm as brisk as General George S. Patton on patrol, hitting the complainer with focused question after question.

- What's the offer you're using? How are you selling that offer to make it motivating to people? (Usually there's no offer.)
- What's your leading client-centered benefit? (Generally, it's a "me-centered" paragraph about how great the company is. Ho, hum.)
- Where are the results-oriented testimonials? (Non-existent)
- Are you promoting your FOD, your home page as a necessary part of your marketing communications... on every piece of letterhead you send, on all those business envelopes you use every day... on your sales slips... and packing bags... and all the other things that ought to be walking billboards for your home page and FOD? ("Well, I haven't gotten around to it yet.")

On and on I go through the many salient points covered in this resource, trying to get at just what the complainant is in fact doing, only to discover once again that it's ridiculously little, or nothing. And yet these creatures have the temerity to tell me that the Internet's at fault, the Web's at fault, the technology's at fault, anyone and everything is at fault except for them and the jejune way they approach the mighty and essential business of motivating people so that their products and services get sold faster. As Cassius said

The fault, dear Brutus, is not in our stars,

But in ourselves, that we are underlings.

Thus, Cassius-like, I pass this truth on to you, asking you to behave accordingly.

I was watching "Wall Street Week with Louis Rukeser" while working on this chapter. On this particular program producers went behind the camera to show how the program gets put together every week. It was most instructive. Rukeser is involved in every aspect of the program. He gets to the set early and stays late, making sure that everything is just so. Such punctiliousness over the course of 25 years has resulted in WSW becoming — long ago — the most highly watched financial show of all times. Yet Rukeser made a point of saying, as he left the PBS studio at midnight, that he's going to "keep on doing it until we get it right." I liked that from such a successful man. It showed just the right spirit and determination to continue working for — if, perhaps not achieving — perfection.

You've got to think just the same way about the marketing communications you produce... your home page, your fax-on-demand. No matter how good, no matter how many sales you make, you can always work for incremental improvement. The person who rests on laurels will soon have nothing else to rest on.

Thus, in both home page and FOD, you must keep working to

- create motivating offers. No home page, no fax-on-demand can be as good, as compelling, as successful for you as it needs to be if you don't provide an offer designed to get your prospects to TAKE ACTION NOW!

- heap prospect centered benefits on each other. Remember, benefits always focus on the all-important prospect/customer. Features focus on you, on what you're selling. Benefits motivate. Features merely explain.

- craft results-oriented testimonials. Prospects want to know they're not alone... that others have walked where they're about to walk... and that they liked the view! If customers are not giving you testimonials, prod them. Ask questions designed to elicit results-oriented responses, like "When you used <product, service> what happened?" Then use what the customers say to motivate new customers to contact you.

- answer prospect questions thoroughly. You know a lot about your business, more than anyone in the entire world. But you're the only one who's ever likely to know that much. Thus, people can and will have questions about your operation. Plan for it. Record the questions you hear... and answer them in painstaking detail.

- ask the prospect to tell you what he wants. I make it very clear in all my materials that I'm no mindreader. I need people to tell me what they want, when they want it, how much they have to pay for it, *etc.* Don't assume. Ask. Good prospects want you to know what they want, so you can give it to them. Only unreal prospects cavil when you start probing for answers. They take umbrage, usually because they've got empty pockets and don't want you to know it. When a prospect says, "No calls, please," it usually means the phone's shut off!

Become a fanatic about

- brainstorming new ideas for each of these categories
- swiping ideas from other people, whether in your business or not
- recording what works, what doesn't
- making changes in your home page and fax-on-demand accordingly.

Some day on my escutcheon I want these three words: "I will persist." It's precisely how I feel about the need to persevere and to keep on keepin' on. Always be clear on where you're going, of course, (that management by objectives approach I advised you to adopt)... but be resolved to do whatever is necessary to get the human beasts we must deal with to achieve success to move... now!

Last Words

Do you think all this exhausting? It is. It can also be frustrating... irritating. However, it's absolutely essential for maximum success.

Maybe you're one of those people who once (not now!) thought that all you had to do was draft a good fax-on-demand or throw some verbiage up on the 'net, sit down in your money wagons to roll on in, success nothing more than our leisure, no fear of love handles!

 very different.

 ige on the Web and you're a store owner! Part Svengali, determined, focused, insistent on turning technology this and you're the Internet store owner who's going

Chapter 8

HOW TO GROW YOUR NETWORK MARKETING ORGANIZATION ON THE INTERNET

So, you're in network marketing. If you're like most people, these are the instructions you've been given for making your pile:

- buy the company's "starter kit" complete with brochures and marketing materials and your first product purchase
- sit down with a pad and pencil and write down the names of all your friends, family, neighbors, co-workers, people in your religious organization, your union, people you went to summer camp with in the 3rd grade, and the guy who bought you a drink in college in 1964
- call them all, tell them about this "once in a lifetime" opportunity
- sit back and count your money as it rolls in.

Isn't this about the size of it?

Well, if this is the pabulum your network marketing company is dishing out to you (and I bet it is), listen up, since what I'm about to share with you is going to wildly alter the way you do business while vastly improving your chance of success.

Why Network Marketing Works

Network marketing works for one and only one reason: leverage. That is, you use other people's time, money and other resources to develop your own increasing monthly income. By getting an increasing number of people to follow a replicatable marketing program, you have to make more money.

Well, friend, the theory's fine, but in practice the vast majority of network marketing companies 1) don't explain the concept very well and 2) want you to implement it mainly by recruiting friends and family. This kind of recruitment is called "warm marketing" and while it has a fabulous pay-off for the companies themselves, it's very, very dangerous for you.

Now think for a minute.

Say you opened a neighborhood service business. Would you rely exclusively on your friends, family, co-workers, neighbors, *etc.* for your business? Of course not! You'd tell them of course... but you wouldn't *rely* on them to make you rich.

The kicker is, when you recruit these friends, family, *etc.* you are making somebody rich — the honchos at your network marketing company — but not yourself... or the people in your organization.

You see, when you sign up, when you sign up your Auntie Susie, the company ordinarily forces you to purchase a certain amount of products and certain "marketing materials," including overpriced four-color brochures, video and audio tapes, and other things that are expensive, if not very helpful. These are all profit centers for the company, so whether you make a dime or not, they get a profit.

What's more. if your network marketing opportunity fails (and over 90% of them do), this "once-in-a-lifetime" opportunity may haunt you for a lifetime, as friends, family, co-workers, *etc.* gently rib and not so otherwise gently remind you that your heaven-sent recommendation was a dog. The more these people invested, the worse their reaction to you. Is this what you want to live with the rest of your life?

Getting Serious

This chapter is about how to incorporate the World Wide Web into your network marketing scheme. However, before we get to the point where I can discuss that point seriously, I need to share certain other important information with you that logically precedes involving the Web in your downline development plans.

I deal with lots of people in network marketing and, sooner or later, information about every single network marketing company ends up in my "in" basket. That's really not so surprising given the fact that I'm both in network marketing myself (I remain the #1 distributor in Ad-Net, Inc., a prospect leads generating company), often write about MLM (multi-level marketing, the phrase trend-setters in the industry no longer like to use but which I continue to find perfectly acceptable), and have clients, through my Sales & Marketing Success Card Deck and Web malls, in most of the existing network marketing companies at any given time.

Most of what I see — most of what's out there — is radio-active, stuff no sensible person should touch with a ten-foot pole but which, because of the unbelievable hype, continues to attract people who would like to believe they're not total idiots.

Thus, my first piece of advice: make sure the company is both legitimate and a reasonable means for making money. This means using your noggin to examine such salient data as:

- its products. The problem with the bulk of products/services being marketed via MLM is that they offer too little value for the price. It's not just that they're over-priced but that they're often valueless. I mean, just how many gallons of body rub do you need before you understand that you've got enough for several life-times given the infrequency with which you use it? Products being marketed by network marketing companies must be products you 1) trust and are committed to, 2) use yourself and feel comfortable advising others to use, 3) which are not available locally in standard stores, and 4) are not overpriced.

Unless what you're looking at meets these essential criteria, avoid the company that provides it.

- its marketing plan. Both a company and its individual distributors must both have complementary marketing plans. The company should be able to tell you, should, in fact, have written down or otherwise conveniently made available (in a home page, for instance) its strategic marketing plan. What is the company per se doing to increase visibility, draw new people in, create and market new products, and generally assist both its own growth and the growth and development of individual distributors? Without such a plan, you cannot possibly tell what's in this company's future and whether it makes sense to join them.

- its financial condition. With the very high failure rate of network marketing companies, you'd be crazy to consider any company unless you knew something solid about its finances. How do you find out? Ask for an audited financial statement. Some network marketing companies, those trading on public stock exchanges, are forced to produce such documents; read them. Others, the good ones, understand that a solid financial statement is a motivating piece of sales literature to attract good independent distributors. Can't get this kind of financial information? Sit back and watch the company sink without a trace real, real soon.

- its personnel. Ever notice who's running a lot of network marketing companies? I surmise the percentage with criminal convictions is certainly higher than the public at large. And you've got lots of other unsavory types. If you see a picture with the CEO surrounded by heaps of his toys, trophy wife, air plane, a fleet of sleek automobiles, hold your wallet. These people certainly aren't into reinvestment. Your hard-earned money is subsidizing their playroom.

The truth is, MLM is by no means an entirely respectable business and one major reason is the "get rich types" who proliferate in it. They know that if they make big enough claims human avarice will cause any number of otherwise fairly sensible citizens to fork over enough dough to keep the "executive" in Moet Chandon until the whole farce collapses... and they can start again under another name, in another state. It's a very disturbing pattern, and the so-called "industry watch dogs" are so often in bed with these promoters that real stories about their financial condition, products, plans, and personnel are as difficult to find in the network marketing media as the proverbial hen's tooth.

For instance, the publisher of one industry publication allows advertisers to buy big glossy and invariably grossly complimentary spreads on their companies... which the advertisers, now sanctified by media, then turn around and peddle to prospects as an indication of how well they're thought of. Another who claims to be an objective scrutinizer puts his children into the companies he recommends, among other tricks, then touts those companies and signs up respondents under his kids. Another runs articles where "heavy hitters" tell what made them successful. Problem is all too often they're filled with outright lies.

I'm looking at an article right now that talks about how the guy being featured is "financially secure" when I know for a certain fact that he's bounced checks lately on any number of suppliers because he 1) doesn't have the money and 2) doesn't mind taking goods and services he can't pay for. Yet this scoundrel makes a great show of being a fine upstanding member of the local church and never has any trouble telling people what a good man, fine Christian he is, either. In reality his manifold faults and mangy condition are not unknown. Yet in the article in my hand he's portrayed as a role model. Why? I suspect it's because he buys ads in the publication in question and wheedles such coverage out as a quid pro quo. Disgusting, it's so common a practice that the words "caveat emptor" should be emblazoned on the forehead of any one daring to go into network marketing! Where are the great Victorian novelists when we need them? Where, for that matter, is "60 Minutes"?

Under these circumstances where you cannot put much reliance in "objective industry sources", you need to review the personnel records of network marketing hot-shots with as much care as you can. Ask for resumés. Find out how long the CEO has been with the company. What was he doing before? Did he mastermind the MLM equivalent of the Titanic's maiden voice, stepping daintily off the deck (like executives of the White Star Line) moments before the enterprise sank ignominiously, to the considerable financial expense of thousands of people who trusted him? Beware, reader, beware. In MLM this story is a commonplace.

- *its independent distributor focus.* With this kind of chicanery a byword in the industry, you need to check — and check closely — to ensure that the company you're dealing with understands that its ultimate success is predicated on the success of individual independent distributors. This fact — which ought to be inscribed in letters of gold where MLM CEOs and other top executives can see it daily — is, in fact, generally forgotten.

Why, when I wrote my book on this subject, MULTI-LEVEL MARKETING, the vice president for marketing of one very well-known network marketing company personally told me that she certainly wasn't going to assist in creating a replicable program for her distributors. No way, José. That, she pontificated, would merely lessen their creativity and initiative and that, she said piously, she would certainly never do! Unsurprisingly, with a nitwit like this in charge of the marketing water cooler, it's hardly surprising that the company she represented has since ceased to be the very visible high flyer it was when she uttered her immortal imbecility. And you don't need to be a rocket scientist to know why, with this blinkered nicompoopery passing for marketing being dished out from high places.

I see this kind of mindless selfishness and myopia continually played out in MLM executive suites.

— the CEO of a health foods company I know is adamant that he will not provide complete descriptions of the products he sells, will not tell people either what's in them, how they work, who they're for, or what they do. To do so, he opines, is to invite the scrutiny of the U.S. Food & Drug Administration, and that would never do. Instead, he fills the columns of his newsletter with snippets from the Bible and with exhortations about praying over his pills and powders before downing them. I wish I were kidding, but I'm not. Sanctimony is obviously preferable to client-centered fact.

— the CEO of another MLM company is equally dim. When people call him to say they're putting together an ad co-op and need to know if others in the company might be interested in participating, he says he cannot help because "all distributors must stand on their own." And, no, he certainly cannot post an announcement about who's looking for other eager beavers to work for the benefit of all because that would be "unfair." (How it would be unfair this 3rd grade turkey can never say.) Unsurprisingly the marketing advice offered by this marketing powerhouse is jejune: "recruit your family and friends" is all he can parrot, thinking he has thereby done his level best to help and priding himself accordingly.

— the CEO of another company used the creation and distribution of marketing materials and prospect leads as a huge profit center for himself, just like most companies do. He sold leads for three, four or more times what they cost him... and made distributors buy grossly inflated four-color printing communications that were big on color, to be sure, but short on client-centered benefits. When it was pointed out to him that his job ought to be to distribute leads as close to cost as possible so as to help distributors build the company... and that marketing materials ought to be, first, loaded with benefits for the prospect and that color, per se, wasn't a big motivator, he blocked his ears to such suggestions. Why? Because the present system benefited him mightily in his pocketbook and changes that diminished that income were anathema... however helpful they'd be to the otherwise hapless distributors.

Dear reader, this is why you must start with the proposition that the company you're reviewing probably isn't prospect-centered at all and certainly hasn't either thought through or developed a replicable system. In such circumstances, it pays to be skeptical — very skeptical — and to have your upline distributor or someone in customer service at the parent company walk you through the replication system they suggest... step by laborious step. Chances are you'll see big gaps in the "system" they propose to you... or the old-fashioned reliance on "recruiting your family and friends," which, remember, is good for them but a ticket to sure-fire money-losing as far as you're concerned.

— prospect-centered marketing communications.

This point goes right along with the one before. There are only three different and interrelated types of marketing communications that a network marketing company needs to produce: 1) materials which describe the benefits of belonging to this particular company, 2) materials which describe the products and services in detail and show why they're substantial and beneficial, and 3) materials which provide distributors with step-by-step instructions about how to build a profit-making organization. All the materials a company needs fall into these categories.

Unfortunately, most materials produced by most companies don't meet the smell test. Why? Because they're focused not on the benefits of the products or how to build a profitable organization, but rather because they're focused on the company itself, how great it is, how "world-class," "cutting edge," "state of the art," and all the other bloated rhetoric they use to disguise the fact that the emperor has no clothes.

I want you to scrutinize the company you're looking at and particularly its marketing message as portrayed in the materials it produces. Chances are these materials will be about the *company* — and not about the prospect or about you. But keep in mind there are really only two important people in the marketing equation who must be considered: YOU the independent distributor and the PROSPECT who will either become an independent distributor and/or product/service user. Companies that focus on the company are companies that don't get the message and which will, in the not so distant future, be part of the giant scrap heap of selfish, self-defeating MLM companies which either didn't get the message... or just chose to ignore it to their (predictably short-term) benefit.

Review the company sales materials closely. Check out just what they recommend to
- motivate a prospect to join

- describe the benefits of the products/services
- allow the people you recruit to replicate the process.

If these materials do not exist, ask yourself whether you really have the time, money and desire to recreate them either yourself or in conjunction with the independent contractors you recruit.

For years I have been pounding home this significant point, namely that when you recruit a person into a network marketing company without making provision for prospect leads, you're ensuring that this person fails. Just as you wouldn't attempt to build a business in the "real world" on the basis of your warm market, so you cannot contemplate doing that in network marketing. It just doesn't work. Instead, look into the following

— card decks and lead-generator cards.

Card decks, like the inexpensive one I publish, are a superb source of leads.

— lead-generating companies like Ad-Net, Inc.

Ad-Net, Inc. is a lead-generating company with a network marketing structure. To get more information, feel free to call me.

— the World Wide Web.

The only dramatically growing source of leads is the Web.

What does the company do to provide prospect leads and creative ideas? Don't take this on faith. Ask. Try to get straight answers about just how many leads the company will help you get… or whether you're going to have to be responsible for generating all your leads yourself. Astonishingly, all too many network marketing companies just don't think it's their responsibility (however much it's in their interest) to assist in supplying prospect leads. Is this sloth? Or just good old stupidity? Or a lethal mixture of both?

Are You the Right Person To Be in Network Marketing At All?

You now know what you must do to determine the right opportunity. However, are you sure you're the right *person* to be in network marketing at *all*? Here are the key points for you to consider:

— Self-Starter

To succeed in network marketing, you're largely on your own. No one is going to stand over you with a whip telling you what to do or how to do it. Frankly, that's one of the reasons people go into network marketing in the first place; the need to be independent and on their own. Unfortunately, many people just cannot handle the lack of structure. Be sure that you're capable of giving yourself the most demanding boss you'll ever have — yourself.

— Good Planner, Good Worker To Plan

One of the major reasons why people fail in network marketing is because they go in without a plan. They just want to "make a few bucks" and don't have a clue how to do even that, much less anything more.

To succeed in network marketing means developing a realistic plan encompassing these key elements

- how much time you've got
- how much money
- how you'll get prospect leads
- how you'll set standards for the people you recruit... and work with them to meet these standards, *etc.*

As you already know, I am a fanatical planner. I like to have at any given time plans of short-term, intermediate and long-term duration. I am a stickler, believe me, for assessing my resources and making sure they are being used to the utmost — and even beyond — to achieve the objective within the time set for the exercise.

Are you this way? Meanderers don't do well in network marketing — or anywhere else in business for that matter!

— Dogged Salesperson

I've read lots of books in my time about sales... and, more to the point, I've done a lot of sales in my time. While I am always looking to perfect my sales techniques and improve my performance, I cannot overstress the importance of one critical element: dogged perseverance.

While I was writing this chapter, I finally made a sale to a person who had over the last several weeks told me "absolutely not" and not just on one, two or even three occasions. Nonetheless we finally made the deal. What it took was these crucial characteristics

- ability to stay focused on the prospect. Would the prospect truly benefit from what I was proposing?
- ability to be flexible (not suicidal) about deal killers like price, terms, and other conditions,
- not letting a "no" be the end of things... but just a renewed beginning. When you're in sales, and when you're going to be the sales champ, the word "no" has no meaning so long as the prospect derives real benefits from what you've got... and so long as he can pay — one way or another — for it. In my mind, only the complete absence of value and a corresponding absence of means to acquire that value on the part of the prospect make a deal "impossible."

If you weren't born with these traits, take heart. Neither was I. I'm not gifted either with a particularly thick skin (the reverse in fact) and I have moments, believe me, when I don't want to do another thing... when neither the flesh nor the spirit are willing. This is the moment when dogged perseverance is necessary... and really pays off.

The next time you're at the end of your wits... your energy... your charm... even your desire to succeed... push yourself to go just a little bit farther. Get on the phone at the end of one of those difficult days and call a prospect. Say, "I'm calling to make a deal with you. I've got an opportunity of value. I want you to benefit. What will it take to get you in?" Reread those essential words "what will it take." Then work with the prospect to see just what he/she wants and whether you want to go that far to make the deal.

Network marketing is populated with some of the greatest ne'er-do-wells I have ever met in my life. Since becoming involved in MLM, I have heard more excuses... more whining... more "do it for me, I can't do it for myself" patheticalness than anywhere else in my entire life. 1) Face the fact that this is going to happen to you, too. 2) Resolve to assess all people as closely as possible to find out if they can-do or not and to drop the time-wasters without a pang. And 3) resolve that YOU will not be deterred from success, despite the legions of flat-worms all around us.

— Appointing Yourself Generalissimo

To succeed in network marketing not only means being goal oriented yourself, well organized, efficient, indefatigable, it also means being the generalissimo for others. Your job is to set standards... and to work with others to enforce them. One of the most discouraging facts of adult life as I have known it is how rare high standards are. The human beast is a lazy, slothful creature, perfectly content to wallow, if the opportunities for wallowing present themselves. However, when you're striving to build a national sales organization — which you most certainly are in network marketing — all that is anathema. This is why you must appoint yourself Generalissimo Sales Director.

In this role, you must

- make it clear that there are no loafers in your organization. No one can just come in for the ride expecting to get rich while doing nothing. While no one need kill themselves with overexertion, by the same token no one is immune from doing his bit to assist in the success of all.

- set quotas. All people in your organization must buy product... and must work with the people they recruit to do the same.

- see to it that all people have prospect leads. Without a continuing source of such leads, remember, your failure is assured.

- stay in touch with people. Network marketing is a people game. And people being what they are, it's your job to ensure that they do what's necessary to succeed. This means regularly staying in touch with them and urging them in all ways to do what's necessary to succeed.

In your role as Generalissimo it would be easy — so very easy — to get discouraged. In our manifestly degenerate times, people think nothing of making promises — and then walking away from them. Breaking promises now is a way of life for large numbers of people who feel, for mysterious reasons, that that is a perfectly acceptable way to live one's life. That may be so for the beasts of the fields, but it's intolerable for civilized beings.

However, you will face such people, early and late. Your job is not to get discouraged by them or give way to wailing and self-pity, as so many in network marketing do. Assess hard. Flush out without remorse those who cannot or will not produce. Work hard with the rest... even though, at first, "the rest" may be the tiniest number. That number will grow... especially when you harness the astonishing power of the World Wide Web to your success chariot. As we're going to do... right now!

Integrating the Web into Your Success Organization

So far, the home-truths in this chapter may have discouraged you. They're not meant to. They're meant to toughen you up and enable you to make a realistic assessment both of your personal ability to succeed in MLM and of the opportunity you have selected to sell and be your success vehicle. If you don't have the personal skills and attributes to succeed... if you have selected the wrong opportunity, the Web cannot save you. Keep in mind that the Web is not a fairy godmother who rushes in to save you when nothing else works. Yet the Web is regularly beaten up by the unsuccessful because it hasn't "worked" for them.

Why, just as I was writing this chapter, a chappie in network marketing called to complain about the Web. Why? Because he'd been on the Web for 7 *days*, and he hadn't received any responses yet. It took this master of convoluted verbiage several minutes to ramble to his complaint, and when I heard it I wanted to pull him through the phone cords and give him a real good shaking. The imbecile gave no thought to the possibility that perhaps the company was at fault, perhaps his offer wasn't motivating (predictably, it turned out that he had no offer), that his company was thin on prospect-centered benefits, *etc., etc., etc.* No, it was the Web and nothing but the Web that was disappointing him. "I suppose it's a scam," he concluded.

Well, I'm not a graduate of the Emily Post School of Sales Decorum. In such situations, I go for the jugular... and I went for it in this case, pointing out in no uncertain terms that what the situation called for was analysis and, quite likely, improvement... and not throwing around a lot of loaded language like the word "scam." Chastened, he got the point; we were then able to proceed in a more orderly, analytical, problem-solving fashion to see what could be done to improve his home page, his copy, his offer, his benefits, *etc.* In short to position him so that the very unjustly criticized Web could do its work for him. Just as it can do its work for you... if you use it properly.

Effectively Using The Web When You're in MLM

Some of what I'm about to say should, by now, come as no surprise to you. However, let's hit the key points from the viewpoint of network marketing, which adds a new, profit-making dimension to my case.

You see the Web should give you *leverage*, that is the ability to build your organization and your monthly pay-checks from the abilities and resources of others. It is with this key concept of leverage in mind (without which there's no point in being in network marketing at all) that you should approach the business of making money from the Web.

Start by Positioning Yourself

You know my motto "position is promotion." Well, here it comes again. Don't even think of putting up an isolated home page. You've got enough to think of in MLM without trying to master all the increasingly complicated Web technology or spend your limited resources in promoting a detached home page. That's a no no. Furthermore, don't make the significant strategic error of putting your home page in a mall that has no traffic and that doesn't have the kind of unrelenting steam roller marketing program that's the hallmark of my Worldprofit malls.

Presentation

Once you've positioned yourself within a highly trafficked mall, it's time to give thought to the objective of your home page… and how you'll present your message to achieve it.

Remember, before you write a word decide just what you want your home page to do.

> 1) Do you want a prospect to call you to discuss your organization, *etc.*?
>
> 2) Or, is your primary objective to get people to complete the paperwork on line and e-mail, fax, or mail you the application?

I suspect most people will decide 1) is the right objective. Why? Because most people before joining a network marketing company want to discuss that company with their prospective upline sponsor. They want to run through the kinds of searching questions presented at the beginning of this chapter to ensure that they're joining not only the right company but the right downline within this company. That's only natural.

However, you should keep in mind that 1) and 2) are really variations on the same theme. If the point of your home page is to get a more qualified prospect to contact you, you'll still surely want to include a sign-up form in your materials. If you're trying to get people to complete the paperwork, you still want to make sure that the prospect is as highly qualified as possible. No dogs need apply!

What Should Be In Your Network Marketing Home Page

Once you've decided just where the emphasis goes in your home page, review this checklist to make sure you're including all the necessary elements:

- offer. I cannot stress enough that successful marketers work hard on their offers. Those offers are the essential bait that gets prospects to take action NOW… which is precisely what you want them to do. When people (in MLM or not) complain to me (as they so often, boringly do) that their home page "doesn't work", I ask, wearily, reader, wearily, "What's your offer?" Most times after a certain amount of tiresome circumlocution, I discover there is no offer. "Well," I say, irked again, "what did you expect?" Offers sell! Marketing communications tell! Here are the kinds of offers that make sense in MLM:

  - free 60 minute cassette.

  - free information package

  - free consultation

  - free prospect leads

  - sign-up fees waived for first <so many> people to respond

  - free marketing communications and guidelines, *etc.*

Note: you don't have to invent these offers. Scan the industry press and see what offers other people are using. There's no law on earth that says you cannot take the most enticing offer you see… and use it yourself! Marketing is and always has been a copycat's game. Play it accordingly.

Another note: don't just push features (as in "60 minute cassette"), push benefits. What's on the cassette? What does the prospect get out of it? What's its dollar value? In other words, push the benefits, not the features. Tra la!

- brainstorm the benefits of joining both your opportunity and your particular organization. Prioritize them. Then use those magic words "You get..." to start them off. Then put them in priority order.

Say something like, "Look at all you get when you join the Get-Ahead Group at World Sublime Enterprises...."

Use bullets to focus the prospect's attention and make sure your sentences are short, action-oriented. Keep hitting the "you get" message.

- always make it clear what you want the prospect to do

There's always an implicit deal in the making in all marketing communications. It goes something like this, "I want you to take <specific action desired>.

I'm not going to be coy about what I want you to do; indeed, I'm going to make it GLARINGLY APPARENT. Then having told you what I want you to do, I'm going to do EVERYTHING I CAN to get you to do it. Your role in this is to, first, consider what I've got to say, then scrutinize it, and if it proves motivating to you to take action now." This implied contract between prospect and advertiser is the essence of successful marketing. When any part of it is missing, or weakened, the essential result of this contract — namely prompt prospect action — will not take place.

Thus, with this compact in mind, make it clear just what you want the prospect to do

- call now
- complete application now
- e-mail, fax or mail completed application now
- ask for free information kit now
- e-mail for free cassette now.

Get it? Marketing never works when all you do is throw words and pictures at people. We're all inundated with words and pictures. It works when you have a clear (and clearly stated) objective... when that objective is equally clear to the prospect... and when, with the medium you're using, you move heaven and earth to secure IMMEDIATE PROSPECT RESPONSE!!!

- make sure you use all the necessary component parts

There are certain things people in MLM want to know, including

- is the company stable? In other words, if I put in resources will the company still be around in six months?
- what makes the company's products better?
- how is the company on customer service, both for people who purchase products and for independent distributors?
- what will you and other members of my upline do to assist me get off to a good, fast, profitable start?

- do you (upline) fully participate in the company's programs? In other words, do you buy product and otherwise engage with the company... or is what you're saying all hype?
- what kinds of ongoing support services do you offer?
- do you offer any assistance in generating leads, including generating leads through the Internet?

Don't be coy about these questions. Don't assume that people will be able to deduce answers themselves from your material. If you're going to succeed in MLM, you must be resolved to discover prospect questions, answer prospect questions, and do your best to anticipate prospect questions and make beneficial changes accordingly. Thus, make sure that you post in your home page all the questions that prospects have... and give them your most client-centered answers.

There are several pay-offs to this system:

1) prospects get crucial information that enables them to make an informed decision.

2) your opportunity will stand out, since most companies are not going to take the time to think through what prospects really want to know and provide the information they need. This gives you a nice competitive advantage.

3) because you've worked hard to provide the information that prospects really need, to answer their questions, you have the right in return to ask prospects what you need to know about them. This is very important. Prospect assessment — determining who you want to work with, who's worth your investment — is a crucial part of what it takes to succeed in network marketing.

— Other network marketing home page elements

In addition to prospect questions and answers, make sure to include the following necessary elements in your home page:

- testimonials. Does your system work? Will real people stand up and talk about their results? (Note: if you're just starting out in MLM and have no results, don't worry. Get testimonials from the company and from your upline. Make sure no one fudges them!)
- complete product descriptions. People want to know what the products are... what they do... and the results real people can achieve.
- product value information. One major reason why so many MLM companies go down in flames is a simple one: the value's not there. As I said, real people don't like to pay more for products just to participate in an MLM opportunity. Overpriced, undervalued products are an ongoing MLM industry problem. Thus, when you find that a company offers products of value... and that these products are not generally available, trumpet the fact high and low.

Finally, don't forget to post all the forms that prospects need to complete to join your opportunity. If the forms are difficult in any way, post instructions, just like airlines do on overseas flights where they provide guidelines on how to complete customs forms. Remember, if the prospect finds it difficult to complete your forms, he'll stop. When he's stopped, he's not working to help build your organization!

Note: oftentimes prospects get confused when facing sign up forms, particularly when there are products to order, marketing materials, etc. Do not hesitate to say something like, "Most people start by doing the following... purchasing <amount> of product... getting <amount> of marketing communications..." etc. In other words, guide the prospect. They need your assistance and recommendations. Provide them!

Similarly, make it clear just how you want the prospect to get the information to you. While working on this chapter, I got some marketing materials in the mail and decided I wanted to take advantage of the offer. However, I could not find the necessary sign-up form amidst all the paraphernalia I was sent. NO I COULD NOT! And I got more and more testy as I wasted my time trying to correct the error of the "marketing" people who put this package together. Don't make this mistake. Provide clear instructions including all the ways you've got for the prospect to communicate with you and send in completed forms, including

- *e-mail* • *fax* • *mail.*

Using Your Home Page As The Headquarters For Your Organization

Members of your organization need a place to "hang out," and since the expense of flying in and lounging around your living room all week-end is prohibitive both to your members' expense accounts and your nerves, you're better off turning your home page into a clubhouse. Here you should post — the first of every month is a good time —

- news about the company and its products. Let the company know what you're doing and that you'll be happy to post whatever they give you of general interest and utility.
- information about how to generate prospect leads (including tips on how to work the Web. Note: remember, if you provide members of your downline with our e-mail address, webmaster@worldprofit.com, members of your downline will get my *Worldgram* newsletter free and it always contains useful marketing information.)
- tips on lead closing
- whatever you've got to help build a bigger, more lucrative organization
- news about the members. People always like to see their names in lights... and there's a thrill about booting up your computer only to find stuff about yourself on-line!

Make your site personal, newsy, fun — and make sure to let your downline know there's always something new up every 30 days and when the posting day is. Putting new things up every day or two becomes too time-consuming and expensive. However bundling all your items for posting monthly is easy and inexpensive. Note: at Worldprofit, we recommend that whenever possible you e-mail your changes to us with explicit instructions both about what you're putting up... and what you're taking down. Remember, every clubhouse needs to be cleaned up occasionally!

Working smart like this enables you to keep in touch with your with-it downline members, wherever they fall in your organization, and is easier and less expensive than using a traditional newsletter. Besides, all too often companies will not supply you with the names and address of people other than those on your first line. This is a superior alternative.

Promoting Your Home Page

Well, it's that time again — time to reemphasize the necessity for constant — and inexpensive — promotion. Let's do a little quiz to see how you're doing.

Grab the materials you're currently using to promote your network marketing opportunity. Yes, every single one of them. Peruse

- brochures
- flyers
- card deck and ads
- fax-on-demand pages
- shipping labels
- business cards
- newsletter, *etc.*

Now, which of these promote the benefit of visiting your home page... and provide that all-important URL address?

Your score, please...

Well, if you're coming up with a big, fat zero you're wasting your money. Reader dear, marketing is and always has been a numbers game. If you want to build a big business, you've got to connect with ever increasing numbers of people. This means thinking smart at all times. Nobody has all the money he needs for marketing (well, maybe Bill Gates does), so we've always got to be searching out the angles that will enable us to connect with more people for less money. That's the game.

As long as you're in business, one of your constant, and growing expenses, will always be the bucks you've got to spend on marketing your opportunity. So... get shrewd about how you spend those bucks and how to derive maximum benefit.

- Make sure that every single thing you send out or use in any way to get prospects includes the prime benefit of visiting your site ("lowest long distance rates guaranteed") and the URL address. Note: including your fax-on-demand number is smart, too.
- If you're using materials the company provides, get a stamp made with this information or develop an insert providing it. Note: if you're paying to have your name and address imprinted on materials, you can pay a few pennies more and get your prime benefit and URL imprinted on those materials, too. Why not?
- Keep a list of all the marketing materials you use (listing them in your computer's a good idea) and, as you re-order, confirm that both prime benefit

and URL are listed. Don't ever spend your money on marketing materials unless you're deriving full benefit from money spent!

These methods are inexpensive and they're guaranteed to increase your home page traffic and thus the number of your qualified prospects. Unfortunately, some people still don't get it.

During the writing of this chapter I was in the throes of closing a quarterly card deck issue (no wonder I have to get up so early to write these books). A network marketer took 100,000 cards, but wouldn't listen to my earnest entreaties about including a home page in the mix. "I don't have a computer... I don't know anything about the Web. I'll get around to it some day," *etc., etc., etc.* Egad! All the man had to do was pay less than a buck a day for the home page and his prime benefit + URL would have been shipped by me to 100,000 prospects. However he was willing to send the card without the message and lose all those precious hits. Not only that, he consigned himself to ensuring that he had to mail out all his expensive information packets, thereby failing to benefit from on-line recruitment... and the synergistic benefits that come through my extensive international mall promotion. What could the guy have been thinking of anyway!!!

The world is littered with ideas that are shopworn, old, no longer valid, but human beings are obstinate creatures. We cling to the past even when that clinging is ludicrous and self-defeating. Clinging, for many, seems more important than succeeding. I don't get it myself... but there it is. What you must keep in mind about technology is this: when technology changes, the rules of success change. And when those rules change, you must change, or you ensure your own failure. When that card-deck advertiser said, "I'm not going to change because I know nothing about the technology and how it works, and I'm not willing to alter my behavior to learn," he made a choice... and it wasn't a choice to help either his business or himself. It was the decision to atrophy, the decision to make his success more difficult to achieve and elusive. Pitiful.

Assessing your prospects

As you begin to use the Web more cleverly (which means scrutinizing every expense before you make it and ensuring that home page promotion is factored into every little thing you do), more and more people will contact you. As you promote client-centered benefits and make it easy for people to do what you want them to do (always presented, of course, as a benefit to them), the world and its brother *will* beat a path to your door. Unfortunately, you really won't want to know or work with everyone who shows up. That's why you've got to become very, very good at assessment. The Web can help you even here.

First of all, post in your home page the requirements you seek in people. One of the fallacies often mooted in network marketing circles is that MLM is the "democratic" form of marketing, that it's something everyone can do. I have never agreed with this puerile analysis. Marketing of any kind is not for everyone; everyone can't be a good, much less superior, marketer. The marketers who succeed are those with brains, drive, ambition, and a never-changing focus on the prospect and the benefit that prospect gets by acting.

This "democratic marketing" idea is promoted by the network marketing companies, of course, because they benefit when the hapless independent distributor signs up Auntie Tammy and her brood. But where does the marketer go from there? That's always been the weakness of MLM, and it's one most network marketing executives still won't bother to address. Frankly, they probably don't know what to do either.

However *we* know, don't we? We know we've got to follow the guidelines in this book to generate maximum prospect leads. We also know we've got to qualify these people to ensure that we're working with the best available tools (for what else are independent distributors after all?)

Start by posting your independent distributor qualifications in your home page. Say exactly who you're looking for and exactly what you want them to do. Make sure your qualifications list includes the following:

- time commitment
- financial commitment
- recruiting commitment
- ad co-op commitment
- product purchase commitment
- contact with downline commitment.

Get the idea? It's your responsibility to think through what you need people in your organization to do to succeed. You're the generalissimo after all. Equally, it's your responsibility to be blunt, direct, and "in your face" about your requirements. Face it, you don't want to work with everyone; (remember the 33 phone calls you made to one loser distributor who never recruited anyone and dropped out cursing you for not doing enough for him?) People aren't equal. They don't have equal skills and resources. They're not all worth working with. Network marketing is about making money, not about saving the world. I wish people would get that straight!

The more you qualify people, the better off you're going to be. Of course, you're going to get fewer people. Only mediocrity offers the prospect of no limitation. Good, by definition, means infrequent. People are always moaning to me about the number of bad prospects they attract. Attracting bad prospects comes with the territory if you don't bother to post the qualifications you're looking for.

When people know what you're looking for — and it's easy to tell them as part of your home page — they'll think twice before contacting you if they don't have what you're looking for. Furthermore, if they don't have what you're looking for and call you anyway, all you have to say, in the nicest possible way, is that you'd love to work with them as soon as they have the wherewithal to make the contact mutually beneficial. End of story.

Placing New Members On The Web

The Web, as you surely now know, is infinite. It has neither beginning nor end. It is unending inner space. It connects now with millions. Soon it will connect with hundreds of millions. Indeed, soon it will connect with anyone of importance anywhere. Those who are not connected to the Internet will be, from a marketing standpoint, absolute nullities. That is the clear direction of events. However you yourself, being just one, with limited time and resources, will not be available to benefit from this astonishing global growth — unless you link the power of network marketing leverage to the infinite connecting power of the Internet.

As I keep reminding you, you are the generalissimo. This means you must turn yourself into the strategic thinker for your organization. In this role, you must position people in your downline so that both they and you prosper. Let me show you how this can be done in terms of the malls at Worldprofit.

To start with, look at the word "Worldprofit" and consider this name in relation to other mall handles. Other owners use cute names, or self-centered names, or names that just cock a snoot at the establishment. In other words, they let you know right from the get-go that they're self-indulgent, self-focused and, yes, self-defeating. In marketing *everything* counts, and a mall's name is your first indication of just where the mall management is coming from... and where they want to go.

Hence "Worldprofit." This is not just a name; no emanation from the limited imagination of some socially challenged nerd. "Worldprofit" is at once a territory, an objective, and a manifesto.

Life is curious. When I specialized in the great age of monarchical expansion and imperialism when I was at Harvard, I thought I was studying the past. Now I find I was preparing for a future in which technology opens up the prospect of international imperialism — of worldprofit — in ways our 19th century ancestors couldn't even dream of. My studies encouraged me to think globally. Technology is enabling me to profit globally. Two significant streams meeting for a single exhilarating purpose.

When you're in MLM, you must use the Internet as your tool to project your benefits into all countries and to all suitable prospects. To do so, means positioning your downline for maximum advantage. You do this, first, of course by selecting the right mall. You know now how to do that. Once you've selected that mall, you examine its categories and keep a list of where your people should be placed as you recruit them, and how they should position themselves for maximum advantage.

At Worldprofit, for instance, we have many, many malls, including a Network Marketing Mall, Money Mall, Total Home & Garden Mall, Better Health Mall, Home-Based Business Mall, Mail Order Mall, Christian Mall, InfoMall, and many others. The objective is not just to bunch up all your people in the Network Marketing Mall where they trip over themselves and fail to produce maximum benefit. The idea, reader, is to position your people in each of the relevant malls and in each relevant section of each mall and then position the message of the home page you put in that mall so that it speaks directly to the people who will visit that mall, that section.

Thus, if you're representing an MLM with health products, you're certainly going to want to be in the Better Health Mall. Within that mall you'll want to be in the appropriate section for children, women, men, families, general health, specialized conditions, *etc.*... so long as your product can produce results for the kinds of people visiting these sections. The key is positioning your message so that it speaks to all the prospects who come.

Dumb marketers use the same message for everyone. However we live in an age of infinitely subdividing markets, of an infinite number of cohesive markets. Your job is not to make one-size marketing fit all... but to shape and craft your marketing message so that it's appropriate to the very people who will visit that site. People who have a specialized health condition, for instance, want to know what your products do for them. If they're happy with the benefits you put forward... then they'll certainly take action to acquire the products that produce them.

You as generalissimo have a duty to

- keep abreast of mall developments to see what new promotional opportunities are opening up for you and your downline
- position people in appropriate categories, and
- assist in focusing their message so that it's entirely appropriate for the prospects who visit.

Does this mean you have to throw out all the marketing materials you've developed? Certainly not! It means you have to tweak them so they address just the prospects you expect to visit that home page. This tweaking is an essential element of what enables you to succeed in marketing as a whole and on the Web in particular.

You cannot simply throw the same marketing communications at all people and expect them to feel equally enthusiastic. People respond to things that scream, "Hey, bub, this is for YOU," when it's clear the marketer has done his homework and that the message really is for that specific prospect in his/her specific situation and condition.

Keeping Your Home Page Up-To-Date

You now know as well as I do that you cannot treat your home page as an advertising dumpster. At all times you must return to first principles and ensure that your home page embodies them so that you derive the most business from your Web experience.

First principles include

- staying abreast of technology and graphical enhancements so that your home page doesn't look old-fashioned, passé;
- remaining resolutely client-centered. Is what you're posting focused on the prospect... or it is just a bundle of words about you and yours? Home pages work when they scream, "Hey, bub, look what's here for you" and then proceed to lay on the benefits thick and fast.
- being clear what your home page objective is. A home page can do many things sequentially, but it cannot do all things simultaneously. Be clear on your objective: are you looking for a qualified prospect... or do you want the prospect to sign up now?
- doing everything you can to motivate the fastest possible action from the most well qualified prospect. Treat this important matter as the game it most assuredly is. Just what can you do to compel faster action? Then, having achieved that objective, what can you do to compel even faster action?
- constantly promoting your home page through all your marketing gambits so that your traffic continually increases. If you hand out so much as one business card without the prime benefit of visiting your home page and your URL address, you are wasting your money and failing to do what you can to generate traffic.

For people in network marketing these first principles apply not just to themselves... but to the people they bring into their organizations or whom people in their organizations bring in. In other words, in network marketing you succeed to the extent that you get others to replicate your actions and leverage their resources on your behalf. Thus, you must ensure that you not only adhere to these first principles yourself... but that you work with members of your organization so that they do, too. Then and only then will you succeed in reaping both the benefits of network marketing and the World Wide Web.

Last Words

What makes network marketing hard is not the tasks one must do; they're actually straight forward and relatively uncomplicated. What makes MLM hard is the too often inferior caliber of people one must deal with and their unrealistic expectations about what they have to do (or not do) to achieve wealth. A sordid "get rich quick" mentality predominates in MLM and as a result, people attempt to do as little as possible while insisting upon maximum results. If, instead, participants set realistic objectives and did everything they could to live up to them, more people would benefit and fewer people would have the pronounced distaste for MLM that they so obviously do.

MLM enthusiasts are constantly throwing around wild numbers of the volume of business done through MLM and how, one day soon, a giant percentage of the world's goods will be sold through network marketing. This, of course, is rubbish. The fact is MLM hasn't begun to live up to the white-hot hype proponents constantly dish out. In fact, for most people MLM has proven to be a bust for reasons which, having read this chapter, you should be able to deduce for yourself.

What's clear, however, is that the Web will become a key element in developing a profitable organization so long as it's used *intelligently* and if you maintain realistic expectations about what it can and cannot do for you.

- The Web won't save you if the company you select is bad; if its products are overpriced and its management corrupt and self-centered. The Web is not penicillin for some debilitating bacillus.
- The Web won't save you if the company has no duplicable marketing program and doesn't understand the importance of client-centered marketing, of stressing benefits (not flatulent hype) in its marketing communications and doing everything possible to assist — in eminently practical ways — its independent distributor corps.
- The Web won't save you if you just throw up a hodgepodge of verbiage on your home page, words that are not at the service of your essential objective, words that don't motivate, words that do not press home the benefits of doing business with you. The Web is a tool, but you are the marketing generalissimo.
- The Web won't save you if you position your home page off by itself or put it in a mall that gets no traffic and where unrelenting marketing is not the order of the day, every day.
- The Web won't save you if you do not integrate the prime benefit of visiting your home page and your URL address into every single marketing communication and prospect contact that you use — and that every member of your organization uses. The Web doesn't work by magic; it only works when you work it.
- The Web won't save you if you think that a single message, never updated, never changed, never improved will produce all the results you want. The Web is not a mausoleum; it's your international department store, forever open to the more

than 60,000,000 people worldwide who now have access to the Web. These people, like all people, are fickle. They are self-centered. They want more and more and more... more and more and more easily and quickly. They want you to show them all the benefits you have... and make it ridiculously easy to acquire them.

But these aren't mistakes you'll make! Not armed with this chapter and this book! For you, as for me, the Web will become the key marketing tool in your armory, the tool that will forever lift you beyond the stultifying constraints of "warm marketing" and enable you to grow your network marketing organization and your monthly checks. Now, even your part-time kitchen-table business will have at its disposal the necessary technology used by the largest corporations and which enables you to

- be a national, even an international business from Day I
- present all the information your prospects need... and get it to them without the expense of faxing, mailing, *etc.*
- update that client-centered message within hours, even minutes, and
- integrate all your distributors into a universal system that enables you to guide them in both selling the products produced by your opportunity and the opportunity itself (even if they don't have computers themselves).

And all for a cost even the tiniest micro business can afford!

What are you waiting for? That fax-on-demand number (403) 425-6049, document #1. Use it yourself. Make sure every member of your organization uses it, too.

Follow-up and Resources

I have many ways to help you build your downline. To get my book **Multi-Level Money: The Complete Guide To Generating, Closing & Working With All The People You Need To Make *Real* Money *Every* Month In Network Marketing**, send $25.95 postpaid to JLA Publications, P.O. Box 38-2767, Cambridge, MA 02238 or call (617) 547-6372. To get information on my card deck, use FOD (403) 425-6049, document #3; to get information on how I can help develop your downline as a consultant, select document #9. And make sure that you turn on all the members of your downline to my *Worldgram* so that every two weeks they'll get free marketing tips to develop their profitable organizations.

Chapter 9

HOW TO USE THE INTERNET TO DEVELOP YOUR AD SALES AND YOUR PUBLICATION

This chapter is for publishers of any publication selling ad space, whether you're printing a magazine, newspaper, newsletter, tabloid, *etc.* That doesn't matter. What does matter is that you face up to the fact that the traditional environment in which you functioned for so long is now in the process of drastic change. You know as well as I do that

- Item. Paper prices have gone up dramatically in recent years. Yes, 50% and more.

- Item. Postage prices have similarly risen steeply and the 1996 Postal Reclassification scheme has caused them to rise even higher for many small publishers. (As more and more people use other alternatives to get their messages to people, the Post Office's business has continued to decrease. Still, their prices continue their relentless rise. This, not natural amity, accounts for their much publicized "customer service" advertising. But, knowing postal clerks as I do, it's clear the post office will not be happy until it charges exorbitant prices for no work at all. Have a nice day.

- Item There's a limit to what people will pay for advertising. Every time higher paper, postage and personnel costs trigger a rise in advertising costs, a certain percentage of advertisers drop out, no longer able to participate.

Of course it pays to advertise, but steeper advertising rates mean that more businesses just can't afford to do so.

Given these facts, it's hardly surprising that we can see the sizes of any number of publications melting away before our very eyes, like the last snowy remnants from the Cambridge Common in late March. What's more, these trends are not going to abate... especially given the fact that now the Internet beckons with its astonishing advantages.

Publisher, behold these advantages and wonder!

- There are no paper costs on the Internet.
- There are no printing costs on the Internet.
- There are no postage costs on the Internet.

If these three biggies don't convince you, here's even more...

- It's easier to assemble a publication on the Internet than in "real life." You can do everything with diskettes, scanners and through e-mail.
- You can add color and other graphic enhancements (like flashing and moving text) to add dramatic emphasis to the words you wish to stress.

- You can add an audio and a video component to your publication, something you cannot do in the standard publishing environment.
- You don't have to do all the marketing yourself. When you run your own publication alone, you and your staff have to do everything... editorial, production, promotion. This isn't true on the Web. If you're positioned in the right mall and get the right technical assistance, you're finally getting what you've wanted all along: SMART HELP and MORE READERS!

Note: If you're in the right mall, you get readers you wouldn't otherwise have gotten. If you set up a solo home page and promote it in your publication, you only get readers of your home page who are also readers of your publication. No increase in readers. But if you're in a popular, high traffic mall you get all sorts of new readers beyond the ones you can generate off your own readership. Smart; very, very smart.

- Your publication is available worldwide... and it's instantly available. No more waiting for the Post Office to get around to mailing it and no more wondering if people actually got it.
- The number of people accessing the Web continues its relentless rise. Every single hour more people are hooked in to the Web. This trend will continue for the foreseeable future. In other words, more & better!

Still not enough?

Well, try this one last significant reason. The cost of posting your publication and all your advertisers on the Web has actually gone down — thanks in large part to innovators like me who have insisted that Web sharks, charging hundreds and even thousands of dollars per home page and hundreds and even thousands of dollars for monthly fees, shall not prevail. When a person comes on the scene as determined as I was to change its pricing structure, it changes. And lest you think I'm saying this out of some sort of philanthropic urge, I'm not. This decision was based on two important principles: 1) high prices should never be a bar to the free exchange of information (what writer or publisher worth his salt could think differently) and 2) lower prices mean a vaster market, including people who otherwise wouldn't advertise. In short, it was good politics to lower prices and keep them low... and good economics, too.

In response to this fast changing environment, publishers have generally taken three points of view

1) Despite all the changes, there will be no changes here.
2) In response to the changes, we'll make internal reforms and hope that that's enough to keep us afloat, and
3) embracing the Internet and its possibilities, with this embracing running the gamut from people who do so reluctantly to those who have taken to this new inexpensive, international technology like the proverbial duck to water.

Let's look at each of these three camps. Publisher, you're in at least one of them.

— *"Damn the torpedoes, full speed ahead."*

Publishers are some of the dumbest people on earth. I know. I deal with them every day. Generally verbally proficient far beyond the run of mortal man, such people are able without difficulty to perceive of themselves as superior, nay godlike. Autocrats of their own (as well as any number of other worthy citizens') breakfast tables, they can — and often do — convince themselves that the world revolves around them and that any trend they have not started or seized upon is just a "fad."

One of these worthies recently wrote an article in which he compared the Internet to 900 numbers and dismissed it with these, to him, withering words: "I use the Internet weekly and have a lot of fun doing so." But as for the Internet being a serious invention with beneficial marketing opportunities, oh, no, he didn't agree with that and he certainly wasn't going to change his habits to make money from it. Just wait, he seemed to counsel, and it will all wither away, just like Karl Marx said about the capitalist state.

Now, reader, I deal with a lot of people who are not Nobel Laureate material but this person is clearly one of the dimmest bulbs around. Self-satisfied, smug, arrogant to a fault, his views, alas, are laughable. If he didn't have the ability to put them in print, they would be of no interest whatsoever.

However because they're in print and because they represent the most backward approach to the Web possible, let's deal with them — if only to laugh.

Reader, the only people who can stand against the trends of their time (and that only relatively) are those so rich they can buy themselves out of them... and those so poor that they no longer count in any way.

If you're a publisher with money to burn, or if you publish as a hobby, or if you'll pay any amount to disseminate your message, you can afford Colonel Blimpish attacks on the money-making phenomenon that is the Internet. Why? Because in these instances, it won't matter to you if paper prices go up, if postage prices rise, if advertising rates soar, even if readership dips. Even so, you can keep playing the publishing game with yourself.

Such publishing pashas, of course, are museum pieces; they just haven't been carted away yet. Behold them — and guffaw.

— *"Salvation through reform."*

If the pashas generally have more visibility than their numbers warrant (they have, after all, colossal egos and the drive and resources to place their generally ludicrous views before the public), most of the publishing community is composed of people who want to make money and who have to live in the real world. For them questions of how to stay alive by cutting expenses without unduly sacrificing quality are the stuff and substance of their daily existence.

Unfortunately, these people did not in college major in technology or even study the role of technology in contemporary life. I know. I'm one of them. Indeed, when I was in college such courses didn't even exist! Thus, whatever we knew of technology we had to pick up on our own. Fine if you're a ravenous autodidact; difficult if you're trying to run a business, raise a family, and even take the occasional day off and loaf.

Such people take a mild reformist approach to the business of staying alive. They consider questions like:

- What kind of paper should we use? Changing paper might save money.
- Can we benefit by changing the size of the publication? If we drop 8 pages, what would we save in terms of dollars; what would we lose in terms of editorial and advertising space. Are we better off?
- What are our postal options? Should we drop people from the mailing list, or barcode our mailings, or try new software sorting techniques to save money?

These questions are intelligent and they, and a hundred like them, are regularly and rightly asked in publishing offices nationwide.

However, these questions are insufficient unless they take into account the Internet, as these publishers, so often without any technical understanding whatsoever, so often fail to do.

Why are they insufficient?

Well, consider this fact. Say you're Publisher A, attempting to run your publication without reference to the Internet. How can you succeed against Publisher B who, however reluctantly, understands the importance of this technology with all its advantages (check them out again, above) and starts positioning at least part of his operations on the 'Net?

Publisher B quickly starts gaining an editorial and promotional advantage over Publisher A by

- selling advertisers not just space in his publication but space in his Internet home page. Indeed, because space on the Internet is so inexpensive (particularly if you're in the right mall), Publisher B can afford to virtually give it away... to get his regular space advertisers to pay full price for their ads.
- posting promotional and editorial material on the Web and telling people, both through his publication and all his marketing communications, to access it there;
- by drawing new readers and advertisers from people who regularly use the Internet, and
- by cutting his expenses because of the ease and efficiency with which Web material can be posted vis à vis traditional methods.

Now the real kicker. Needless to say Publisher B, a devotee of my marketing books, starts promoting these advantages to all the advertisers in Publisher A's publications; (there is, you know, no more assiduous reader of Publisher A's stuff than Publisher B). Shortly, as these advantages are hammered home to Publisher A's corps of advertisers, these people, insistent upon their own advantages, get the message and start moving from A to B. This is very much in their advantage. After all, Publisher B can give them both Internet and space advertising. Publisher A cannot. It's hemorrhageville chez A.

What can the well-meaning but hapless Publisher A, still trying to save his publication without reference to the Internet, do? He can keep worrying about and fiddling with

- paper prices
- the cost of personnel
- the size of his publication
- cutting mailing costs, *etc.*

But, as must be clear to you if not to Publisher A, these steps, while not unintelligent in themselves, must and always will be insufficient when Publisher B has such dramatic advantages thanks to the Internet and keeps pounding them home to, among others, Publisher A's advertisers. When even a small number of A's advertisers have walked... as they certainly will in the face of the many advantages propounded and stressed by Publisher B, all Publisher A's reforms, each and every one so intelligent in itself, will count for nothing... for Publisher A, so otherwise intelligent, liberal in spirit and genial in manners, will be gone, kaput, out of business, a statistic.

You see, when technology changes, the game changes, and merely making changes within the context of the prior game (where state-of-the-art technology did not exist) will never be enough.

Think of this. In my day (and remember, I'm not even fifty yet), there were still ice sellers on the streets of Boston. These were people who harnessed up their horse and wagon (yes, that, too) and rode through the streets selling pieces of ice for home ice-boxes. Ladies of the house leaned their heads out of upper windows on hot days and shouted down for a nickel's worth or, giddy with life's possibilities, a dime's.

When the refrigerator came along, you may imagine the consternation amongst the ice sellers and the companies employing them. Some, rich (and stupid) enough said, "Refrigerators are a fad. We'll just wait it out." Others, well meaning but missing the big picture, said "We'll keep on making customer-centered improvements." They thought such improvements would enable them to compete against the refrigerator.

Did it work, friend? Well, this spring or summer come to Boston and walk the streets. Or, on a hot day walk around your neighborhood. You'll want ice, of course, for your favorite concoction. But you won't have to wait for the ice-man to pass your door and sell you a dime's worth. No, friend, all you'll have to do is walk to your kitchen and open the ice-box.

And this, as the ice-sellers could have told you, is why reforms enough, no matter how many, no matter how well-meaning, can never be sufficient in the face of sweeping new technology that changes the game altogether. In such an environment, reforms are fine in the short term, and disastrous in the long. "Any ice today, lady?"

— *"Embracing the Internet."*

If you're like me you didn't find yourself naturally at home with technology. Indeed, the reverse. I'm not like my gifted Worldprofit colleague George Kosch, an astonishing techno-wizard who can pick up a new piece of software and make it hum before I've even figured out how to boot up the machine. Those are not my gifts.

One gift I have discovered rather late in life, however, is that I can not only adapt to but see the potential of the fast-speeding technology and embrace it, even if I've got butterflies in my stomach when I do. If technology came easily to you, you might not rate this very highly. But, if like me, you came to technology without a shred of native aptitude, you'd be right to think well of this skill. It has enabled me to see one thing very clearly, publisher: the Internet has entirely changed the game. You must change to adapt yourself to it... so that you won't follow in the steps of the Boston ice sellers.

Start by reviewing what's happened to your publication in the last year or two. Is it more expensive to run? Is it smaller? When the shoe starts pinching, it's usually a good time to get another pair, but most of us are more inclined to overlook the annoyance than promptly do what's necessary to end it and make things better. Therefore, you need a good self-review.

Complete this little questionnaire to give an idea of your present situation and the trend of events over the last year:

number of pages printed one year ago _____

number printed today _____

number of ads printed in average issue one year ago _____

number printed today _____

volume of advertising revenues in average issue one year ago _____

volume of advertising revenues today _____

number of articles published one year ago _____

number of articles printed today _____

cost of printing the publication one year ago _____

cost of printing the publication today _____

cost of distributing the publication one year ago _____

cost of distributing the publication today _____

profit from standard issue of the publication one year ago _____

profit from standard issue today _____

cost cutting measures you have instituted in the last year in the following categories:

  – paper   _____

  – printing   _____

  – postage and other means of distribution, *etc.*_____

You get the idea.

You need a snapshot of your situation. I bet you've never done this before, and I suspect you'll find the experience unsettling. What these data will probably show is that you're worse off today than you were just a year ago.

The question is, will you accept that as a given, or will you do what's necessary to improve matters?

Factoring in the Internet

You're not alone in the leaky publishing boat; every other publisher is suffering from these trends just like you are. Every other publisher, that is, except the ones who have decided to add an entirely new dimension to the traditional publishing environment, namely the Internet. For such people the game has changed... they have resolved not just to try to get by making petty reforms, no matter how sensible. They have resolved to prosper by making the new Web technology their particular success tool. The sad fact is that unless you join them, their success will come in part at the expense of your very existence. Why? Because once they're positioned on the Web, with its far greater advantages to traditional publishing and far less expense, they'll have a competitive advantage that you just cannot match and which will strongly work to your disadvantage — unless you, too, embrace the Web.

Priming Your Brain

We live in an era of titanic economic struggle. The interests of hundreds of millions of people are at stake and most of them have very little say in what happens to them. That's one reason for the mass frustration that currently distinguishes the political scene and which causes so many upheavals. We say we are a culture where the individual is significant and yet the economic trends that batter us laugh at the very notion that an individual is of any consequence whatsoever.

In this environment, the first thing you must decide is that you will be a winner, not a casualty like so many millions of people most certainly are… and will continue to be. You must resolve to use technology to fashion an environment in which you can prosper, not be crushed. This takes cunning and shrewdness. It also takes a personality that can live with a certain degree of calculated risk and can ride out the inevitable ups and downs that accompany massive societal transformation.

In this environment, priming your brain is the most important thing. You must

- see your situation clearly and unflinchingly
- not attempt to defend the customary merely because it is the comfortable
- seize the new technology and use it to promote your own interests, and
- diminish the interests of your competitors.

In short, you must realize, as Mao once said, that a "revolution is not a tea party." Willing or not, we are now participants in a revolution with far greater consequences for the way we live than the seventy-year interruption of Communism ever was.

Getting A Home Page In A Well Promoted Mall

The road to improve your situation and give you a mighty competitive advantage starts by taking a home page on the Internet. But not an unattached home page. You already know why that's a big mistake. While writing this very chapter, a well-known publisher signed up in one of my malls. What made this particular sign-up sweet was that months ago he told us in his own vastly superior way that he didn't need the benefits of a mall, any mall, and our malls in particular. He could do it all himself. When after six months his total traffic count stood at the level we customarily get in one day at Worldprofit, he saw that, well, arrogance was no match for unrelenting collective marketing. And so, swallowing more than a dollop of that overweening pride, he signed up with us.

Why? Because your job is publishing… you don't need the job of becoming a master of all the ins and outs of micro technological development. Leave that to the techies. You need to know how the technology works and how it applies to what you're doing, what it does, and how it can help you. But, frankly, you don't have the time to keep abreast of every little nuance. That's our job.

Over the course of many years, you've built up a loyal readership, people who look forward to receiving your publication. No doubt you're engaged in strenuous outreach to increase this readership. All that's to the good.

Now imagine that you could be planted in an environment that's connected to tens of millions of computer owners worldwide. Only the foolish think that all these computer users will look in at your site even once. But only the stupid argue with the notion that your traffic will not increase once you're positioned… not just on the Internet but in an aggressively promoted mall. All of a sudden your readership and your advertising prospect universe must increase… often dramatically.

Getting Your Advertisers In Your Home Page

The idea of putting yourself on the Internet is to make money. Never forget that. It's not a status symbol (those are important only to people who have no status to begin with). It's not a toy. It's a tool. A tool which must make money, or be a tool of no importance.

To make money on the Internet for a publisher means, first of all, getting all your advertisers in your Web site.

Right now you sell traditional space advertising. This you will continue to do. However, when you go onto the Internet you immediately can sell the following options:

- Option A. Traditional space ad.
- Option B. Internet classified ad.
- Option C. Internet space ad.
- Option D. Combination of space ad and Internet ad.

Immediately, your profit picture expands... and so does your competitive advantage.

How much should you charge for these services? Well, that depends on your competitive environment. But you'll at least double the cost of the space you've purchased on the Internet.

Targeting Your Competitors

You should, of course, be among the most faithful readers of the publications produced by your competitors. You need to stay abreast of what they're doing, prices, circulation, articles published, number of advertisers, advertising rates, *etc.* You do this, don't you?

Once you're on the Internet you must move quickly to leverage your advantage by stripping advertisers away from your competitors. How do you do this?

- systematically develop a list of the names and addresses of these advertisers. This isn't difficult to do. Even if the contact name for the company is not in the ad, there's usually a phone or fax number... or at least a company name and address. This information is most valuable to you.
- develop a sales letter that goes something like this

Dear <Advertiser by name, if you have it>,

Right now you're running space ads. That's good...

... What's better is to promote what you're selling through space ads and through an ad on the World Wide Web.

We can make that happen for just pennies a day.

Yes, the ad you're running now can be posted on the World Wide Web within 24 hours.

But not just posted... promoted!

As you may know, anyone can post an ad on the Internet. However, if you post it without promoting it, no one will visit and you'll waste your money. That's why you must insist upon having your ad placed in a Mall that's unrelentingly promoted. Look how we promote the mall to create your traffic.

- regular ads in <name of your publication>
- Dr. Jeffrey Lant's quarterly 100,000 circulation Sales & Marketing Success Card Deck

- over a million other cards run annually in other card decks
- Dr. Lant's quarterly 140,000+ Sure-Fire Business Success Catalog
- mention in his two internationally syndicated columns, "Sure-Fire Business Success" and "Qwik Smarts w/ Dr. Jeffrey Lant." These columns reach over 1.5 million people monthly!
- the twice-monthly *Worldgram* newsletter, circulated exclusively via e-mail transmission. Through the *Worldgram* all advertisers with e-mail are provided with detailed marketing instructions on a regular basis so they can bring more traffic to their sites and thus increase the mall traffic, to everyone's advantage!

In addition, we utilize all intra-Internet means to promote the mall, such as registration with search computers, postings at newsgroups, *etc.*

Here are the key points to keep in mind:

1) getting you this much coverage is in your interest whatever you're selling
2) you cannot get it from a publication that only offers space ads.
3) merely advertising on the Internet isn't the solution. Your ad must be in a mall that's heavily promoted
4) all this costs just pennies a day!

An order form accompanies this letter clearly outlining all the beneficial alternatives. Mail, fax or e-mail back today so we can start promoting your business through our pages... and through the World Wide Web!

Sincerely,

Forward Looking Publisher

P.S. Act now and get a free subscription to Dr. Jeffrey Lant's twice-monthly *Worldgram* newsletter. This free newsletter — worth $125 a year — is packed with information you can use now to sell your products and services and build a more profitable business. You get your subscription free now. <Note: you must provide an e-mail address for your subscription.>

Comments on this Letter

Several things are happening in this sales letter which are worth drawing your attention to:

- whenever possible address the letter to a specific person. Once you've got an advertiser in your publication, this could easily turn into a long-term relationship worth thousands of dollars to you. Treat it accordingly right from the start.
- never just tell prospects they can advertise on the 'net with you. Make it clear that any idiot can advertise on the Web. What makes Web advertising significant is placement in an aggressively promoted mall. Do not hesitate to list the means the mall uses to promote itself. These means, as the example above clearly illustrates, would be prohibitively expensive for all but the wealthiest advertisers if paid for individually. But even the smallest micro business can benefit from this collective marketing when it's part of a mall. That's crucial and will enable you to pick up advertiser after advertiser!
- make it clear that what you're offering is something others cannot offer. It may be in a few years that even the most reluctant publishers will have significant presence's on the Web. But as of now, they do not. That means that you can

move in now — like a sooner into the Oklahoma Territory — and grab the best stuff, including creaming off your competitors' advertisers, a very shrewd stroke indeed!

- stress how little all this costs. The truth is, Internet advertising — if you don't fall for the inflated prices of the sharks — is inexpensive advertising. I know. I set prices on the Internet... and I've set them low... and thus passed them on low to my advertisers. I'd rather take a few pennies a day from a million advertisers than a hundred dollars once from a few hundred. Always make it clear to your advertisers just how little it costs... and how much they get!

- use my *Worldgram* newsletter as a free motivating offer. Let your prospects know that twice each month, they'll be receiving a free newsletter from me, packed with the kind of hard-hitting, substantial advice you're reading right here. Remind them they never have to pay a penny for it... so long as you (or they) supply us with an e-mail address at webmaster@worldprofit.com

---

Note: always use the free <u>Worldgram</u> *subscription offer to stimulate faster response. It's better if you take down the e-mail address at the time of the sale (include a space for it on your order form) and transmit to us (by e-mail, remember). The free subscription starts within 14 days! If the advertiser protests that he has no e-mail address, say that the offer will remain open. As soon as he has one, he should transmit his e-mail address to you or to webmaster@worldprofit.com directly, mentioning your name.*

Remember, as a customer of my Malls, you can also place short paragraphs (we call them modules) in the *Worldgram*. Thus, we'd be happy to publish information about your specials, sales, news items, *etc.* This is a good way of inexpensively connecting with your customers. It's just *another* service you get through Worldprofit which others don't offer. Simply transmit the paragraphs you want us to publish, including full follow-up information so readers can get in touch with you.

Making Your Home Page Riveting

Reading this book, you already know what I think of a large majority of Internet sites. They're *b-o-r-i-n-g*! One thing successful marketers learn is that you can't bore people into buying things. It just doesn't work.

If a prospect makes the effort to visit your site, you must be prepared. And you must be prepared so that if he comes back within 30 days (as you most assuredly want him to do), you're prepared for that, too — with updates, new information, a different look, a special, sale, new offer, *etc.*

Again, as I have previously told you, the problem begins with how most people conceptualize their site. They think of it as a fixed advertisement, something static and unchanging rather than as a retail store. Think of the computer screen as your main window... think of each section of your home page as an aisle, an infinitely expandable aisle.

Now think of yourself when you shop. Do you like to see the same things all the time? Or do you, when you visit an establishment, like a little variety, like to feel that you're actually enjoying yourself, getting benefits, broadening your horizons? In short, that it's not just the same dull old thing? Obvious, isn't it?

Yet the majority of home page — and mall — owners simply dump text on people like some sort of puritanical cyber-librarian. My advice? GET OVER IT!

Publisher, here are some ideas to make your home page sing:

- Start with the name. The name, of course, should be the name of your publication, to reinforce the connection between your print and Internet operations. Add a descriptive phrase indicating what people will find when they visit. This phrase, of course, should summarize your major benefit such as, "Offering you the best in profit-making business development information every 30 days." A beneficial summary like this lets people know 1) what kinds of things you offer (so they know if this site should be a regular hang-out for them) and how often they should pop by to see what's new. (The key is to establish a good mix between offering your visitors new, updated information... and not going crazy trying to update your site every single minute. For most people monthly changes are sensible.)

- Open with a paragraph welcoming your visitors and giving them a clear sense of what they'll find and the benefits of continually visiting your site.

- Provide an index of what's available. When visitors click on different entries in this index, they'll go directly to them and find the detailed information promised.

- Your index may include (but is certainly not limited to)

  —an article or two from your current issue. (Looking for authors? Make an announcement to that effect here, including complete follow-up information.)

  —news items and useful information. (Remember, whenever possible you want the prospect to find data he can use right now. The more useful, valuable you make your site, the more interactive, the better. The visitor should come to rely on you for stuff he can use — right now!)

  —files for your advertisers. Just don't call them advertisers. Say, "Check out our business opportunity and development listings. Hundreds of money-making opportunities and business-to-business products designed to save you money and provide value right now!" Provide zippier headings for your advertisers than the dull ones most publications (myopic as the day is long) continue to (wrong headedly) think will draw in traffic. Instead of saying "Business opportunities," say "Money-making opportunities." Instead of saying "Office supplies," say "Bargains on must-have office supplies." See the difference? Publisher, your job is always to accommodate your advertisers, to help them sell more, and thereby keep them loyal to you. If your advertisers are happy and prosperous... you're going to be happy and prosperous, so gild the lily!

  —information on how to post an advertisement at your site. People are copycats, always have been, always will be. When they see someone like them posted on your site and see the amount of creative energy you've put forth to presenting them for maximum advantage, they're going to want to be presented there, too. Thus, always make sure to provide complete details about how they can... including an on-line application form (and/or fax-on-demand number where they can get it) and e-mail, fax, and mail response options.

Stay abreast of new graphic and text enhancement devices (remember, in our *Worldgram* we provide this kind of information to you twice a month) to soup up the site and make it interesting. Use tools like

- flashing text
- marquees
- text that moves in from the left or right, up or down
- audio clips, *etc.*

These are all things you cannot do in the traditional print environment that you ought to be using to improve the drawing power of your Web site.

I have a private theory that one reason people's publications are dull... their marketing communications dull... their home pages dull is because they're dull. But worse than that, they don't want to really connect with anyone. When you really want to motivate another fickle, capricious, far-from-satisfactory human being, you can't just dip a toe in the water, offering a bland message or tepid welcome. You've got to hone your benefits and pound them home, refusing to take no for an answer, committed to doing WHATEVER NEEDS TO BE DONE to get that blasted animal to MOVE!

When you do this, of course, a certain percentage of people will complain about what you're doing. They'll call it a "hard sell", as did one woman I spoke to when writing this chapter. *She* didn't want to sell anyone anything, and *she* didn't want to push anyone out of their comfort zone to buy anything. Egad! What she was really saying to me was this:

- I don't want to get up close and personal with anyone.
- I don't believe much in my products.
- I am not willing to do everything that needs to be done to get my product into the prospects' hands and get paid for doing so.

If you really have a product that transforms the lives of your prospects, makes them better off, if you really want to help them, then you're duty bound to do everything you can to get those prospects to buy it. Including turning the Internet into a international client-centered tool of amazing outreach, energy and connecting power.

If you learn nothing else from this book, learn that the Internet is not some giant bulletin board. That's truly a useless way of considering this fabulous phenomenon. The Internet is your opportunity to have your own retail space wherein you can showcase every single thing that's important and motivating about your business, your publication. It's a retail space that's

- infinite in scope
- universal in outreach
- never closed
- able to accommodate an infinite number of visitors simultaneously
- direct, intimate, accessible.

And which, remember, is so inexpensive that at the malls at Worldprofit, you can have it (along with fax-on-demand service) for only about a buck a day! Amazing!!!

Promoting Your Home Page In The Pages Of Your Own Publication

Keep this in mind: your home page should support your print operations... and your print operations should support your home page. Both must work to sustain the other. Thus:

- include a "This month on the Web" column in every print issue you produce. (Just as you'll include a comparable column on the Web puffing your print publication.)
- always tell your print readers about new technical and graphical enhancements you have available. (You can take these, of course, right out of our *Worldgram* newsletter.)
- let readers know that you've posted additional articles and other useful information in your home page.
- let potential advertisers know they can download your posted forms from the 'net as well as calling and e-mailing you to get them. (They should also be able to get your advertising information via fax-on-demand.)

No issue of your print publication should go to press without promoting your Web site. By the same token, your home page should never be without promotional information on your print publication. And both should cater to the needs of advertisers so that these advertisers buy space in both media.

Promoting Your Home Page As Part Of Your General Marketing And Operations

I trust what I'm about to say will be redundant, for by now you should already know that home page promotion must be integrated into all marketing and administrative operations to the maximum extent possible. To do this

- brainstorm a prime benefit for reading your publication and visiting your site. Thus, "your first source for creating a profit-making home-based business."
- draw up a list of every single marketing communication you use.
- as these marketing communications are revised, ensure that both your prime benefit and URL address are printed on them. Thus, when you renew your Yellow Pages ad, make sure you don't renew without including this information! (Including your fax-on-demand number makes sense, too!) Remember, using your money to buy advertising and other marketing communications without using them to promote your home page is just plain dumb.

Similarly, review your operations to see which things you produce that are seen by either prospects or customers, including

- invoices
- shipping labels
- cartons
- package stuffers

- advertising specialties
- general business correspondence, *etc.*

Whether you fully appreciate the fact or not, each of these is a tiny messenger that should deliver a client-centered marketing message designed to increase readership and home page traffic. Make sure they do!

Make sure each carries your prime benefit and URL address! Remember, the short (but potent) client-centered message you put on something as seemingly innocuous as an over-due bill reminder could be the tool that gets

- a new reader... who writes to the author of the article complimenting his work,
- provides one of your advertisers a crucial sale that causes her to renew, or that
- finally decides a wavering prospect to take out an ad after all.

In marketing, you see, everything counts. Nothing is neutral. Either the item in question — from full-color ad to shipping carton — either advances your interests by reinforcing in the prospect's mind the benefits you have available and how to get them — or they fail in this task. In business, *every* thing, *every* action that doesn't assist the sale is something that is merely an expense, and mere expenses, as every smart business person knows, are anathema. So you'll be careful, won't you, to do EVERYTHING you can to ensure that EVERYTHING you use, EVERYTHING that touches a prospect or customer in any way carries home your message and so helps develop both your print and on-line operations?

Last Words

Publisher, sooner or later some or even all your publishing operations will be on the Internet. Far from being the fad that some determinedly myopic publishers wish it to be, the Internet is a trend that has already changed the environment in which you work... and will end up finally changing that environment completely, irrevocably.

It's easy to see why.

If you knew that you could benefit by

- publishing without paying for paper
- not paying for printing services
- not paying the increasingly onerous costs of postage
- adding the potential of thousands, tens of thousands, even hundreds of thousands of readers without having to spend the resources to bring them to your attention
- expediting the production of your finished product (and accordingly lowering your costs for producing your work product)
- having immediate international transmission of your own editorial and marketing features thereby increasing not just your readership but your influence
- giving your advertisers additional national and international exposure so that they could sell more products
- posting information about the benefits of doing business with you that would reach a host of new people and bring you new advertising revenues

- enabling people to learn about you and get the message you wanted them to have about you — of whatever length — 24 hours a day, 365 days a year
- being able to accommodate an unlimited number of people who might decide, at any given time, to access that message
- creative linking with other, similar operations reaching the same kinds of people you reach so that the marketing resources of each could be pooled and used for the greater benefit of all...

... If you knew all this... and you knew that you could do it for just about a buck a day, what would you do?

Would you continue to turn your Nelson's eye to these pivotal benefits and to the fact that other publishers, publishers who compete with you, are not so obstinate? Are, in fact, determined to take advantage of every single competitive advantage to boost their own prospects and, if that's how the cookie crumbles, hurt yours. Or will you scrutinize this crucial new tool that is the Internet and see just how it can assist you and just what you have to do to step lightly from the end of one publishing era into the dawn of another?

Unfortunately, for all publishers the answer is by no means obvious. You see, being a syndicated columnist, a book publisher, a card deck publisher, selling other people's books through my paper and electronic catalogs, I deal, most days, with other publishers. I know these people inside and out. Bright, cultivated, fun at a party, always *au courant* with something you want to know, all too often they suffer delusions that they are somehow, as astute observers, immune from the winds of history and their fateful consequences. Nothing, of course, could be further from the truth. The refuge heaps of history are stacked high with people who, blinded by their civility and graces, by their intelligence and verbal agility, thought that change could never wash them away. But it most certainly did. Just consider the aristocrats who danced at Versailles in 1789 or the Commissars in the Kremlin just the other day.

But not you, publisher, not now. For in your hand you hold the roadmap, the essential exit instructions from the outmoded practices of the past to those which will enable you to thrive in the thrilling new world in which, like it or not, we are all going to live. The question is, will we dance upon this wave... or be dashed to oblivion by it? I, for one, intend to dance for all I'm worth. And so should *you*!

Chapter 10

HOW TO PROFIT FROM YOUR OWN MALL AT WORLDPROFIT

This entire book is about making money on the Internet. But this chapter offers a different perspective. Until now, what you learned in each chapter could be generally applied on the Internet. Here, however, I'm going to tell you now to make money in association with *me* on the Internet, by having your own specialty mall at Worldprofit.

Let me say right off that this chapter is not for everyone. It's only for people who truly want to make a truly substantial sum of money from the Web and who are willing to take the time and make the commitment to build a valuable property and long-term business. To do this takes the usual elements for business success, namely

- ambition
- focus
- energy
- organization
- creativity
- financial resources, and
- the ability to leap tall buildings in a single bound.

I'm not going to discuss these factors in detail here; hundreds of business books — including my own — have already done so.

What I am going to focus on are the two essential elements to succeed in establishing a valuable mall property on the Web that produces substantial annual and ongoing profit: technical skills and marketing expertise.

Some Background

In the early days of Internet development, Microsoft CEO Bill Gates announced, in his usual bold manner, that thousands of millionaires would be created from the Web; indeed, that he'd help create most of them! When Bill Gates, the richest person in the richest nation on earth, speaks, it behooves other ambitious people to pay close attention. I did. Gates' remark fermented in my brain.

At the time he said this, the Internet was fairly rudimentary in many ways. It was largely run by geeks for geeks and these 'netderthals delighted in retarding the development that can only come when commercial people with commercial vision take charge. I bided my time... and continued to await developments while brainstorming possibilities.

Now, I'm one of those entrepreneurs who believes in the reality of kismet, fate. I believe that if I posit the problem and begin mulling over solutions that fate will throw into my path just the people I need to meet and that these people will, just then, be looking to meet me, too. And so, as in so many other aspects of my life, it proved in this pivotal case.

In the far West of Canada a big strapping fellow named George Kosch was in the process of transitioning from being a young captain in the Canadian Air Force to civilian life. A techie from early days, Kosch had distinguished himself in the Air Force by his mastery of computers, a mastery he thought that would, along with his other skills, carry him to a general's rank. However, Kosch had what all true entrepreneurs must have to succeed, namely the insistent desire to run one's own show, taking the risks and reaping the rewards that only come when the enterprise belongs to oneself. He knew the Internet... he had the technical skills... he wanted the control that entrepreneurs insist upon... but he needed the other half of the success equation: marketing skills.

Thousands of miles away in Cambridge, Massachusetts I had a marketing machine... the country's single largest card deck, two internationally syndicated columns... a catalog... books, *etc.* It was clear to me that once the primitive squatters on the Internet lost the ability to handicap the Web's development and that the technology advanced so that it was easier for real people to use, a veritable gold rush would take place. I could get to these people in staggering numbers. What I needed was a techie with a vision, someone who loved the technology... but liked making money more than playing with the 'net.

It was then that kismet intervened, for George Kosch bought one of my books and did what many smart people have done over the years... he picked up the phone and called me, to bounce some ideas around.

I'm not going to tell you that the first, second, third or even fourth time we talked everything fell into place. It wasn't nearly as simple as that. For one thing, there were no models to follow; there still aren't. True pathfinders, we had to find the way ourselves. But with each party bringing both essential skills and a willingness to keep working until the pieces fit together, there was always progress, progress that accelerated as the technology — and therefore the value of the Internet — developed, improving its prospects as the world's premier connecting device.

Now, I ask you, what else is business but a connecting phenomenon, of linking a person with a want... with a person who has the ability to satisfy that want? Starting as a novelty, a toy, a techie's playroom, the Internet was on the road to becoming what it will ultimately be, the world's premier merchandise mart, the most accessible, democratic and cost effective form of marketing and personal communication the world has ever known.

But how to take advantage of this astonishing development?

It's All In A Name

Throughout my life, I've been good at thinking up catchy names for things. This small talent stood me in good stead when it came time to christen this new enterprise. My competitors delighted in calling their Web sites after themselves... or in giving them techie or cutesy names. I thought that was both stupid and self-indulgent. The name, you see, should define the purpose. It should possess, at once, clear market focus and a vision of who you are, who you want, what you're doing, where you're going.

I brainstormed many names before the obvious one occurred to me: WORLDPROFIT. It was exactly the right name... for it combined in not even a dozen letters a clear indication of the purpose of our enterprise and our focus. The value of the Internet is that it opens up markets internationally to even the smallest micro business. It forces people to think less provincially... to see the opportunities available to them wherever they exist. Bingo! That's precisely what we wanted... the *world*... and its *profit*, for our advertisers and for ourselves.

The question was how.

The Mall, The Whole Mall, And Nothing But The Mall

While I was writing this chapter the final issue of a newsletter I have read with interest for many years arrived. On the front page was another sour article about the Internet. One entrepreneur wrote, "I know what you mean about on-line marketing. We've done a lot, including hosting our own home page (on a joint basis with two others) and found results to be dismal." And this, the fellow implied, was all there was to be said about the issue; he'd washed his hands of the Internet, oh yes he had.

However that, dear reader, was most assuredly not all there is to be said. The creature in question made one of the most crucial mistakes about the Internet... he tried to go it alone. He tried, that is, to be simultaneously the master of developing technology, content, presentation, and marketing. No wonder it didn't work. This scenario is doomed to failure — for reasons with which you are now well acquainted. Nonetheless, bright people, like the fellow featured (a fellow, by the way, who has written many articles on marketing and really ought to know better) and the publisher of this newsletter who printed this drivel, persist in not getting the message, indeed of trashing the tool because they don't understand it, use it incorrectly and then moan (oh, how they moan) when it doesn't work the way they want. Thinking themselves smart, they "leave the Internet" and run away to run a soup kitchen in Arizona.

Of course, this is all nonsense.

Man is a social animal; we work best when we can work together. There is, of course, in the American experience the myth of the unfettered individual, the individual who does things alone, his or her way, damn the torpedoes, full speed ahead. This is the way even today most people approach the Internet, convinced that they can do everything, need nobody, and can succeed doing it "my way."

The more I thought about this modus operandi, the more obvious it seemed to me that this was the stupidest way of approaching the Internet imaginable. I've been around the block a time or two, and I can count the people with both technical Internet skills, marketing know-how, and a marketing machine on the fingers of one hand. They're a very rare breed. Most people have one set of skills or the other.

One word offered the solution to this problem, and that word was MALL. A mall enabled people allied by a common theme to link together and promote both that theme and themselves simultaneously. It enabled a percentage of what they paid to go for the technical maintenance of the mall and another portion to go for the marketing of the mall and the overall increase in traffic, thereby benefiting everyone.

In this model, Worldprofit, our domain site, became a network. This is where people tune in to see which channels are available. These channels are thematically unified (like the Network Marketing Mall or the Money Mall or the Total Home and Garden Mall). Within each channel, each advertiser offers an individual program. To enhance the visiting experience for each person visiting the channels, the network also provides amenities (like *Worldprofit On-line Magazine* or the *Worldgram* newsletter). Conceptualizing this model caused a whole series of elements to fall into place:

1) our job as network owners was to promote visitorship to Worldprofit. The reasons for visiting would develop as the different channels developed, but the one overriding goal would remain the same: visit Worldprofit... and could be promoted accordingly.

2) by creating a series of specialty malls, we immediately avoided the problems that continue to bedevil other malls, namely stacking advertisers willy nilly one on another. When someone goes to a mall, they don't want to have to wade through a lot of stuff they're not interested in. A person looking for a network marketing opportunity doesn't want to have to work hard to find that information. That's why the Worldprofit system makes sense: people go to the Main Menu, discover just what malls are available for their profit and enjoyment, and go where they want to go without troubling with thousands of other things, valuable in themselves but of no use to that prospect at that time.

3) each individual home page owner could promote his/her site directly without having to spend a lot of money doing so. At Worldprofit, we have never advocated that advertisers spend a ton of money promoting their home pages. That's daft. What we have advocated is that advertisers take advantage of all the money they're currently spending on marketing and include the prime benefit of visiting their site and their URL address in everything they do.

If you don't band together in a mall, this inexpensive marketing will never be enough to create substantial traffic... but where the network owner and *each* individual advertiser are all working together to increase traffic... your individual traffic is going to increase. This point is so important that in those instances where Worldprofit advertisers don't bother to integrate their home page promotion into their general advertising I get quite cross with them, reminding them that success is possible only if *everyone* does his bit.

4) costs could be kept to the barest minimum. Scarcely a day goes by but an advertiser doesn't pop up exclaiming about how low, how fair our prices are. It's true. Our prices are low, indeed the lowest in the industry. However this didn't just happen. I knew that Internet prices were ridiculously out of line with what they should have been. I also knew that if I offered fair prices people would desert the competitors (or not go to them at all) and would do business with us. Each time an advertiser comes in to a mall willing to follow the directions, add his mite to the overall marketing effort, bring more traffic to the malls, it ensures the success of the model and enables us to continue offering the low prices that continue to bring in more people, thereby perpetuating the model and making Worldprofit always new, always different, always interesting, always compelling.

5) Finally, this model enables us to add an infinite number of new malls to the network, to work with bright, ambitious people who, like us, see the tremendous growth possibilities from the Web and are determined, like us, both to mine them and to make them available to targeted groups of advertisers.

And this, as they say, is where you come in.

The Technical Skills & Equipment You Need

To succeed on the Internet means having just the right mix of technical and marketing skills. Here is a brief run-down of the technical skills and equipment you need.

- Pentium computer or equivalent Macintosh
- 16 megabytes RAM
- 1 gigabyte hard drive
- 1200 dpi (minimum) color scanner
- 28,000 baud modem
- printer (laser printer with at least 2 MB RAM recommended).

In addition here's the software you'll need:

- Windows 3.1, Windows 95 or equivalent Macintosh Operating System
- Word 6.0 (or 7.0 for Windows 95) with HTML editor or equivalent Macintosh
- HTML browser. (As of this printing Netscape 3.0 or Microsoft Internet Explorer. (Browsers not supporting HTML 3+ tags are not acceptable.)
- Graphics software to manipulate images from scanner (Photoshop or Corel Draw 6.0 are highly recommended.)
- Relational database management program (MS Access, Foxpro, *etc.*)

Note: Your database program must be able to track the following:

- customer information including client names, accounts, file names, directory listings, work orders, status, renewals, invoicing, *etc.*
- your program must be dynamic and able to provide daily Home Page Status Reports to include the following information: home pages in production, home pages needing copywriting, home pages requiring client approval, *etc.*
- lead tracking.

In addition you will also need an Internet connection through a local service provider (PPP account), not through an on-line service such as Compuserve, America On-line or Prodigy. While we're at it, you're also going to need merchant Visa/Mastercard status!

We're Working Along With You!

It is important to point out, however, that you are not working in a technical vacuum. No way. When you have a specialty mall at Worldprofit, you benefit from George Kosch's continuing oversight. He is and remains your technical liaison Here's how he works with you:

- To start with, he provides you with a domain address for your mall. It will be http://www.worldprofit.com/<your directory name>.
- He gives you a file name for your mall's Main Menu page. This filename is limited to 8 characters. This file will be loaded automatically when people type in your domain address.
- You'll get the naming convention for your directory files and client files.
- Once you've finished one of your advertiser's home pages, you'll e-mail it to our office. These pages are posted daily on the Internet!
- You'll get a fax-on-demand number. Remember, your fax-on-demand can have up to three pages of sales information in it. You'll want to use your FOD number along with your domain address in all your marketing materials.
- George will e-mail you our graphic files in a zipped file called graphics.zip. You will place these in a directory/folder (Macintosh) for use on your home pages.

Finding A Programmer

If what I've just written seems daunting or if you're too busy to do it all yourself, you're going to need a programmer to help launch and operate your mall. That's fine. A good mall, as I've previously pointed out, is an alliance between programmer and marketer. Their skills are very seldom found in the same person.

Your programmer will handle the conversion, typing and uploading of all customer files. He'll also need to track the Web sites on a database to handle file maintenance and removal.

To find the programmer you need, start with your local service provider, the people who provide access to the Internet. Check in the Yellow Pages under on-line services, computer services, or just plain Internet. You'll want to work with someone local who understands what you are trying to accomplish, has the time to assist you, is reasonably priced (programmers cost about $50 per hour), and can provide satisfactory references. Once you've got a selection, introduce your candidate to George Kosch. He'll put him through his paces and give you an opinion of the programmer's technical skills and ability to assist you.

Note: whether you get an outside programmer or not, we're going to ask you to e-mail us a functional home page so we can assess your skill level. This home page must include these elements:

- *mall directory home page*
- *linked to a URL*
- *linked to e-mail*
- *linked to local files (then linked back to mall home page)*
- *button graphics*
- *headings, block quotes, bullets, and a table*
- *background color or graphic.*

You may e-mail this file to sandi@worldprofit.com

Once you know how to do this, you can create Web sites. Then the game becomes selling them!

Marketing Your Mall

The second key element to success with your own mall is how you market it. Successful marketing begins by selecting the right mall to market.

Take a look at some of the malls we already have at Worldprofit:

- Business to Business
- Network Marketing
- Mail Order
- Health
- Money.

Why these subjects?

My criteria for Mall success are simple:

1) the theme must be timeless. Remember, you're developing a long-term property. You don't want something that's going to be hot today, cold tomorrow. You won't have enough time to generate recurring income.
2) it must be a "big" subject, something with a lot of prospects.
3) it must be clear-cut and coherent. People looking at the theme must be able to say in an instant, "That mall's for me, either as an advertiser or as a visitor, or both — or it isn't." Imprecision is costly.
4) it should be something you feel passionate about. If you're not excited about your own mall site, why should anyone else be?
5) it must offer a subject that has plenty of advertising vehicles, including specialized publications (for free publicity), mailing lists and Web newsgroups (where you can post messages). You're going to need to get to your prospects. Just how do you intend to do that?
6) the people you want as advertisers must have the money to purchase the space you want to sell them.

Based on these criteria, there can be literally thousands of specialty malls, including

– geographic malls

These malls focus on a particular, coherent geographical place. They're both for people already in this place and those interested in it. Such malls may include

- U.S. state malls
- Canadian provincial malls
- country malls
- large city malls, *etc.*

– religious and ethnic malls

These malls are of interest to people who self-identify themselves as members of a particular religious or ethnic group. Such malls include

- Islamic mall
- Afro-American mall
- Hispanic mall, *etc.*

– business malls

As the world's premier merchandise mart in development, the Web is a superb place for business malls such as

- barter mall
- industrial parts and tools mall
- hardware/software mall
- real estate
- arts & crafts mall
- careers/work mall, and
- nonprofit organization mall

– personal development malls

Smart people always want to improve themselves. Specialized Internet malls offer them the opportunity to do just that.

- educational and training mall
- social assistance mall
- travel mall, *etc.*

– avocations malls

Just how people will use their leisure time in the future will continue to be a topic of significant interest.

- sports mall
- family entertainment mall
- antiques and collectibles mall, and
- gourmet and other foods malls.

I must stress that these are just a few mall ideas. You need to brainstorm the ones you like and assess them with my 6 key criteria in mind.

Note: Both George Kosch & I are available to review your mall ideas. We'd like to hear what you've got in mind and why you think it will become a major property. Remember, we are looking for things with long-term, sustained growth prospects, not a "flash in the pan."

Once you've made a tentative decision about which mall property you want to develop, before getting too involved take that idea to a few people who you feel would be advertisers in such a mall. Tell them you're considering starting such a mall and that you want to know whether they'd participate in it. If so, find out why (there may be reasons you haven't thought of). If not, find out why. These reasons may be helpful in either structuring your mall or shaping your marketing communications. The important thing is to make sure that real people will pay real money to participate in your mall. Once you're sure you've got a winner, then you need to march smartly ahead.

Setting Up Your Mall, Walking Things Through

At this point, you need to do two major things:

      1) actually set up your mall.

      2) walk through your procedures to make sure you know what to do when prospects and advertisers start asking you questions hot and fast.

— Setting up your mall

Establishing a mall at Worldprofit is surprisingly easy once your theme/subject has been approved, and we know you've got the necessary technical/programming and marketing skills. You get in touch with George Kosch, pay the very reasonable mall fee and sign our simple forms. Now you're a mall owner — and you're working with us to develop the most lucrative Internet property possible!

— Walking Things Through

As soon as you've set up your mall, take a moment to congratulate yourself. You deserve it. You've taken a big step towards creating a long-term lucrative property. You've got a subject that only one person (you!) can have... and if you play things properly you'll be able, with our help at Worldprofit, to take over this subject in such a way that you dominate this market. This is an important thing to realize. At Worldprofit, we don't want anyone to create a puny mall. We want all our malls to be the pinnacle of mall-dom for that particular subject. We don't accept a subject unless we feel that the resulting mall will be both superior and lucrative... and that you're the right person to produce both conditions. Thus, congratulations at this point are very much in order.

After patting yourself on the back, walk through everything that's going to happen with your prospects and customers. Create a check list like this:

- prospect e-mails me for information. What do I send?
- prospect calls fax-on-demand. What marketing communications do I send back?
- prospect calls. What do I say? What do I send?
- prospect sends in material for his/her home page. What do I do?
- prospect material is posted but prospect wants changes. What do I do?
- prospect needs instructions about how to promote his/her home page. What do I do?

Let's look at each of these in more detail.

– The prospect e-mails you for information. What do you send?

For your mall to succeed you must become comfortable handling marketing and customer relations in several formats. One of these is e-mail.

You can count on it that once you've got a mall your e-mail traffic is going to rise. Learn to handle this increased traffic as promptly as possible.

To do this, make sure you have templates of all your marketing and standard business communications. Use these to get your prospects and customers the promptest possible response. Customize these responses as necessary, of course, but transmit them fast. What kinds of templates will you need?

- basic prospect information about your mall
- welcome to new customer with instructions about how you work (including instructions on how to change home pages when desired)
- acknowledgment for when you have received a home page text change and that you have done this, *etc.*

In other words, you should make sure that you have templates available for *all* your standard prospect and marketing situations so that you can promptly transmit your responses. This kind of efficient, client-centered service is one good reason why people on your mall will stay with you for years to come and recommend you to others.

Note: every time you face a situation where don't have a template document, take the response you must first create to handle this matter and file it for later use as a template. This way you're ready for the situation the next time it occurs.

— The prospect calls fax-on-demand number. What marketing communications do you send back?

You start, of course, by reviewing the fax-on-demand transmissions that we already use. You may cannibalize what you want. Your fax-on-demand communications must contain:

- information about your mall
- the kinds of advertisers you want to attract/who will do well in the mall
- the low prices of both Worldprofit generally and yourself in particular (this is, obviously a big selling point)
- the state-of-the-art technical assistance available (George Kosch is available to assist you with this portion of your communication)
- details on the unrelenting marketing program provided by Worldprofit (any extra information you want on this is supplied by me)... as well as the specific marketing things you are doing that are unique to your own mall.
- commonly asked questions and answers.

You also want to stress the fact that

- we can design the advertiser's home page for them
- files go up FAST (generally within 24 hours), and
- changes can be made at any time and are reasonably priced.

You should also emphasize that when they sign up, they will get a free subscription to the *Worldgram* newsletter, so long as they have e-mail. No e-mail? "As soon as you have it, let us know!"

Finally, of course, you need a sign-up form that presents all the options and gathers the kinds of information you need to establish an account for your client. Don't hesitate to adapt the form from the existing Worldprofit fax-on-demand (document #1) or which appears in my Sure-Fire Business Success Catalog.

You can handle all this in three pages, including

- (page 1) client-centered selling information about the mall and about Worldprofit in general.
- (page 2) commonly asked questions and answers about your mall.
- (page 3) sign up form so prospect can fax you back an order with credit card information.

Note: You will find that about 50% of your business is done with credit cards, so as soon as you can make arrangements with your bank to get a merchant MasterCard/VISA account.

— The prospect calls. What do you say?

Your new advertiser wants clarity from you... clarity and a sense that you know what you're doing! Thus, think through the situation from the prospect's standpoint and give her what she needs to feel entirely comfortable. Your prospect needs to know:

- what options she has for the duration of her Web site. Six months? One year?
- what charges apply
- what forms of payment you accept
- what mall sections you have available
- how you handle the development of her home page if she has everything ready and doesn't need copywriting assistance. (At Worldprofit, we have templates available for this situation. Our programmers insert the text into a standard templates and place on the Internet — fast!)
- how you handle the development of her home page if she does need copywriting assistance
- how you prefer to receive both material for a Web site and a finished home page. (At Worldprofit, we prefer to receive material by e-mail. We will also take a camera-ready typed page and, if no other means is available, a fax.)
- how she can change her Web site when necessary, what charges apply. (At Worldprofit, we make changes any time. If they're small, we don't charge for them. If they're things like adding a new paragraph, there's a nominal fee of $10. If the changes are more extension, we charge $40 an hour to make them. To completely change and ad and list it in another mall costs $45. If it's a new ad with no relisting, the charge is just $25. Again, we prefer to have any change by e-mail, mail, or fax.)
- how long it takes to provide copywriting assistance. (If our Worldprofit copywriters handle the assignment, it takes about a week, or less, from receipt of material to posting the completed home page on the Internet. The only thing that slows this down is customer delays, incessant modifications (yes, there are such

customers!), or just procrastinating about providing the necessary home page approval.)

- when her home page will be posted after you receive her material.
- how long home page registration and indexing takes. (At Worldprofit, advanced search registration takes 3-6 weeks.)

As you see these questions, you should be thinking about how best to present this information. Obviously, I suggest you start with a "Commonly Asked Questions & Answers" page as part of both your fax-on-demand (which can also be e-mailed, of course) and with a home page posting.

My personal belief, and one I have long used to develop my business, is that it is the business owner's responsibility to think through all the reasonable questions a prospect will have and to provide the answers in the most accessible form possible. The Internet has improved this process enormously.

By the same token, it is the responsibility of the prospect to consult this information so as not to burden the business owner with lots of questions that are fully and conveniently answered elsewhere. In other words, the prospect should be respectful of the business owner's time and other responsibilities... just as the business owner should always be respectful of what the prospect needs and do everything possible to satisfy them in the most accessible formats.

As prospects ask you questions, add them and your answers to the Q & A documents you have available, so your responses are always complete and up-to-date.

Thus, when a prospect contacts you, do this:

- first get the prospect's name, address, phone, fax, and e-mail. You always need this information for follow-up.
- next ask whether the prospect has reviewed your Q & A materials. If so, the discussion can quickly focus on specific points on which the prospect wants more information. If not, you should direct the prospect to places where her specific questions will be answered.
- even when you've directed the prospect to another place, make sure to find out when the prospect will review these materials and how the next contact will take place. In other words, be clear on when and how the next step will occur. Then follow up accordingly.

— The prospect sends in material for his/her home page. What do you do?

Just what you do when you receive material for a home page depends on what you see.

If the prospect is sending you material that needs copywriting assistance, your job is to get what you've received into the hands of the copywriter ASAP. This means

- having copywriters available to assist your customers (at Worldprofit we have such people readily available)
- alerting them as to when you expect material to be ready. (You can always let a customer needing a copywriter know that you've got a copywriter available NOW to handle his work... but that if he waits to make a decision, he may well have to wait for copywriting assistance; in other words, use the current availability of a copywriter as an inducement for faster prospect action.)

- sending the material over to the copywriter promptly and monitoring the situation so that the home page is finished in a reasonable time (a week is perfectly acceptable) and the client is happy with the result.

Note: as your mall grows you won't be able to review the content of every single home page. However, you should regularly review a few home pages to make sure they are as sleek and client-centered as possible. Review Chapter 3 and make sure that every single home page posted in your mall has what it needs to attract the maximum number of prospects.

By the same token, if an advertiser sends in a home page that he regards as finished, whenever possible review it to make sure it really does contain the necessary elements for Web success. In this connection, I suggest that you recommend this book to all your prospects and advertisers. It will help them in many ways, of course, not least in crafting just the right Web site content.

If what you see can be improved and the changes are small, make them gratis. Before posting them on the Internet, however, make sure to get the client's approval for what you've done. Some people are so attached to their (poor quality) work that they'd rather keep it than make any sensible changes you might recommend. In the final analysis, "the customer is always right," even when the customer's suggestions are just plain wrong. Be sure to let the customer know, however, just why you've made your suggestions; this may prove helpful latter if his results are not what he expected!

On the other hand, if major changes are necessary (this definitely happens), outline what changes you think need to be made, your reasons for these changes, and the charges that apply. You need never apologize to a client for making suggestions on what will improve the response of his Web site. Every client won't necessarily leap for joy at what you tell her, but at least you've done your duty by using your experience as the basis for certain beneficial suggestions. Again, of course, the customer will have the last say, right or wrong!

— they send in the wrong amount of money for the material they send

Customers are often confused about just how much money to send for the services they desire. For such situations, develop a template that enables you to list the services you've provided and the amount the client needs to send to pay for them.

Ask the customer either to send in a check for the amount owing or send you a note authorizing you to charge this amount on one of the credit cards you accept. Keep this authorization on file in case the customer later questions the charge.

If the work in question is more than $100, I suggest calling the customer first to get approval for the work you'll be doing before you do it.

Note: make sure to inform the customer that his Web site cannot be posted until all outstanding charges are paid. This is one of the great advantages of having an Internet mall. You need never have any outstanding receivables. You do the work when you're paid... and nothing gets posted to the Internet until you're paid. You'll never be in the situation of companies scrambling for money that's owed them and going through all the irritation and difficulty of bill collecting.

— The prospect's material is posted but the prospect wants changes. What do you do?

I've already spoken to this above, but I would like to reinforce my point. The great thing about the Internet is that you can change your message every single minute of the day, if you like. Unfortunately, people do like… not so much because their message is changing but because they forgot to include certain crucial information the first, second or third time they made alterations. Thus, you need to think through how you'll handle all the changes customers want you to make. Here are some suggestions:

- make small changes free. It's good PR, and besides, your advertisers will soon come to resent paying for minor word changes.
- e-mail your changes to Worldprofit. Make it clear (by including client name and URL address) just what home page needs to be changed and precisely what changes need to be made. Your instructions need to be precise so that our programmers know just what to do.
- if you're making the changes yourself, use your downtime to do them. Make all your changes at the same time for maximum efficiency.
- if a client keeps pestering you to make changes, establish your ground rules. "I'll make one small change a week for you without charge. Thereafter, I'll bill you at the rate of $40 per hour." In other words, be client-centered but not a door mat. There are advertisers who will try to run over you if you let them.

— The client needs instructions about how to promote his/her home page. What do you do?

Don't think for one minute that your advertisers are going to know what to do to promote their home pages. Yet only by everyone working together will the traffic increase to the maximum extent. Thus, it's crucial that you provide them with instructions on what to do.

Start by sending a welcome letter to all advertisers. The best — and cheapest — way to do this is via e-mail the day the advertiser's home page is posted. This letter should

- welcome advertisers to your mall and to Worldprofit
- ask them to provide an e-mail address so they receive the *Worldgram* newsletter. Remember, one crucial aspect of the *Worldgram* is to provide continuing information on how to get the best results from a home page… which includes continuing promotional tips.
- advise the advertiser to select a prime benefit for their home page ("Bargain prices for all office supplies.")
- tell the advertiser to put this prime benefit and URL address on ALL marketing communications and ALL documents any prospect or customer sees. Provide some examples like office stationery, business cards, shipping labels, brochures, media kits, *etc.*

Finally, this letter should provide any details you wish the advertiser to have about how to make corrections and additions to an advertiser home page. In other words, explain how you work with your clients.

Along with this welcome letter send a disclaimer form like this.

DISCLAIMER FOR THE WORLDPROFIT MALLS
COPYRIGHT NOTICE AND AGREEMENT
DISCLAIMER OF WARRANTIES AND LIABILITY

Due to the number of sources from which information on the Worldprofit Malls is obtained, and the inherent hazards of electronic distribution, there may be delays, omissions or inaccuracies in such information. Worldprofit Malls and its affiliates, agents and licensers cannot and do not warrant the accuracy, completeness, noninfringement, merchantability or fitness for a particular purpose of the news and information available through the service, or the service itself. Neither Worldprofit nor any of its affiliates, agents or licensers shall be liable to you or to anyone else for any loss or injury caused in whole or part by its negligence or contingencies beyond its control in procuring, compiling, interpreting, reporting or delivering the service and any information through the service. In no event will Worldprofit, its affiliates, agents or licensers be liable to you or anyone else for any decision made or action taken by you in reliance on such information or for any consequential, special or similar damages, even if advised of the possibility of such damages. You agree that the liability of Worldprofit, its affiliates, agents and licensers, if any, arising out of any kind of legal claim (whether in contract, tort or otherwise) in any way connected with this advertising service or the information in this advertising service shall not exceed the amount you paid to Worldprofit for use of its service.

One reason for our lack of problems at Worldprofit is the fact that we do not knowingly post anything that reasonable people would find obscene or objectionable. You won't find material that's prurient, distasteful or harmful at Worldprofit. We are not part of the murky Internet subculture and never will be in any way.

Resellers agree to abide by this policy and our high standards and to ensure that their advertisers agree and adhere to them, too. That's why you must get a signed disclaimer from each advertiser before posting anything from them on the Web, and you must let them know that their files will not be posted until you have such a disclaimer on hand. In the age of fax and e-mail, this is hardly an onerous condition. However, if an advertiser does e-mail or fax you the document, while you should post his home page immediately, you should nonetheless request a signed hard copy of the disclaimer document for your files.

The Marketing You'll Be Doing

The welcome letter you send advertisers is, of course, a marketing communication as well as a way of transmitting important housekeeping details. You need to create a list of all the marketing activities that you'll be using to promote your mall and bring in advertisers. This marketing breaks down into two major components: marketing to recruit advertisers and marketing to promote your mall.

— Marketing to recruit advertisers

To bring in more advertisers, you need to do the following:
- develop an 8 1/2" x 11" flyer. This is a variant of what you'll use on the fax-on-demand and should contain the major selling points about both your mall and Worldprofit and an order form. You may design this as a self-mailer flyer, for a business envelope, or to be printed as a two-page space ad. (If you'd like, you can simply adapt the 8 1/2" x 11" flyer we've already developed as part of the Worldprofit Dealer Kit.)
- develop a series of space ads. These ads, in various sizes, should stress the benefits of your mall and Worldprofit (never forgetting both the low prices and constant promotion) and invite prospects to contact you by phone, fax, fax-on-demand and e-mail. Again, you can adapt ads we already have available.
- create modules for the *Worldgram*. At Worldprofit, we are happy to help you get new clients. E-mail modules about the benefits of joining your mall to George Kosch, and we'll run them as space allows in the *Worldgram*.
- keep a list of all the relevant newsgroups on the Internet for your mall. As you develop modules for the newsletter, make it a point to post these items at the newsgroups, always inviting visitors to these groups to "drop by" to see what's new on your mall.

Note: once you have a fully operating mall at Worldprofit, we help get advertisers for you by running information about your mall and your fax-on-demand number in my Sure-Fire Business Success catalog. This way, you're getting details out on what you're offering to hundreds of thousands of people… and it isn't costing you a dime!

— Promoting your mall

When you're a mall owner you have two objectives: getting the maximum number of advertisers into your mall and getting the maximum number of visitors to your mall. These two objectives are symbiotic.

Brainstorm what you'll do to promote your mall and increase traffic. Obviously, the many suggestions in this book will help you. Here are a few:

- again, use the Internet newsgroups. Post regular notices about what's new at your mall and why people should come see. Every time you add a new advertiser, you have the basis for another newsgroup module.
- make deals with other sites for cross promotions. Tell them you'll list information about their mall or home page in return for a similar listing. Always make sure that your listing is highly promotional and includes complete follow up details. Always stress the benefits of participating in your mall as well as the value of what people will find when they visit.
- make sure that all your marketing communications include your mall name, prime benefit and URL address. You won't be a very credible model for other marketers if you're not doing what you should yourself.
- send media releases to relevant trade, technical and other publications. The same kinds of modules that you're posting in the *Worldgram* and in the newsgroups should be sent to print publications. Always include your phone, fax, fax-on-demand, and e-mail addresses for prompt response.
- Drop a note to the editors of publications listing home page addresses and ask to have your mall listed. Invite them to visit and suggest an article. (*The Boston Globe*, for instance, regularly lists Web sites of interest.)
- remind advertisers to include their URL address in all their media releases. This kind of leverage costs you nothing and, as these stories are printed, necessarily increases your traffic.
- whenever you speak with your advertisers or otherwise communicate with them, quiz them about what they're doing to promote their home pages. You'll find as we have that many advertisers still don't conceptualize their home page as a retail site needing constant promotion but rather as a kind of electronic bill board where you simply post a message and abandon it. Nothing, of course, could be further from the truth. To be on the 'net means to be in the promotion business *every single day*!

Fortunately, when you have a mall at Worldprofit you are not in the promotion business alone. No way, we're working right along with you to increase your traffic.

What We Do To Help You

As you already know promotion at Worldprofit takes several different forms:
- all advertisers do what they can to increase the traffic to their individual Web sites.
- all mall owners do what they can to increase the traffic to their individual mall(s).
- Worldprofit management does what it can to bring people to the malls generally.
Each is a key component in continually increasing the traffic at Worldprofit.

A Wish

I am a very aggressive, indeed an unrelenting promoter. I live, eat, sleep and breath promotion. Why? Because without continuing promotion your business — any business — will die.

If the genie in the bottle came along and gave me a wish, I'd wish that every advertiser at Worldprofit approached the business of promoting his or her home page with the same single-mindedness that I do. That they'd look for and use all the no-cost, low-cost promotional tools available to them and that they'd make it a point to inform all their prospects and customers about their Web sites and faxes-on-demand. *And* that they'd do what they could *before* moaning to me and having it clearly pointed out that no one has a right to complain who hasn't first followed the directions that make the complaint unlikely to occur in the first place.

Well, I may wish all I like... but the reality is that too many people on the Web, even, I must admit, in my own malls, sit back, relax, and enjoy the flight without doing what they're supposed to do to make it successful.

If I were that way, our mall at Worldprofit would be like the lackluster malls where promotion is an afterthought, if it's thought about at all. But I am most assuredly not that way.

A Marketing Empire At Your Disposal

When you take or your advertisers take a home page at Worldprofit, you benefit from the following marketing tools that I have laboriously created over the course of nearly 20 years now, all of which are designed to target the maximum number of people with prospect-centered offers of all kinds and to get these same people to take IMMEDIATE ACTION to acquire them. Let's look at each closely:

- Sales & Marketing Success Card Deck
- national advertising campaign
- Sure-Fire Business Success Catalog
- "Sure-Fire Business Success" and "Qwik-Smarts w/ Dr. Jeffrey Lant" columns
- *Worldgram* newsletter
- deals bringing periodical publishers into association with Worldprofit
- marketing instructions to all Worldprofit advertisers.

– Sales & Marketing Success Card Deck

When an individual receives the card deck, he/she's looking at 102 cards. That's the number we've been running now for several years, every 90 days. That individual probably doesn't even know that 100,000 such decks go out every quarter. This means that every 90 days, I pay for the printing and mailing of 10,200,000 post cards! It's an enormous number.

There are several things to keep in mind about this number.

- I run several cards promoting the Worldprofit malls. Cards like this:

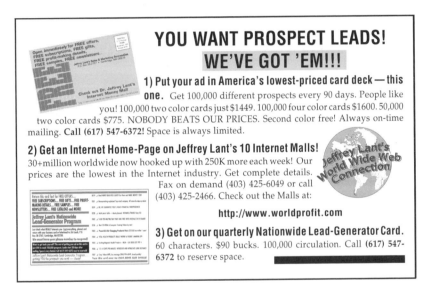

- these cards are strategically placed so that they get a very high readership.
- at least 2/3's of the cards in any individual issue run Worldprofit Web site addresses.

Now, it's important to know that only the traffic at the Main Menu is counted, not the traffic that goes to each individual home page, where the advertiser may not have a counter. Thus, if an advertiser in, say, my card deck runs a card with his Worldprofit URL address featured... when his prospects visit this home page, they're not counted! The daily and ongoing count at Worldprofit, therefore, is always *substantially* higher than the already high numbers at the Main Menu suggest.

When you and your advertisers place an ad at Worldprofit, we'd obviously like them — or you — to purchase a card in the card deck. However, even if they don't purchase a card, they're still benefiting from all the card deck cards that mail. Why? Because when people visit a mall, they don't just visit one home page… they visit many. Moreover, they visit many different *malls*, thereby benefiting many different advertisers.

Before leaving this section on the card deck, I think you should know a few key facts about it that you may wish to share with your advertisers. Remember, putting a card deck at the service of building Web traffic gives Worldprofit a sizable competitive advantage. It's an advantage we mean to maintain… and which should be easy to do given these considerable advantages:

- lowest prices in the card-deck industry. From the first day of business to this, my card-deck prices have been lower than any one else's. The only time others even come close to my offerings is when they're desperate to fill a card deck and reluctantly come down in price. With me, you get low prices every single day, no haggling, no "specials" that some people get and others never know about.

- always on-time mailings. Other decks often mail days, even weeks late. Late mailing is epidemic in this industry. We mail when we say we will. Period.

- card-deck responsive names. I've worked hard over the years to develop just the right mix for who will get the deck. The names, of course, are different with every issue… but in every issue one thing stays the same: they're card-deck responsive. In other words, the deck goes to people who respond to card deck offers. Obviously, that improves your response.

- more four-color cards. Some decks think they can bore you into buying by being stingy on the color. Not me. I know that color attracts and color sells. That's why I price four-color printing at cost and do everything I can to make it easy for people to run a four-color card.

- copywriting assistance. Few people in the world have written more card-deck cards than I have. That's why, for a very low cost (which I purposefully keep below my regular copywriting fees), I'm available to write your card *personally*.

- camera-ready art assistance. The same can be said for my long-time designer and pal John Hamwey. He is available for any kind of design, of course, (including elaborate Web sites on the Internet), but he's developed a real expertise in producing card-deck cards that get results. You may call him at ABC Publications at (617) 575-9915.

- top positions at no extra cost. Other decks charge you more for a top 10 or top 20 position in the deck. Or they reserve these spaces for their pampered favorites. Not me. Democratically, I open them up to anyone — at no extra cost. You pay early, yes, but not more. Top 10 positions are allocated to people who pay no later than the day the previous deck mails. Top 20 positions are allocated 30 days prior to the published closing date. It's easy, fair, and gives everyone a shot at the cards prospects will see first and which have a marginal advantage over those falling later in the deck.

The InternetConnect Card

I developed this unique card so that advertisers on limited budgets who cannot afford a full card could nonetheless direct more traffic right to their home pages. This card, unique in the industry, consists of 60-character ads concluding with the advertiser's individual URL address. (See page 84 for example)

All Worldprofit advertisers can run on this card which is sent out quarterly in each Sales & Marketing Success deck. The cost at this writing is just $90 per issue, which isn't bad for a guaranteed 100,000 circulation. Note: tell your advertisers about this service and have them call me to get on this card.

— National Advertising Campaign

Every single day, some awed prospect calls us to say, "I've got to get into your malls. I see your ads *everywhere*." It's true. One of the benefits you and your advertisers get by participating in the Worldprofit malls is the ongoing national ad campaign organized and run by me.

We run lots of ads. Here are a couple of examples:

You've probably seen them.

These ads have several objectives, to

- increase traffic at the malls
- get people to become advertisers, and
- build up our e-mail list so that more prospects receive our highly promotional *Worldgram* newsletter.

I make creative deals with many periodical publishers, publishers we also encourage to take their own Web sites at Worldprofit (see below).

— Sure-Fire Business Success Catalog

If you receive my Sure-Fire Business Success Catalog (and if not, you can call me at (617) 547-6372 to start your free subscription), you already know that each issue contains several pages devoted to the malls and critical developments therein.

This catalog, which I have been doing now for many, many years, goes out to 140,000+ people each time. Some of these people are part of my house mailing list. Others come from my lead sources. Either way, I make it a point to send it to people who are interested in entrepreneurial subjects and living better.

The catalog has several purposes beyond the obvious one of selling my merchandise, including.

- directing all recipients to visit the Worldprofit malls
- selling card deck cards (which obviously translates into mall development benefits)
- telling people to send in their e-mail for a free *Worldgram* subscription, and
- increasing fax-on-demand traffic.

1-(403) 425-6049

Dial this 24 hour fax-on-demand number from your fax phone. Press the document number listed below on your telephone key pad and the information you want will be faxed back to you immediately. If you want multiple documents, press them in as prompted.

Document #	Description
1	Put your home page in the 10 Malls at Worldprofit! http://www.worldprofit.com
2	Profit from our money-making fax-on-demand system. Tell your prospects to call (403) 425-6049 and get all the information they need to know about what you're selling at *their* expense.
3	Promote your company, product, or service in Jeffrey's quarterly 100,000 circulation Card Deck.
4	Publishers: Complete details on running Jeffrey's two syndicated columns, including article titles.
5	Get your own mall at Worldprofit and really make Internet profit!
6	Have Jeffrey's International Copywriting & Netvertising Center do all your marketing communications. Retain Jeffrey as your marketing consultant.
7	Join The Worldprofit Dealer Program. Make $ selling Worldprofit home pages!
8	Improve your Web results! Get more hits, more leads, motivate prospects and make more $$$$$$$$!
9	In MLM? Discover how Jeffrey works with you to build your commissions... and the opportunity you're in!
85	Promote your Native American craft, business, or cause on the Native Internet Mall!
184	Looking for a LOW COST & NO RISK, PROFITABLE home-based business? Here it is!!!
186	Get a Web site in the new Worldprofit Tech Mall. Sell your technology products worldwide. http://www.worldprofit.com/techmall
189	Solid business opportunity. 6 figures first year with #1 Nutritional Authority

Obviously, all these build mall traffic and thereby benefit you and your advertisers.

— "Sure-Fire Business Success" and "Qwik-Smarts w/ Dr. Jeffrey Lant" columns

I've always been a writing machine ever since those early days, nigh onto a half century now, since I published my first article. Going into print is as natural to me as breathing, and I hope this felicitous state of affairs remains with me for life.

I wrote my first regular column back when I was about 10 or 11 in the newspaper I created and published, *The Belmont Star*. I went to two high schools and had a column at each one. I wrote another in college. And for the last 15 years or so, I've written, first, "Sure-Fire Business Success" and then "Qwik-Smarts w/ Dr. Jeffrey Lant." These fast-moving, very personal and, I hope, ultra-practical columns deal with specific subjects designed to help people get ahead in our tricky, tumultuous world.

Nowadays about 200 publications (the number is always fluctuating) around the world print these articles in both traditional paper format and, of course, on the Web. We also feature them in my own *Worldprofit On-line Magazine* that comes out monthly and does much to attract continuing traffic to Worldprofit.

What's important for you and your advertisers to know is that each article ends with a "Resource Box." This is a blatantly promotional section of each article. Here's what one looks like:

Resource Box

Dr. Jeffrey Lant runs a complex of 10 malls at Worldprofit. These malls include the Money Mall, Better Health Mall, Business to Business Mall, Mail Order Mall, and Network Marketing Mall. Get information on participating by using 24 hour fax on demand (403) 425-6049 document #1 or calling (403) 425-2466. Get your own specialty Mall at Worldprofit and cash in on the Internet. Same fax, document #5. Get a free subscription to his twice-monthly *Worldgram* newsletter, packed with marketing tips to build your business by sending your e-mail address to webmaster@worldprofit.com Access the malls at http://www.worldprofit.com Get a free subscription to his quarterly Sure-Fire Business Success Catalog by calling (617) 547-6372.

The purpose of this Resource Box is to sell merchandise and build prospect lists, both on and off the Web. These articles run in publications and circulate around the world. Every time one runs, the traffic at Worldprofit increases, new advertisers sign up (who, we hope, do their bit to increase the traffic), and — you benefit, without every having to lift your pretty little finger!

— Worldgram newsletter

Can parents love all their children the same? I doubt it. Certainly, in my case, my *Worldgram* newsletter gives me a special thrill. It should do the same for you.

The *Worldgram* is published twice-monthly and sent out solely by e-mail transmission. Like most newsletters it has its on-going departments, including

- promotional tips for your home page
- TechAdvance, tech modules from George Kosch
- the E-Mart, with products for sale
- news notes from all our resellers
- promotional modules from mall advertisers, and
- other business building information.

What's neat about the *Worldgram* is that it uses no paper. It's a total electronic publication. What's also neat is the speed at which it is both compiled (remember, we use my handy module format) and transmitted. Within minutes of when we've finished any given issue, people around the world have it. Fabulous!

The *Worldgram* offers you many advantages:

- First, you can use it as an offer to all your prospects and advertisers, using words like these

    DR. JEFFREY LANT OFFERS FREE SUBSCRIPTION TO HIS ON-LINE
    WORLDGRAM NEWSLETTER

Got an e-mail address? If so, Dr. Jeffrey Lant will give you a free subscription to his twice-monthly *Worldgram* newsletter. Packed with business-building information you can use right now, this newsletter has a marketing focus. Unsurprisingly, given Jeffrey's 10 Internet malls it also includes a ton of useful stuff about how to profit from the World Wide Web. Get your subscription started by sending your e-mail address to webmaster@worldprofit.com Tell them <your name here> sent you! Check out Jeffrey's malls at http://www.worldprofit.com

- by inserting regular modules into each transmission, you can bring your own sales messages and news notes to the attention of both prospects and advertisers. You can also encourage advertisers to submit the occasional news notes.

- you can use it to transmit marketing and promotional tips to your advertisers. Just in case this isn't pellucidly clear by now, let me say again that one key reason why the traffic at Worldprofit grows like it does is because we not only encourage all advertisers to do their part to promote their Web sites but because we provide them with ongoing tips for doing so — and my own distinctive brand of insistent motivation.

I encourage all mall resellers to regard the *Worldgram* as their newsletter, too, and to use it to build their traffic. I certainly do. Here's just one of the many ads I run, this one from my card deck, designed to build our e-mail list and thus the number of prospects we market Worldprofit to.

Side 1 shown

— Deals Bringing Periodical Publishers Into Association With Worldprofit

Because of my long involvement with print publishing, I am aware of both its value and impact. I also have productive relationships with many such publishers. As a result I am convincingly able to emphasize to publishers the value of being associated with Worldprofit and just what they need to do to make the association mutually profitable.

My objective is simple: if a periodical wants to reach the kinds of people we attract to Worldprofit, I want that publisher to be a part of Worldprofit. There are many mutual advantages to such an association:

- the publisher gets a new profit center with a large, expanding audience, and
- Worldprofit gets another means of promoting the malls and bringing in a host of new advertisers.

It's a win-win-win situation, with the new advertisers themselves dramatically benefiting, too.

Because of these advantages, I make a point of reaching out to publishers and explaining why they should associate with Worldprofit. Predictably, some of these publishers, long familiar with the traditional publishing environment, are loath to change. Indeed, with a few, it would probably be easier dealing with mules, so little do they want to hear about the changing environment, much less adapt themselves to it. That's predictable.

The traditional publishing environment has existed for a long time, and, for many, it's a lot easier to hope that the radical new publishing environment won't impact them than to take the pro-active step of understanding that environment and changing operations to profit from it. I understand how difficult it is to make constructive changes... I also understand that in an environment of far-reaching change, one is going to be affected by events whether one wants to be or not. Better to embrace the change constructively than to watch helplessly as one's universe crumbles, without doing what's necessary to survive the change and prosper from it.

In this situation, I keep chipping away at the publishers who ought to be in Worldprofit, letting them know and letting them know again that it's in their interest to work with us... and that we'll continue to approach them until they get the message. You see, I am a very persistent and, when necessary, a very patient man. Once I have made up my mind that a prospect will be better off in association with us than without, I will keep gnawing away at that prospect so long as any advantage is to be gained by doing so. Most salespeople are not like that. They give up. I get motivated, determined to be successful, a marketing Mounty, who always gets my man (or woman)!

No wonder! The stakes are high. When a publication comes into association with Worldprofit, its publisher is going to do the following:

- tell his/her readers why
- run the Worldprofit address in every issue of the publication and supply reasons for visiting
- contact all current advertisers and advertising prospects to induce them to advertise at Worldprofit.

As a result, they will:

- dramatically increase their reading public

- enter into a publishing environment where there are no paper, print, or postage costs

- benefit from all the promotional gambits we do at Worldprofit and from the steadily increasing traffic that results.

When a new publisher associates with us he immediately gets a competitive edge publishers outside Worldprofit can never have and will never beat. Net result? The far-sighted publisher in association with us prospers with a new profit center; the other, having stultified himself, hands his competitors the advantage that will, in due course, destroy him.

Fortunately, despite the mules, *many* far-seeing and entrepreneurial publishers have joined Worldprofit as you'll see by searching the malls. And more will come in the future, because I do not intend to rest until every appropriate publisher is not only in Worldprofit but consistently brings the benefits of Worldprofit home to both his readers and advertisers and so helps increase the life-giving mall traffic every single day.

— Marketing Instructions To All Worldprofit Advertisers

In the middle of every night, George Kosch sends me a list of the new Worldprofit advertisers who have signed up that day. By 9 a.m. I have sent them all detailed instructions on what they need to do to make their involvement with Worldprofit profitable. These letters go out with the first mail of the day, every day.

I get the distinct feeling, from constant perusal of other malls, that their owners treat their malls like a kind of storage facility. An advertiser comes in, posts an ad, and disappears, hoping for the best from the message left behind. The valuable Web site property is not husbanded, not overseen, not developed for maximum benefit. It merely is.

Things couldn't be more different at Worldprofit.

As should now be clear to you, I believe that malls prosper because *everyone* does their bit to make them prosper, mall owner and mall advertiser. However mall advertisers don't come into the world instinctively knowing what to do. They need guidance. And that, every day, is what I provide them in their welcome letter… in regular transmissions of the *Worldgram* newsletter… and now, of course, in this resource.

These instructions, as you won't be surprised to learn having read this book, cover all aspects of what advertisers need to do to promote their Web site thereby increasing its traffic and that of the malls generally.

I deal with

- how to create prime benefits
- where to promote your URL address
- how to integrate Web site promotion into all your marketing communications
- making sure nothing that touches prospects and customers leaves your office without prime benefit and URL address, *etc.*

The kinds of topics, in short, which we've been discussing throughout this book.

When people come into Worldprofit, they come into a combine where the resources of all are put towards the good of all. As I write this book, there are many hundreds of companies in the malls at Worldprofit. This, in time, will become many thousands… and then, a little further along, many tens of thousands of companies.

My grand design is simple and compelling: to work with tens of thousands of businesses worldwide. To let them know that they can achieve a meaningful, profitable Web presence at modest price. That I expect neither technical insight nor marketing heroics from them. What I do expect, however, is

- a client-centered message. I want prospects who come to their sites to know at once what units of value the advertiser is offering them, what reason for prompt response.

- promotion of their Web site to be fully integrated into their other marketing activities, so that they inform the maximum number of prospects and customers about that Web site and its prime benefit for the least possible cost, and

- that these self same clients keep their sites up-to-date so that people who visit are not forced to wade through outmoded, irrelevant data to get to the few meaningful nuggets.

Is this too much to ask?

I certainly don't think so, but whether it is or not I shall continue to urge, prompt, push, wheedle, and cajole all Worldprofit advertisers to assist the general good by implementing these three key points.

Thus, these hundreds, thousands, and ultimately tens of thousands of advertisers working together, relentlessly, sensibly, consistently, thoroughly, will produce a series of associated malls that will astonish the world by the client-centered simplicity of their approach, the clarity of their presentation, and the value of all the information. As a result, growth (already so far so fast) will be inevitable… and so will the general prosperity!

Last Words

This chapter has had one unabashed objective: getting you to develop your own lucrative mall at Worldprofit. I am looking for a select band of very special people who don't just want to live in the future, but want to have an active hand in shaping it… as well as profiting from it. Such people are both rare and precious.

You will know after reading this chapter whether you wish to join us at Worldprofit, whether you have what it takes to develop a valuable property and seize a subject to be marketed around the world for the advantage of yourself, your advertisers and Worldprofit itself. If so, call (403) 425-6049 and get document #5 now or e-mail webmaster@worldprofit.com to request it. You will get up-to-the-minute information on our Reseller Program.

It is in the nature of things that fewer people will respond to this chapter than others. Creating, developing and managing a mall is, after all, a serious commitment. While all people who read this book and seriously follow its suggestions will prosper, those who work with us to create their own malls will prosper most of all.

Chapter 11

HOW TO PROFIT AS A WORLDPROFIT DEALER

When you finished the last chapter did you have the feeling that while you might someday like to have your own mall that you weren't quite ready for it now? Yet that you'd like a way of profiting from staggering growth of the Internet beyond just having your own Web site?

Well, this chapter is for you. It explains how you can profit by becoming a Worldprofit Dealer. It is the third major way you can profit through your association with me and with Worldprofit... the first being to get a Web site of your own; the second by developing your own lucrative mall property.

Why I Established The Worldprofit Dealer Program

As you already know, growth on the Internet is astronomical... and growing every day. *The Wall Street Journal*, for instance, says that home pages on the Internet will explode from a current level of about 18 million to over one billion in just three to four years. *USA Today* says emphatically, "Every business will have a Web site." A recent program on PBS had an Internet expert talking about 5 *billion* Web sites within ten years. Having read this volume you know why so many people are flocking to the Web.

I established the Worldprofit Dealer Program for one simple reason: to enable people worldwide to cash in on this exponential growth without having to own a computer or a Web site, much less create a mall and find a programmer, as described in the previous chapter. Thanks to my dealer program you can profit from the Internet without going anywhere near the Internet!

How Does The Worldprofit Dealer Program Work

We have purposefully made the Worldprofit Dealer Program as easy as possible. When you become a dealer, you get

- a Lifetime Dealer Number.
- all the marketing materials you need. I've personally developed the 8 1/2"x 11" flyers and all the prospect ads you'll need. These marketing communications explain the considerable benefits of being part of the malls at Worldprofit. These benefits include:
- STATE-OF-THE-ART TECHNICAL ASSISTANCE. Our highly skilled technical staff provides advertisers with full professional Web site development. We offer free technical consultation during the entire set-up process. Advertisers can take advantage of our full spectrum of Internet capabilities including color graphics,

electronic order form, sound clips, and advanced multi-media. We produce professional interactive Web sites with the emphasis on our customers getting results! We stay abreast of developments in the fast-moving Internet environment and translate these developments so that you profit from them. You don't need to know anything about technology... the Web... or even own or operate a computer. We do everything for you to make sure you profit now from current technology.

- FREE SUBSCRIPTION TO OUR TWICE MONTHLY *Worldgram* newsletter. We'll give every single person you refer (assuming they have an e-mail address) a free subscription to our twice-monthly newsletter. This newsletter is packed with useful marketing and business building information, including suggestions on how to create a money-making Web site.

- UNRELENTING MALL MARKETING & PROMOTION. We have the most aggressive marketing program in the Internet business. We know that people with Web sites want increased traffic. Here are just some of ways we promote the malls to increase that traffic:

  - Jeffrey Lant's quarterly 100,000 circulation Sales & Marketing Success Card Deck. At least 60-70 cards per issue promote the Worldprofit malls in one way or another.
  - marketing in many other card decks
  - quarterly 140,000+ Sure-Fire Business Success Catalog
  - through *Worldprofit On-Line Magazine* (you can access this at worldprofit.com to see for yourself)
  - through two internationally syndicated columns "Sure-Fire Business Success" and "Qwik-Smarts w/ Dr. Jeffrey Lant." These columns reach over 1.5 million people monthly.
  - through the *Worldgram*.
  - through Internet search computers and newsgroups, and
  - by providing detailed marketing suggestions and recommendations to all Web site advertisers at Worldprofit. It's no surprise that the traffic goes up significantly every single day. Want to know how much? There's a counter on the Main Menu at worldprofit.com so you'll know as fast we do!

- REASONABLY PRICED PROFESSIONAL COPYWRITING ASSISTANCE. We know that advertisers may not be expert in creating client-centered home pages. No problem! Our expert copywriters can do it for them... at prices others just cannot (or will not) match!!!

- LOWEST WEB SITE PRICES ON THE ENTIRE INTERNET. Business people are always interested in value. At Worldprofit, we give it to them in spades! Our prices are the lowest on the entire Internet. Advertisers can have a one-year Web site with state-of-the-art fax-on-demand service (so their prospects can get all the information they want by calling a central number) for a year for just about a buck a day!!! That's right, just about a dollar a day. Given the fact that others charge hundreds, even thousands of dollars a month (and that additional per-lead costs are common), you can see now why the prices at Worldprofit are such a bargain... especially given our fast-rising traffic level. We give advertisers high traffic and low cost... which is just the way they like it!!!

How You Get Compensated As A Worldprofit Dealer

Anytime anyone takes a Web site at Worldprofit providing your Lifetime Dealer Number, you derive a commission check. Your customers may complete the sign-up form (which has your number printed on it), or they may call or e-mail us to sign up and provide your number to us at that time. So long as they give us your Lifetime Dealer Number you're entitled to the commission, which is paid monthly.

Moreover, when your customers renew you get another commission check — for as long as they continue to be Worldprofit advertisers. Moreover, we do everything we can to keep these advertisers happy, not least by regularly communicating with them through the *Worldgram* and making sure their experience at Worldprofit is a profitable one.

Note: because you can benefit from a customer's renewal for years to come, once you've become a dealer it's essential that you keep your address, phone and e-mail records with us up-to-date. Otherwise, your commission checks will be undeliverable!

Who Should Become A Worldprofit Dealer

The number of people who should become Worldprofit dealers is immense. They include:

- anyone with a house mailing list or regular mailing program reaching the kinds of designated prospects for the Worldprofit malls. In other words, if you have a mailing list of home-based business owners, you should become a dealer so that you can bring these people information about the Home-based Business Mall. If you have a business to business service such as printing and maintain a house mailing list... you should become a dealer, too.

- anyone with a periodical publication catering to the same kinds of people we cater to in the Worldprofit malls. Are you a publisher reaching people in mail order? Why, then, you'll want to become a dealer and refer mail order types to Worldprofit and profit accordingly. Do you have a publication reaching network marketers? Ditto.

- you are a book publisher. There are thousands of book publishers who can profit as Worldprofit dealers right this minute. How? Simply by inserting our flyers into their outgoing book packages.

- your customers are Worldprofit's customers. Consider the kinds of customers you reach. Then consider the kinds of customers for each of the Worldprofit malls (a complex, by the way, which is constantly expanding, thereby adding new targeted customer and prospect groups). Think how you get to these people... by mail, with a newsletter, with packages, through e-mail. Wouldn't it be easy for you just to insert the Worldprofit marketing materials — always remembering they feature your Lifetime Dealer Number — and reap the benefits therefrom?

- you give workshops and other talk programs to the kinds of people who should be in the Worldprofit malls. If the people attending your talk programs are the kinds of people who should be in the Worldprofit malls, give them our marketing communications and make more money!

Other People Who Should Be Worldprofit Dealers

- Are you selling a network marketing opportunity? Then you're reaching a ton of people one way and another. Why couldn't you ask your prospects, at a convenient moment at the end of your conversation, what business they're in and whether they have a Web site already. Say the person responds, "I'm a florist and, no, I don't have a Web site." They you say, "Let me give you some information that will be helpful to your business" and give them the Worldprofit marketing information!

- Are you in sales, calling on different accounts either in person or on the phone? You do the same! What's great about the Worldprofit Dealer Program is that it's simple and straightforward. If the person you're communicating with should be on the Internet and is part of the numerous (and expanding) target groups we cater to at Worldprofit, then you're doing that person a favor by telling them about Worldprofit.

And if the person is already on the Internet? Then tell them they can get a link at Worldprofit and start benefiting from our major promotion and daily increased traffic. Bingo! A new advertiser joins the group of satisfied Worldprofit customers… and you get a nice commission check!!!

But, you say, I don't have any of these things in place. I'm just starting out. No problem. Especially for you, we created the prospect-generating ads you get as part of your Worldprofit Dealer Kit. These ads come in various sizes, strongly point out the benefits of going on the Internet, and ask people to contact you. All you do is add your name, address, phone, fax, *etc.* in the space provided and run in whatever publication(s) you like. We even give you suggestions on where to get appropriate lists of publications you may wish to consider running these ads in.

As you can see, there are literally hundreds of thousands of people worldwide who should become Worldprofit dealers. This number is constantly increasing as we add new malls and, therefore, new targeted prospect groups.

On the average day, I identify dozens of new dealer sources just from the people who call and write to me. Many of these people have lost sight of the forest for the trees. The other day, for instance, I was talking to a guy who has a catalog of office supplies. When I told him about the Worldprofit dealer program he was initially disinterested, even hostile. Why, he sold office supplies. He wasn't on the Internet… knew nothing about it… wasn't planning on going on the Internet. And that, as he practically stomped his tootsie, was that. That, of course, wasn't that. As you're not surprised to learn, I don't take no for an answer when I know there's money to be made through a little behavior modification (and I don't mean mine).

I asked the fellow if he'd give he just 120 seconds of his time to show him how we could make money together. He reluctantly agreed. I then pointed out that he was reaching the

kinds of business people who could easily find a home in our Business to Business Mall...
and our Money Mall... in our Home-based Business Mall... in our Information Mall, *etc.*
That while it was true that selling office supplies was indeed his primary objective, was he
averse to adding another service that would enable him to make still more profit from his
primary customers... all by

- printing a notice in his catalog
- inserting one of our flyers in his outgoing mail or
- doing so in the packages he sends to his customers?

Just as I thought, in a minute the guy was interested in becoming a dealer... and in
under five he said he'd give it serious consideration. The next day when I called him, I
closed him and now he's promoting Worldprofit and making himself some nice extra money!
(He's still not on the Internet... but that, too, will happen. Believe me.)

What You Need To Do To Profit As A Worldprofit Dealer

My own personal belief is that profiting as a Worldprofit dealer is about the easiest
thing to do in this world — if you do what's necessary to profit.

- Set an objective. As you already know, I'm a committed management-by-objec-
  tives thinker. Thus, decide how many people you want to turn on to Worldprofit
  in the course of a week, a month, how much extra money you'd like to make.
  Then write down your objective and post it. Now you're really on your way to
  success.
- You're more likely to profit if you're familiar with the Internet and have a Web
  site at Worldprofit. Why? Because you'll understand how the Internet works and
  because people are most assuredly going to ask you (if you talk to people about
  the Internet) what your own experience has been like... and whether you have a
  Web site at Worldprofit. In other words, if you're not in Worldprofit yourself,
  they may well dismiss what you say as entirely self-serving. As I've previously
  said, to be a Worldprofit dealer you don't have to have a computer, don't have to
  have to be on the Internet, don't have to have a Web site at Worldprofit, and
  don't have to know anything at all about the Internet. You could become a dealer
  and simply stuff our marketing communications (the very ones we use and which
  have been so profitable for us) in your outgoing packages. That works... but it
  doesn't work as well as it could because you're not using all the tools that you
  could be using.
- Integrate the Worldprofit Dealer Program into every aspect of your business life.
  One of the most irritating things about dealing with people in business is how
  myopic they are. Billions of bits of useful information go to waste every single
  day because people don't attempt to gather these bits and make use of them. It's
  infuriating. I was talking to a fellow in network marketing yesterday who says
  he wants to get rich. But, you now, he never asks the people to whom he talks
  what they do for a living. I told him that information was priceless. Why? Because every time he talked to someone in business, for example, he could turn
  them on to Worldprofit and make a nice commission check for himself. He's paying to make sales calls, either in person or on the phone; he's paying to send out

information. He's paying to stay in touch. However, he's not maximizing his return on investment because he's not getting all the information he needs to profit, much less working on it. Stupid!

Or take the silly mail order dealer I talked to the other day who was determined not to be persuaded to become a Worldprofit dealer. Every day this fellow mails catalogs and letters and books to people who are perfect for various Worldprofit malls. The fellow has no Internet line and currently has no way at all of benefiting from the Internet. He has no Web site, no mall, and no Web materials at all to bring to his prospects and customers... despite the fact that he's reaching — every single day — the precise sort of people who should be profiting from the Web.

When I spoke to him he kept saying over and over, "I don't know anything about the Internet," as if that were some kind of magic mantra. Look, people, ignorance is no excuse. Face it, it would be better for the guy if he did know something about the Internet. It would be better if he did what was necessary to give himself an Internet presence (lots of people, after all, do very well, thank you, selling information products over the Web). It would be even better if he thought about how he could really cash in on the Internet by developing a mall property. Failing all this, he could *still* profit by merely referring his prospects and customers to Worldprofit and letting us set them up in the profitable Web sites that this bozo wouldn't take the time and trouble to make use of for himself. But, no, "I don't know anything about the Internet, I don't know anything about the Internet."

You know, when I was younger, I was as softly muddle-headed and kind-hearted as any liberal in the world. However, over the years I've now dealt with millions of people one way and another, and I've come to the hard and fast conclusion that people are their own worst enemies; more often than not they deserve what they get, including Mr. "I don't know anything about the Internet" who is determined to go down with his ship.

Refer A Person To Worldprofit, Put Some Money In Your Pocket

When I set up the Worldprofit Dealer Program, I recognized that the dealers would never know as much about Worldprofit as I do... that they would never be as enthusiastic about it as I am. I had to take into account their lesser knowledge and enthusiasm and still create a program that meets our mutual objectives.

Thus, when you're a Worldprofit dealer

- if a prospect asks you a question you can't answer about what Worldprofit is or how we promote the malls... or how to set up a state-of-the-art home page, if you don't know, you simply say, "I don't know. But if you talk to the folks at Worldprofit they'll tell you." I learned one thing from my experience in network marketing: that independent distributors will never know as much about the companies they represent as full-time people in those companies themselves. It would be nice if they did, but in this world it's just not going to happen. Thus, I make it clear to the dealers to refer all questions to us... and that we'll work along with you as your senior partner, if you will, not just to answer the prospect's questions... but to *close* the prospect into the appropriate mall. In other words, we'll work with you to get you your commission. What could be fairer than that?

> Prospect: "I have already have a home page on the Web. Can Worldprofit provide a link?"
>
> You: "I don't know. But here's the Worldprofit phone number, (403) 425-2466. They can tell you! Just be sure to give them my Dealer Number when you call."
>
> Prospect: "I want to have my Web site in full color with an audio clip. Can I have that?"
>
> You: "I don't know. But here's the Worldprofit phone number, (403) 425-2466. They can tell you! Just be sure to give them my Dealer Number when you call."
>
> Prospect: "I want to put my entire catalog in one of the Worldprofit malls. What's the best way to do that?"
>
> You: "I don't know. But here's the Worldprofit phone number, (403) 425-2466. They can tell you! Just be sure to give them my Dealer Number when you call."

Get the drift? We work with you. Day in, day out. However as the Chinese laundryman says, "no tickee, no washee." If the person you refer doesn't give us YOUR Lifetime Dealer Number, how are we going to know to cut a commission check for you? If we don't have a current address for you, how are we going to get you that check? In other words, do your part!

Tips For Profiting As A Worldprofit Dealer

There are literally hundreds of thousands of people who can profit as Worldprofit dealers. Their situations are all going to be a little different. However, here are some tips to get you thinking so that you can make money every single day working with us and putting us to work for you.

- Consider the mailings you already do to your customers. About every business in the world mails to its customers from time to time. But do you know how much your mailing weighs? In the United States just now, a one ounce letter goes for 32 cents. Say your package contains just three sheets, a two-page sales letter and a standard three-fold brochure. You've got room for TWO more 8 $1/2$" x 11" pages — four sides. You could EASILY fit in one of our standard back-to-back 8 $1/2$" x 11" flyers. What do you have to do? Take our camera-ready art (with your Lifetime Dealer Number on it, mind you) to a quick copy shop and print up the number of copies you need. You've just added a dandy new profit center without costing you an extra dime for postage. Smart.

- Think about your catalog. Do you produce one? Well, why not either run one of our standard flyers in it, or, if your space and format do not permit, how about one of our space ads to generate prospect leads? Ask people who are interested in profiting from the Web to call you and then send just these people the marketing materials?

- Consider the questions you ask prospects. If you want to sell, you need as much relevant prospect data as possible. How about adding one question to your repertoire: "Do you have a Web site <or Internet home page> yet?" Whether the answer is yes or no doesn't much matter. If it's yes, you simply pitch the prospect on going into the HEAVILY PROMOTED and HIGH TRAFFIC Worldprofit Malls. If it's no, why, then, this is certainly a candidate for a Web site. Remember what *USA Today* wrote, "Every business will have a Web site!"

- Mull over the talk programs you do. I don't know about you, but before I speak I want my audience sitting there reading my materials. That's why I always hand out (personally, whenever possible) marketing flyers, catalogs, *etc.* to people in my audience as they come in. Since there are always early, early birds, this is a good way to get them started on — buying! By the time the inevitable late-comers arrive, you should already have made a pocketful of sales. Thus, when you're speaking to an audience where the people in it should be in at least one Worldprofit mall, make sure to distribute the materials with your dealer number.

- Shipping packages? I do. Except for Sundays and holidays, I ship packages every single day of the year. I regard every shipped package as an opportunity to make more money. That's why packages never leave my office without a host of additional offers. What about you? Shipping is a very considerable expense these days. Why not do everything you can to minimize it and increase your profit? In other words, why not insert Worldprofit materials into every single outgoing package — the single relevant criterion being that that package is going to someone who ought to be in a Worldprofit mall in the first place. (Remember, we are always adding new ones.)

- Upgrade customers. Do you make sales every single day. I hope so. But do you try to upgrade every single sale you make every single day??? Many marketers are remiss in this area. Say, however, that you've just finished selling a customer a display unit for exhibitions. You know they sell high end photocopy equipment. Did you think about asking them if they're on the Internet? WHY NOT??? The objective is not just to sell to a customer once... that's far too expensive and time-consuming. The objective isn't just to sell to that customer once in a day. That's not using your noggin, either. The objective is to identify as many customer wants as possible... and to satisfy as many of them as you can. So instead of congratulating yourself that you've made just that one sale — and heading to the bar to celebrate — you say instead, "Have you thought about advertising those photocopiers on the Web?"

Objections You May Hear And How To Deal With Them

Face it. There are a lot of snarly people in the world who don't purchase without being pushed, pulled, and prodded to purchase. These are The Objectors... and they often delight in being as difficult as possible. So be prepared for them!

- ◆ "The Web doesn't work." These people haven't read this book. Suggest they do. Also find out if they're got a client-centered Web site in a heavily promoted mall. Or did they make Mistake #1, namely trying to go it alone, forcing themselves to be responsible for everything — content, promotion, technical advances? When you ask people who groan about the Web how they got to that point, you find out — not just occasionally, but always — that they did it wrong. Unless they're defeatniks, determined to fail, they might just listen to what you have to say on the subject. If not, refer them to us and let us work them over. They deserve to profit from the Web, even if they're among the obstinate ones.

♦ "The Web's expensive." We hear this a lot and for the unwise it's true. The Web can cost a lot... way too much. However, as you already know from this volume, our fees at Worldprofit are just a fraction of what others charge. These days there isn't a day that goes by that I don't receive a phone call from someone exclaiming about the low prices at Worldprofit. These people are usually the dazed and bloody ones who have found out that sharks always go for the jugular. Their sincere gratitude at how we've arranged matters at Worldprofit (very, very differently) sincerely touches me. The Web doesn't have to be expensive. Show them our prices... or refer them to us and we'll happily do so.

♦ "I don't need to advertise worldwide." Rightly, people don't want to pay an extra nickel for their advertising. They want to target just the people they want and not spend any more getting to those they don't. But the Web doesn't work like traditional advertising. You're not going to pay any more to advertise worldwide (unless you unwisely select one of the expensive Web content providers) than you pay to advertise in Mobile. People who are selling locally and only want to sell locally should say so — in their home page. All advertising is about qualifying. If you need to provide your prospects with information on just who you want to deal with (which includes a whole lot more factors than just where they're located), why, then, do so. What's great about the Web is that you can say precisely who you want to deal with, get access to them for a low, low price (assuming you're in the right mall) and provide them with all the information they need about what you're selling. What could be better?

♦ "I don't own a computer." Lots of people have a very crazy notion about the Internet. They think *they* have to be on the Internet to profit from the Internet. Well, let's be clear about this. Of course it's better for you if you're on the Internet. There are more things you can do that way, more benefits you can get. (No Internet access, for instance, means no free *Worldgram* subscription!) However, you don't have to be on the Internet. "But," people wail to me, "how am I going to get my leads if I'm not on the Internet." This question betokens a shocking ignorance about how the Internet works. "How, indeed," I reply. "By providing your prospects with your phone number, fax, address, whatever you're using now!" Lack of a computer is no excuse for not having a Web site.

♦ "I'm not comfortable with technology." Another stunner. The Internet is a series of technological advances. However you don't need to understand them any more than you understand how your toaster works. Think of all the technological advances you use every single day that you really don't understand. What you need to understand is that the Internet is a marketing tool... and you need to consider how best to use it to reach your marketing objectives. There are people, of course, people like George Kosch, who make it their business to stay abreast of breaking technological developments. Be grateful they're there. Because when they're at their posts understanding developments and putting them into a form you can use... you can focus your attention on the infinitely more engaging business of using the Internet to make more money every single day.

You'll hear other objectives, too, but don't let them get you down. Most of them stem from a complete misunderstanding of the Internet and failure to use the Web properly. Sometimes, of course, you have to pinch yourself from not laughing aloud at the howlers people come up with. From my studies of social history, I can tell you the same sorts of questions and comments emerged when automobiles first hit the road... and when radio made its appearance. The important thing is to do your best to answer these objections... or just to refer the people to us. We've heard it all before.

How We Assist You To Make Money As A Worldprofit Dealer

By this time, you already know that I'm an activist. During the writing of this chapter, I got a call from a fellow in Australia who was astonished to talk directly to me about his plan to launch a huge information-product emporium Down Under and how he could integrate a Worldprofit dealership. Why so astonished? It was 6:30 a.m. and I was at work putting down these words as fast as I could before they escaped into the ether. So, understand, that while the world and his brother are snug in their beds I'm up working to build an international empire of which the Internet is a very significant piece.

Understand, too, that I want *you* to become a dealer, whether you're reading this book in Albuquerque or Bombay — as people most assuredly will. I want you to know, too, that we at Worldprofit are committed to doing what we must to ensure your success, which begins by creating the quality product — our malls — on which that success must necessarily rest. So, let me share with you just what we're going to help you... so that you'll not only be comfortable as a Worldprofit dealer but make as much money as you want to.

— Mall Development

We will consistently build the product base that constitutes the malls at Worldprofit. When you visit Worldprofit today you'll be impressed by the scope, diversity and value of the Malls. But, as Ronald Reagan used to say, "You ain't seen nothing yet." Perhaps the most important thing we offer at Worldprofit is a vision of what an Internet mall complex should be... and the determination to turn this vision into profit-making reality. Thus, we always have new malls in development... and are constantly assessing new mall ideas for future development. We are happy to hear from people like you... either with suggestions about malls we might like to develop... or malls you might like to develop in association with us. The important thing is that however good the malls are today, I can assure you they will be better — and more numerous — tomorrow.

— Unceasing Promotion

I like to think back to the early days at Worldprofit. Several scoffers (they're always around getting their jollies by unloading as much bile as possible) asked me just why I thought my malls would do well when there were so many other malls out there. My answer, in two words, "Unceasing promotion."

Apparently other mall owners didn't know these words... or weren't willing to do what it takes to build constantly escalating traffic. Unsurprisingly, these malls have bitten the dust at a rapid rate. Such people believed that just because 30 million or 40 million or 60 million people have access to the Internet that all they had to do was post a few notices on a few bulletin boards and the success of their malls (and presumably their advertisers) was assured. I knew that was a load of rubbish.

If you want traffic, whether for a traditional retail store or for your Internet Web site, you've got to become the consummate marketer. You've got to do everything to bring traffic to your site... and you've got to work with a mall owner who is, in his turn, doing everything to bring traffic to the mall as well as supply each Web site owner with guidelines on how to increase that traffic still further. In other words, you need to associate yourself with a certified marketing fanatic.

Personally, I exhibit this desirable fanaticism in any number of ways:

- I insist that as many advertisers as can be cajoled, wheeled and, if necessary, bullied into running Worldprofit Web site addresses on their cards in my quarterly 100,000 circulation Sales & Marketing Success Card Deck, do so. The result? 6-7 MILLION cards per issue have that address. Look at the (relatively few) other card decks that have an Internet presence and look at the cards in their decks. They go out regularly without getting their advertisers either in their malls or using their URL addresses on their cards; (believe me, I check this). This is madness. It's also the difference between mall (and advertiser) success... and failure.

- I ensure that all my columns... now reaching well over 1.5 million people monthly... feature our malls in the Resource Boxes at the ends of the articles. Moreover, I constantly make deals with periodical publishers to give me better article and ad placement in return for various benefits that I can provide them. Why? Because I know, like William Randolph Hearst knew, that if you want maximum promotional results, you cannot just wait for them to happen... you've got to use every little thing at your disposal to leverage better placement, more space, and hence better results. Other columnists write columns. I use columns to drive traffic and build an empire. I trust you see this very significant difference.

- I keep pushing and prodding and nudging all the hundreds of advertisers at Worldprofit to do their bit. I don't expect heroic marketing actions from anyone but myself. What I do expect is daily progress. When I see an advertiser who isn't putting her Worldprofit URL address on her stationery, I don't let it pass. I say something. Why not? Every single sheet she sends should be working for her to increase traffic to her Web site... and it should also be working to increase the overall traffic at Worldprofit. When I find that an advertiser is mailing a brochure without his URL, I'm not polite... I send a note saying, in effect, "Get with the program." I offer no apologies for being blunt, direct, a pocket generalissimo implementing, through small tactical alterations, a grand strategy. Do the advertisers always like these notes and suggestions? I doubt it. Did you like it when your father told you to polish your shoes or wash the dishes? Yet when they stop and think about it most (they tell me later, always later) are grateful for the suggestions. They just wish there weren't so many of them!

But, friend, that's the point. There are many of them. Each thing that we do at Worldprofit is designed to increase traffic. We're committed to that. However we're not committed to running an advertiser rest home. We're not in the coddling business... we're in the marketing business. That means not only doing everything we can to increase the traffic... it means getting our advertisers to do what they can — every single day — to achieve the same result.

— the Worldgram

I've got to tell you, I love my *Worldgram* newsletter. There's something thrilling about coming up with a great marketing idea... or finding a tip to improve a home page... or being able to transmit a piece of technological intelligence to our readers NOW... and not in a week or 30 days or whenever that thrills me. I am in love with the idea of being able to send, with merely the push of a few buttons, client-centered marketing intelligence worldwide all from the comfort of my computer command center.

This is what the *Worldgram* is all about. It's not your staid traditional newsletter in customary format. It's as direct, pungent and urgent as a telegram, packed with tips to help you build a profitable business, particularly a profitable business with a Web component. If what we have to say is pressing, we do a special edition. We compose what we have to say... and we send it IMMEDIATELY. We can get ideas to our readers and advertisers with unbelievable speed — and you can start profiting from them immediately.

More usually, we send our editions out every other week, packed with tips, information, guidelines and suggestions to help you succeed. You and your advertisers. For, you see, the *Worldgram* is a major way we help keep the people you refer to us at Worldprofit in the malls. One of the sins of marketing is to sell someone something... and then never connect with them again. This doesn't happen at Worldprofit... unless advertisers don't have e-mail (thus being unable to get our transmissions) or never visit the Internet. Even these hermits, however, cannot escape: if they've got an address, they still get my four-times a year card-deck and catalog. In other words, advertisers who give us what we need to communicate with them hear from us over 30 times a year! Now, really, who does more "connecting" than that?

— Worldprofit On-line Magazine

What do you spend on magazine subscriptions yearly? $35? $100? More? Well, how would you like to receive a slick, glossy, full color magazine dedicated to your personal and business success for FREE! That's what you — and your advertisers — get every thirty days in the *Worldprofit On-line Magazine*.

Each issue is packed with the intelligent commentary, tips, guidelines and useful suggestions of people who have something to say about the significant topics they're writing about. Again, this is an activist's publication. We want you — and the people you refer to Worldprofit —to dive into each issue, grabbing one useful idea after another. We construct this magazine to improve lives... those of our advertisers, our dealers, and the people these dealers daily refer to us. Oh, yes, and our own lives, for we ourselves assiduously peruse the magazine's content for ideas that will enable us to be better, better, better.

When you speak to a potential Worldprofit advertiser, you should stress that they not only get a Web site... but tangible benefits like the newsletter and the magazine. We're not in the business of posting information for people... we're in the business of improving lives one valuable suggestion at a time. We do this in lots of ways... *Worldprofit On-line Magazine* is one of the best.

— Technological Development

The Web isn't today what it will be tomorrow. And tomorrow's advance may well look positively primitive compared to what is coming down the pike next year. The key to this is staying abreast of breaking developments and translating these into profit-making guidelines and suggestions you can use right now not merely to develop a Web site but to increase your sales. That's our job... and thanks to the masterly hand of George Kosch we do it very well.

Who benefits from this hand at the throttle? All the advertisers at Worldprofit... and thus YOU. Every single day Kosch is at his command center translating arcane bits of technological information into profit bytes you can benefit from right now. Our system is constantly upgraded thanks to new technology upgrades... and, thanks to George's "TechAdvance" notes in the *Worldgram*, we're constantly letting you know what's available to improve your site... and your results.

This dedication not to technology but to translating technology into usable, results-oriented guidelines for your benefit will not change. We do this for many reasons... but one of them is to make our dealers' lives easier and to enable them to sell more Web sites at Worldprofit effortlessly.

— Up-To-Date Marketing Communications

In an environment as fast-changing as the Web, the marketing communications that worked so well yesterday will not work tomorrow. One of the things that astonishes me is how slow other malls and mall owners are to keep their marketing documents in a state-of-the art format. There are malls I could tell you about right now whose marketing communications we laugh about, they're so outmoded and, well, naive.

Let me tell you about the Worldprofit marketing communications and the spirit behind them. Our goal is to keep all marketing communications easy-to-read, easy-to-understand and entirely client-centered at all times. We don't use jargon or techie words. And we never keep the discussion focused on the malls and Web sites... only on what your prospects will GET by doing business with us.

Thus, when you hand someone one of our marketing communications, you have the certainty that we are helping you make the strongest possible case as to why this prospect should do business with Worldprofit... and earn you a commission! As we develop new benefits at Worldprofit (and that, after all, is one of our continuing objectives) we incorporate these into our materials... fast.

— Superior Prospect Service (To Help You Close)

But what if the marketing communication, however good, doesn't close your prospect? What if you cannot answer the prospect's questions... what if the marketing communication doesn't finally do the job, either? We know there are going to be people with questions. We know that you as a dealer are not necessarily going to know the answers... and we know that we cannot address every single concern of every single prospect in every single marketing communication. That's why we encourage you to encourage your prospects to call us. We'll answer their questions... and we'll work with you as a team to help close your prospects.

Have you ever been in a network marketing or other commission-sales "opportunity"? If so, you know as well as I do that in 99% of those situations, the company abandons you, essentially saying "Sink or swim," Pontius-Pilot-like washing their hands of you. It is because we despise that way of doing business that we operate in a very different way.

Of course, we want you to know as much about Worldprofit and our malls as possible. That's why we go to such dramatic lengths to provide you and your prospects with useful information and make it as easy as possible both to get and to understand it. However, we also know that you've got other things on your mind (imagine!) and that you're never going to know as much about the malls as we do. No one sells the malls at Worldprofit better than we do. Personally, I have an extremely high closing rate for the people I talk to. This is no surprise. I know that people will be better off with a Web site at Worldprofit than without one, and I don't let any petty arguments or objections get in the way of my demonstrating to prospects just how true that is. Besides, I'm more persistent than you can easily imagine!

We put these skills at your disposal by encouraging you to get the prospects who need extra time or information to call us. So, refer them to us and we'll work as part of your closing team.

Note: if you fail to persuade your prospect to join Worldprofit, have them get this book. Then have them send us their e-mail address so we can start sending them the Worldgram. If this isn't enough, get them to visit the malls directly. Need still more help? Have them call. We're willing to help, of course, but we've provided lots of ways for people to get the information they need. We like it when they do their bit to get and to understand it. Then we're not taking calls with questions like, "What is the Internet anyway?" These, I must confess, do lose their allure after you've received, say, a few thousand of them.

— Superior Customer Service (After We've Closed)

When it comes to the Internet people have questions. Boy, do they have questions. If you think they've got questions *before* they take a home page... you should be around *after* they've got one. Obviously, they want to have the greatest results from their Web sites; equally obviously we want them to have those results. This cannot happen, however, without superior customer service.

The first thing you'll notice about Worldprofit is that we're actually *available* to answer your questions. Try getting through to other malls. You might as well be the prince fighting through the thorny growth of a hundred years to get to Sleeping Beauty. It's tough, if not impossible. With us, you call, we answer. Different.

Note: when you call, don't be surprised if we don't want to listen to every single event in your long life. We're activists, remember. We want to help you. We don't have time to chat. So, be prepared for the call.

- *Have a pen and paper handy. Or, better yet, call us from your computer keyboard.*

- *Don't be surprised if we direct you to one of our answer-already-available tools, like the Worldprofit malls themselves, or the fax-on-demand, or even this book!*

- *If you can, e-mail your question to webmaster@worldprofit.com We go through the e-mails several times a day.*

- *If you don't understand what we say, say so. We'll try to be a little clearer. We make a real effort to avoid speaking in complicated technical language.*

- *If you need to do something to achieve the results you want, then do it — promptly. One of the most infuriating things is when people say they're going to do something and they don't, especially when it necessitates us following up to go over the same ground yet again. For instance, if we say "use the fax on demand to get document #1 for Web site details," we're saying this to be helpful. Please do your bit before calling back again!*

In other words, we see superior customer service as a two-way street. We're there for our customers… if our customers work *with* us… and not just dump everything on us. Here, just as in all other aspects of Worldprofit, customer service is a cooperative venture. We believe in helping each other achieve the desired objective. This doesn't include shouting at the top of your voice and making demands which make the "customer from hell" look like a pussy cat. Okay?

— The Lowest, Fairest Prices

As you already know, prices on the Internet can be astronomical. People, being people, are going to sock you for whatever they can get. It goes something like this. Most people, the sharks reckon, don't know anything about the Internet. They don't know what's a fair price and what isn't. Moreover, most people, although they know better, don't shop around. They're lazy shoppers. Furthermore, the sharks know that most people are only going to establish a single Web site, that there's not going to be a lot of additional business from a single customer and that if there's a profit to be made, they better make it right away.

At Worldprofit we do things differently. To start with, we believe that the Internet is the most democratic marketing forum in the history of the world. Through human history right up to and including the present people have been both systematically and episodically prosecuted for their beliefs. Yet, human development can only occur when people are allowed to express their beliefs in socially appropriate ways and not have to suffer for them. Thus, we believe it crucial that as many people have access to the Internet as possible… not as few. That means keeping prices fair… and not trying to finance a yacht by assisting an élite and denying access to the many.

High prices on the Internet are the result of human greed and an inability to conceptualize how to make a reasonable profit by performing superior work at a fair price. Now, we may be no less greedy than the next guy (Worldprofit is not, I tell you, run by saints)… but we have figured out how to make that reasonable profit. The key to the system is cooperation.

Each and every person with a Web site at Worldprofit wants more traffic. We, the management, work every day to increase that traffic. However we do not believe we are entirely responsible for providing maximum traffic. We believe that each Web site owner, doing the kinds of both systematic and continuing marketing tasks outlined in this book, is responsible for doing his or her bit to increase traffic. When all people do this, all people benefit. And we're here to remind the non-cooperators that they have a part to do, too, no matter how grand or important or "busy" they think they are. If everyone expects to benefit (as they do), everyone must do what's necessary to ensure the beneficial result.

When traffic is higher, people want to be in a mall and therefore we don't have to "sell" anyone on coming in. Instead, we discuss the best options available to them to achieve their objective. Now, most businesses spend a very large amount of the money they bring in on marketing and overhead. Not us. By keeping our overhead expenses well in hand and by insisting that all people in Worldprofit do their fair share of the overall marketing (thereby limiting what we have to spend in that department, too), we keep our expenditures within appropriate limits... and can keep our prices to the bare bones, too, thereby benefiting all.

There isn't a day that goes by that someone doesn't call up and thank us for our prices. I got used to this kind of appreciation when I set up my Sales & Marketing Success card deck which has always offered the lowest prices in that very competitive field. Still, I'm always glad when people say "Thanks for keeping your prices so much lower than all the others I've found. How do you do it?" Well, now you know.

Personally, I hate selling people stuff. It's demeaning. Instead, I like helping people. I like offering them value, value they can truly understand and benefit from, and working with them to maximize their results. In other words, I like structuring success. I don't want to have to learn about clever closes and sure-fire sales techniques that always work to catch the customer. A lot of that, so prevalent in American business writing and history, strikes me as low-grade bunkum, infinitely distasteful. Instead, I like to present real people with real value and let them make up their own minds. Of course, I'm going to do everything possible to motivate them to act NOW. However, I want that motivation to be within a framework of real value designed to enhance the customer's life.

That's what you get at Worldprofit. We work hard to figure out what our competitors are up to — so we can beat the pants off them. We work hard to create solid value for our customers — so they won't want to go anywhere else and so that they will understand the benefits of doing business with us without our having to "sell" them, which we despise. We work hard to do what's necessary to make Worldprofit the best malls in the world... so that we have the moral standing we need to tell you and the people you refer to us to get off their backsides and help themselves. We're not sitting around with our fingers in our ears all day sipping cognac and planning our next outing to the South of France. We're up and at it, building an astonishing international empire accessible by tens of millions of people worldwide, helping all our customers tap into this mother lode and profit from it as soon as possible. Working this way, we insist that you do what's necessary both to help yourself and to aid the general cause. When you and the people you refer to us do this... we can do what we like: keep the prices far lower than anyone else's... and offer service and an intensive marketing program that they cannot even imagine.

Investment, Profit

So, you may be asking, how much does it all cost? The price to become a dealer is just $100. That's it.

And how much can you make? Best answer: as much as you want. One major secret to making money is to be in the right place at the right time. Money is always being made; money is always being lost. The key is timing. Right now and for the foreseeable future the Web's the place to make money. Why? Because general economic and cultural movements all over the world are assisting you. Every single day in virtually every single media source you hear about the Web. These sources are doing your selling work for you. You don't have to pitch people on the benefits of being on the Web. They've got an idea about those benefits. The question is whether they grab for them now... or later. You simply have to direct them to an appropriate place where they can derive these benefits. In a word, you simply have to tell them about Worldprofit.

Think of the money to be made as the number of home pages jumps from the few millions... to the hundreds of millions... to the billions as all businesses (and the most intelligent and go-ahead portion of the general population worldwide) becomes Web-literate and Web-integrated. Well, friend, it comes down to this. Do you want to sit on the sidelines of this avalanche of cash... and this critical transformation of the way we'll live and do business, knowing, even as you fail to take advantage of the situation, that your life is going to be transformed by it anyway? Or do you want to catch at least a part of the action?

For me, there was absolutely no difficulty about answering that question. Ex-tech-phobe that I am, quintessential university humanities major, I resolved to be a player at this fast-expanding feast. Now I urge you to be a player, too, by

- putting up your own Web site at Worldprofit (fax on demand (403) 425-6049 (document #1)
- creating your own mall (document #5) and/or
- cashing in as a Worldprofit dealer (document #7).

You may also e-mail for the information at webmaster@worldprofit.com, or call us at (403) 425-2466 to sign up. Or, if you prefer, you may mail your one-time $100 dealer processing fee to:

Worldprofit, Inc.
ATTN George Kosch
9010-106 Ave suite 208
Edmonton, Alta T5H 4K3
Canada

Your Worldprofit Dealer Kit goes out the day we hear from you.
Now would be a great time to get started, don't you think?

Commencement

Other books may conclude.

This one is a commencement, a launching pad thrusting you into cyber-profit.

To begin with, how could any book on the Internet just stop? Why, the very essence of this medium is continual, even breath-taking change and transformation. Thus, the first thing I'm going to do is stick my neck out and make 10 predictions about the near-term future of the Internet. I'm not, ordinarily, in the fortune-telling game, but the unstoppable growth of the Internet turns even the most cautious observer into a pop-eyed prognosticator. So, here are the things I think that will happen in just the next couple of years, by the time this book goes into a second edition.

Prediction #1 — The Staggering Growth Of The World Wide Web Will Continue

Predictions about just how much the Web will grow are all over the map. I've read guesstimates of a billion home pages by the year 2000 to a staggering high of 5 billion by 2010. Any way you slice it the growth is going to exceed anything we've ever seen.

A year ago when you talked about the Internet you got a "What's that?" Today it's more likely to be "I know I've got to get on that." In this connection I apply my Barber Test. My barber is very much the "man in the street." He hears a lot from the garrulous men who treat him like a low-priced therapist. He has glib opinions on everything. Last year when I said "Internet" to him, he didn't know what it was and was sure that this "tech-head" idea was definitely not a part of *his* future. Today he's at the "I've got to check that out" stage… with a hint that he'll be on it soon.

As this book goes to press, only about 11% of the U.S. market is hooked up to the Internet. Canada's behind that in second place with Western Europe just beginning to take off. All this means growth, growth, growth… and, of course, when Russia and Asia get into the act you'll see a true global marketplace of staggering proportions. All I can say is that I'm ecstatic that I lived to see the day that all this happened.

It's thrilling!

Prediction #2: Most People Getting A Home Page On The Web For The First Time Will Make The Classic Mistake Of Trying To Go It Alone

The staggering growth of Prediction #1 will be accompanied by the staggering problem of Prediction #2. Tens of millions of people will put up a home page... but it will be in the wrong place, off by itself, all by its lonesome. Reading this book, you can now suggest just why this will occur; you also know that it's a big, big mistake.

Getting a home page without knowing just how traffic will get to it... without being part of a focused, aggressively promoted mall is just plain stupid. Yet millions will do it. They'll put up their "in business" sign somewhere in the galaxy and wait for the hordes of prospects and buyers to drop by... only to be grossly disappointed when they don't.

Thus millions who get on the Internet will, in short order, be frustrated with the small volume of traffic dropping by; they will never experience the amazing connecting power of the Web and fully profit from it. Unsurprisingly, though entirely unfairly, many of these will blame the Internet itself for their problem when, of course, they're entirely responsible.

Prediction #3: Everybody And His Brother Will Get Into The Mall Game

This prediction doesn't put me too far out on the limb; I already see the distinct signs of this. In my daily conversations with entrepreneurs, I'm already hearing the "I'm gonna git me one of them malls" comments that indicate the lemmings are beginning to move towards the cliff for one of their regular rites of mass suicide. Interestingly enough I'm one of the people who's causing this to happen.

Tens of thousands of bright people have already visited the Worldprofit Mall Complex. A goodly number of them have watched it develop from nothing to the point where, in just a matter of a few *months*, the properties are huge, thriving and clearly more valuable every single day. It doesn't take a rocket scientist to figure out that other people, lots of other people, would put two and two together and get... why not me, too?

Thus the most unlikely people in the world are popping up on a regular basis, sniffing around, asking me clumsy questions about what I'm doing, how I do it, what's going to happen next... while simultaneously trying to pump George Kosch, technician extraordinary, on the finer points of mall management. These people think they're being clever, of course, but, really, do they think that Kosch and I were born yesterday? Yes, we've got a good thing going... yes, other people are going to want to have something similar... no, we're not going to tell them how to do it.

This, of course, doesn't stop these (fool) hardy entrepreneurs. Over the last months I've talked to the following people who told me they were going to make their fortunes by developing Internet malls *just like mine*:

- a woman with a small newsletter of 5,000 circulation told me that because she had a publication and because she "knew about promotion", she was certain to make a success of her mall;

- a guy who started a mall and then, lacking all knowledge of how to arrange it, simply went into ours and stole a lot of our editorial material. A quick legal letter to him about copyright violation not only caused him to have second thoughts... he canceled his mall altogether;
- another fellow with a tabloid started a mall and announced his BIG, BIG plans for it on the Internet. Six months later (remember, we monitor these sites closely) there's still NOTHING in his mall... although he continues to advertise it with the same BIG, BIG plans.
- still another entrepreneur started his own mall with the usual hoopla and big noise. However, his price structure is so complicated and charges so inflated that, while about the same age as the Worldprofit Malls, his size and traffic are not even 1% of ours.
- another guy with a magazine started his mall by hooking up with another content provider. When that combination promptly failed, he hooked up with yet another company. As we go to press, his second attempt to launch his worldwide, earth-shaking, can't-be-topped mall is dead in the water, too.

I could go on and on and on.

In this phase of the Internet, we're going to see a lot of this as people, understanding that developing a solo home page on the Internet connected to nothing is dumb, rush to create malls where, so they say, people can combine forces and increase traffic. What ticks me off about them is that they're constantly stealing my ideas, even the very wording of my marketing communications.

Prediction #4: Over 80% Of These Malls Are Death Traps

The corollary to Prediction #3 is that most of these malls will collapse fast. It's easy to see why.

Running a mall is NOT a piece of cake. First off, as this book has made clear, you've got to have a crackerjack technician. I know. In case I haven't already made this single fact abundantly clear, I want you to know that I've got the best guy in the world — George Kosch — handling all the myriad of technical matters that have to take place to make a mall successful. Not only does he know his stuff... he understands that a mall isn't about technology, it's about client-centered market focus. The malls doesn't exist to showcase technology... the technology exists to assist advertisers achieve their objectives simply, easily, and profitably. What's more, Kosch has a military management background; (he was a dashing jet test pilot for the Canadian Air Force). He's one of the few people I have met in my life who's as goal oriented as I am... knowing the importance of getting each thing done as promptly and cleanly as possible. This is so different from others I have worked with (who thought it was a sign of their importance that nothing was ever done right, on time, on budget, or without hassles) that I simply cannot praise these habits enough. If you don't have a technician like this, you're not going to have a successful mall. Period.

Secondly, you've got to have superior customer service that parallels the state-of-the-art technical components. Lots of malls are run by people who are either 1) young tech-heads who specialize in being jerks to customers or 2) by people who have other, full-time jobs, thus leaving them precious little time to handle customer service. Both are these are tremendous problems.

One of the things that most infuriates people like me about dealing with techies is how arrogant and condescending many can be. They don't know about Lord Acton... but I do: "Power corrupts. Absolute power corrupts absolutely." These techies see themselves as the priests of a new religion... as a certified élite... as people who, while still wet behind the ears, hold the fortunes of the planet in their hands. Too often their social skills are rudimentary, at best, and as for understanding client-centered behavior why that is simply too much to hope for. I blame educational establishments like MIT, Cal Tech and others for this. They make no effort to explain that techies need some human skills as well as state-of-the-art expertise to make successful lives. In this connection here's a section of a letter I received while writing this book. It's about customer service at one of our competitor's:

> "I'm allowed to talk to only one person at <the establishment in question> — apparently a very young person, very arrogant, his views already set in concrete, who sometimes tells me I don't know what I'm taking about and who constantly talks down to me." (Unsurprisingly, this fellow, having had enough of this arrant condescension, decided to become a Worldprofit Dealer... and recommended that a number of other clients from the erring company do so, too.)

In addition, there is the phenomenon of people running malls in their space time. This creates many, many problems. The whole idea of the Internet is linking up people of similar interests worldwide and promptly, accurately disseminating information to them. However if a mall manager is only able to put in 6-10 hours a week managing his property how is this possible? In this connection, I've heard from frustrated advertisers who tell me that they've tried to get customer service from various malls, leaving message after message, sending fax after fax... getting hotter and hotter under the collar because they're ignored.

At Worldprofit things are different. In this connection, I want to toss a bouquet of roses to our sterling customer service representative Sandi Hunter. What a charmer! And, again, what an organizer. Every day Sandi fields dozens of calls that range from, "How does the Internet work?" to "I need a home page designed" to "I want to try the new technical features I just read about in today's *Worldgram*." Sandi handles them all with congenial aplomb. If her blood pressure ever rises, she never shows it (unlike poor Jeffrey who has been known to get testy when the questions border on idiocy). I think her previous incarnation as a Canadian social worker is responsible for such consistent grace. Unsurprisingly, the advertisers send me compliment after compliment about her.

Then there has to be marketing expertise. These days every two-bit publisher of a penny-ante publication has visions of himself as the Rupert Murdoch of the Web... the Internet's William Randolph Hearst. They reckon that all you've got to do is throw up a mall... post a couple of announcements in the various newsgroups and run some ads (preferably just in your own publication)... then make arrangements for Brink's to drop by daily to pick up the loot.

If only it were as easy as this...

About the time I started my malls, back in August, 1995, lots of other entrepreneurs were hopping on this bandwagon, starting their own malls, too. One or two, who had been in the Internet business longer, actually sneered at me, essentially saying that they'd wipe their floors with my mangled corpse. Something along those lines. In such situations, I smile... because I know that behind this still-boyish visage lies... an absolute determination to be the best at whatever I do.

While the braggarts were showing off at their local pub, I set to work with a will establishing beneficial alliances with card decks and hundreds of periodical publishers, doing what was necessary to get them into the malls, showing them just how much better off they'd be at Worldprofit than elsewhere... and demonstrating just what they risked by either 1) doing nothing, 2) going on the Internet alone, or 3) making the really foolish mistake of going into another, less technologically superior and less aggressively marketed mall property. Within a matter of weeks this kind of deliberate focus started paying off as both the number of advertisers and the volume of traffic picked up.

Then, as soon as we'd developed the properties to the point where people's reaction was, "Wow, I want in," we started the Worldprofit Dealer Program... understanding that for the malls to grow to the size and prominence that I insisted they become... we needed a huge cadre of people working with us to promote the malls... while taking their cut of the profits. Within literally hours of announcing this program, our first dealers started to sign up. These people — and all who have followed — understood that if they were going to take a cut of the gigantic phenomenon that is the Internet, it was very much in their interests to work closely with the team that, in record time, not only established but developed the profitable Worldprofit Mall Complex.

The big talkers were still talking... only now every word they uttered had an ironic aspect that, frankly, they just didn't comprehend.

Thus, while you're going to see one mall after another be created... you're also going to see the vast majority of these malls collapse. Unfortunately, as they do, they are going to hurt hundreds, maybe even tens of thousands of people who trusted the promises made by these big talkers and forked over their money (often quite a lot of money) accordingly.

Prediction #5: Advertising Prospects Will Get Smarter About Quizzing Mall Owners

The roller coaster ride that will see vast numbers of people jump onto the Web by themselves (with unfortunate consequences), see unprepared mall owners create rickety properties and also equally see the wholesale collapse of these properties, will at least have one good consequence: Web advertisers will get smarter about where they'll put their home pages. Such advertisers will start asking the kinds of questions that emanate from a knowledge of this book and of what it takes to really make money with an Internet home page. You should know these questions as well as I do by now, questions like:

- how do you keep abreast of the changing Internet technology?
- how do you communicate these changes to me?
- how do you market your malls?
- how to you increase the mall traffic?
- how do you work with me to give me traffic-building suggestions?

The Internet is about three major things: changing technology, enabling advertisers to benefit from this technology, and establishing an aggressive marketing program, both on the Web and off, to increase prospect traffic to advertiser Web sites. As more and more advertisers get savvy about these points, they are certain to ask the mall owners and managers just what they're doing in all three areas. That will lead in due course to fewer weak malls... and fewer disgruntled advertisers.

Prediction #6: Web Sites Will Become More Like 24-Hour A Day Television Shows

We are rapidly moving into the period when every Web site will become, due to improved video technology, a 24 hour a day television program. While listening to the PBS special I mentioned above, I literally let out a whoop of joy when one of the experts said that within a decade there would be 5 billion channels on the Internet, each capable of broadcasting a separate program. In other words, each Web site will have the capability, with enhanced video, of turning you into your own international television producer.

Some of the results of this development will, of course, be ludicrous. Lonely people with problems aplenty will go before a video camera and start burbling on about why their lives are a mess. Ever more intimate facts will be retailed before a (hopefully small) international audience. People will relate their sexual fantasies... and (worse) their sexual realities. Every conceivable neurosis will be generally aired in detail, fascinating only because (to those of us who still believe in personal privacy) we could never believe anyone would actually *say those things*.

Better, from a business standpoint you will have the opportunity to do one or a series of video programs which cycle one into another. For 10 minutes you can demonstrate your latest widget and make sure prospects have complete order information. This program will then cycle into another on Widget 2, then another on Widget 3, *etc.*

People will become obsessed with finding both the best and cheapest video production and a whole new micro-industry will spring up catering to the Internet video script and production needs of business.

Needless to say, as this development takes place, unless the advertiser's Web site is properly positioned in a high traffic mall, what that advertiser spends will be lost. Thus as advertisers spend more on creating their own video programming, they will be forced to look much more seriously at the question of traffic... and where they're going to get the best bang for the buck.

Prediction #7: Telephone Calls From The Web Will Be Commonplace

If you want to turn the hair of executives white at AT&T, Sprint, MCI, *etc.* and hear their transatlantic shrieks, just say "Internet." Right now, just a few people are using the Internet to make their long-distance calls. The software is comparatively primitive and there are some drawbacks in terms of quality and the fact that the person you're calling has to have the same software that you're using. It's a nuisance. But then it was a nuisance when I was growing up in the 'fifties that you had to share a telephone party line. I still remember my thrill as a small boy listening in on the lives of others and my parents' horror that a son of theirs could do such a thing. Yes, even then I enjoyed the voyeurism of eavesdropping on other peoples' lives that has never left me.

Just as party lines now seem a bit of remote telephone history, so much more shortly will today's primitive Internet phone connections. Soon, people will quite easily be able to make both domestic and international calls over the Internet for pennies. You can be certain that the big phone companies will do everything in their power to block this development; you can be equally certain that the government will side with the big corporations while all the while claiming that they are, of course, for the technical developments taking place and for "democratizing" phone connections. In short, you'll see a gigantic battle royale for the billions of dollars the phone companies represent. Yet, in the final analysis, cheap phone calls will be made over the Internet, since I do not see our government or any government (despite the immense pressures that will be brought to bear on them) oppressing millions of private citizens who regard it as their right to use the phone and use it cheaply.

Prediction #8: Access To The Internet Via Cable Channels Will Vastly Increase Viewership

One of the reasons why smart people are moving as quickly as they can to get their share of the Internet is because we're just steps away from a huge increase in viewership: getting access to the Internet via your television set.

Trials are already underway in various states and in Canada to work out any remaining bugs in this huge technological leap that will vastly increase the numbers of people with access to the Internet.

Imagine this scenario: you have a Web site in the Worldprofit Mall Complex. One of our millions of promotional pieces lands at the home of Citizen X who leafs through it while lounging in bed. As in millions of homes the television's going, although she's not paying attention. However upon seeing our Mall information and URL, she decides to turn the channel over to the Worldprofit Malls and, seeing your fascinating, client-centered Web site, she responds to what you're offering... all without getting out of bed!

Or, try this variation on the theme. The same viewer goes to Worldprofit and sees our free offer to get an e-mail subscription to our *Worldgram*. First she leaves her e-mail address, then she drops in on one of our malls. Within a few days, the latest issue of the *Worldgram* is automatically transmitted to her. She sees a module about the great offers in your client-centered home page... and pops by to check them out, responding by requesting your information or buying your product on line in our credit card secure environment.

You want to know what kinds of fantasies I have? They're not about nymphs and cocoa butter. You've just read two of them! I dream of the day — now so near — when every single person with a television set not only has a Web site at Worldprofit... but can access those Web sites without ever shifting position in his recliner chair.

Prediction #9: Secure Credit Card Transactions

I feel almost guilty putting this in as a "prediction," because this development is imminent. Nonetheless, because we don't have secure credit card transactions yet, it still qualifies as a prediction.

What is this kind of credit card security going to mean? Well, take my illustration above. With my card deck, the hundreds of full page ads we run at Worldprofit, the catalogs I send out, the hundreds of publications carrying my column, our e-mail publication and on-line magazine, *etc., etc., etc.*, literally millions of people hear about the malls at Worldprofit and hear about them and hear about them and hear about them. When they drop by and find something they want to buy (a function of the relentlessly client-centered marketing we insist our advertisers provide to present their products/services), the customers can BUY IT NOW with whatever credit cards the advertiser accepts.

Again, picture our Madame Recamier on her chaise lounge surfing the 'net. She visits our Total Home & Garden Mall and finds a darling thing for her night stand. It's pictured in full-color… and offers a complete, compelling description. The Web site also includes full credit card purchase information. Madame knows the transaction is secure… and, thus, she buys, happy with her purchase and the delightful effect it will add to her celebrated boudoir.

Now picture every single product and service on earth being presented in Web sites and every single player in the economic universe (that is people with money and credit) being able not only to access them on-line but to purchase them, too! It is any wonder that some of the world's smartest people are falling all over themselves to get this technology in place and to start profiting from it? Look for it very, very soon!

Prediction #10: More & More People In The "Left Behind" Culture

Benjamin Disraeli, once a boyhood dandy, latter England's epigrammatic Prime Minister, in one of his silver-spoon novels coined the phrase "Two Nations," to describe the separation of Britain into the two forever-divided parts of the rich and poor. Since then humanists have regularly bewailed the divisions of society that keep us from universal brotherhood. These divisions, however, are permanent and the galloping growth of the Internet is certain to exacerbate them.

So far I have talked about, and been entirely fascinated by, the number of people who are flocking to the Web and all the delicious growth that's still to occur. There are those who say that the Web is doubling in size every 5 months. Just think how immense that makes this growth!

However at the same time, two other groups are being created: 1) those who cannot get onto the Web either because they do not have the technology or cannot afford it and 2) those who will not go onto the Web.

I intend to say little here about the first group. The fact is that a permanent underclass is being created and that failure to have access to the information and resources on the World Wide Web will keep the people in it permanently out of the sophisticated economic world the rest of us inhabit and profit from. While writing this book, for instance, a graduate student from Zaire visited me. He had no clue about developments on the Internet; had never, indeed, heard of it. No wonder. There is no Internet in Zaire, so that even a member of what must be regarded as that nation's educated élite was ignorant about and unable to profit from it.

Someday, of course, there will be an Internet there, but the class of people who will have access to it will be minuscule. Deduction? The terrible problems of Zaire, and countries like it, will be compounded because these nations and the people in them will not have access to the latest technology and will not be able to benefit from it. They will be increasingly irrelevant, whole nations counting for nothing. Humanists will decry this development but economic reality has a way of reducing such complaints to the outermost fringes of our consciousness and concern.

I am more concerned about people who might have access to the Web, who might be profiting from it, but who have quite deliberately determined not to do so. I am not just talking about poor people in the United States, about people without education or technical training. I am talking about business people who have taken the incredibly foolish position that the Internet will have no part in their lives, now or ever, damn the consequences.

As I write I am thinking about the editor of a newsletter I know. This fellow has prospered to the degree that he has by sending out a mail-order publication stuffed with various low-grade offers. He knows just how many pages he can mail for a given price and to make the most of his printing and postage money, he crams everything he can into his mailing, uses the smallest possible type (I'm nearly 50, remember, and every year I find it more difficult to read type so small) he can... and generally waves off easy readability as completely unimportant.

I call this fellow every so often to twit him about developments in my malls, the number of new advertisers we have, new dealers, *etc.* In short, to brag. I do this, first, because I enjoy the effect it produces on him and secondly, to see what he'll say. I regard him as the mouthpiece of all the dinosaurs, educated people who are not without either intelligence or resources, but who are resolutely determined to eschew the greatest connecting and commercial tool in history and so decline and wither away. As a man who exults in the experience of lusty prosperity, I find such people as interesting as a superior museum exhibit and when I have the chance to talk to them, I take it — if only to get insight into a state of brain I most assuredly do not share.

My acquaintance tells me things like this:

- The Internet doesn't work.
- I cater to low-end mail-order buyers, and these people aren't knowledgeable about the Internet, so why should I be interested?
- I'm making as much money this year as last year, so what's the big deal?

Then we end the conversation the way it always ends, with him saying (he thinks shrewdly), "If you're so interested in having my business, why don't you give me a free home page?" I then laugh and we hang up.

Sadly, this man is a candidate for the economic underclass. The market he's catering to (the people he calls the "low-end mail order buyers") is a shrinking market. The smart people in this cadre are steadily moving their operations to the Internet. As they go onto the Internet, they experience the delight of being able to say what they want to say, how they want to say it. Tiny print with primitive graphics on low-quality paper quickly lose whatever allure they once possessed. With such people gone, he's left with fewer and fewer prospects and those of the poorest quality. It's a prescription for a painful wasting sickness.

Curiously, lots of educated people have deliberately put themselves in this position. Whether they truly don't believe in the already demonstrated promise of the Internet (with so much more to come).. or that they are thinking they can still make a go of it without being part of the World Wide Web... or just hoping that their current operations will see them out for the duration of their lives... they have nonetheless determined to cock a snoot at the Internet. As such they have shot themselves in any number of bodily parts.

I observe these people, whom I regularly encounter, with the most deliberate scrutiny and interest. I note a querulous, embittered defensiveness in many of them. I think many know they've selected a very risky route and feel angry at being forced (so they think) to explain their choice. They have gone from feeling confident about their place in the cosmos and their overall prospects to the distinct possibility of being an obvious also-ran.

In the spirit of science, I let these people ramble on about why they've made such a poor choice. They tell me things like:

- the Internet's a fad like 900 numbers (a particularly witless comment from a man whose idea of how to sell things has not progressed beyond holding house parties, yet who regularly brags about his place on marketing's "cutting edge")
- it's time to "smell the roses and relax." I don't want to learn anything new. I know enough already.
- my brochure and other marketing materials tell our story well enough, *etc.*

All this is rubbish, of course. Moreover I think many of them know by saying such rubbish and choosing such a course that they've chosen to fail. They try hard for self-justification, of course, but not so far under the surface they know they're selecting a route that cannot possibly benefit them. That is why that note of aggressive, sour defensiveness intrudes and is so obvious. They've chosen the death of doing things the way they've always done them over the life that's represented by the astonishing developments on the Internet. Perhaps even they don't really know why they've done something so self-defeating, why they're being so foolish. This makes them interesting, of course, but only from the psychologist's standpoint. In any other ways it just makes them sadly pathetic.

My Last Prediction: The Worldprofit Mall Complex Will Grow & Grow & Grow!

Since I've made so many predictions about others in this final chapter, I feel duty bound to make a prediction about the Worldprofit Mall Complex. I can do so in just three words: more and better!

From time to time in one's life, things happen that are so right that you begin to believe in the concept of destiny; not just destiny as an abstract force that exists in the universe, but destiny as an active agent in your own life. I have felt that force in my life. I felt it when I arrived in Cambridge in the fall of 1969 to attend Harvard as a graduate student. I had never been to Massachusetts, never seen Harvard, but when I walked down Massachusetts Avenue into Harvard Square on the Friday of Labor Day Week-end that year I knew I had come home. I knew I was in the right place at the right time. No one told me. My heart told me.

This same thing occurred when the crucial moment came when McGraw-Hill wanted to publish my book **The Consultant's Kit** and I declined their offer, telling them that I'd publish it myself. Their representative was rudely dismissive. "What do you know about publishing?," he scoffed, as if that were the final word. I told him I knew nothing about publishing but I knew everything about myself. Since then I've grossed well over a million dollars from that book alone — even though I was ignorant of the niceties of how to do business as a publisher!

I felt the same way when I started my card deck. I knew that that industry was badly run; that a few people were raking in vast sums at the expense of advertisers who generally didn't know what they were doing. Card decks were an advertising Augean stables, and they desperately cried out to be cleaned. As usual, I knew next to nothing about how the industry worked but, upon doing my homework, I knew that a successful business could be started merely by offering advertisers good value at reasonable prices. Predictably, the other deck owners howled with outrage when I got started. Some even engaged in dirty tricks to derail my enterprise before it succeeded. All that was irritating, of course, but in the final analysis when people get value at reasonable cost they provide wind for any entrepreneur's sails. And so it proved for me, now owner of the nation's largest card deck!

I felt this crucial, thrilling feeling again when George Kosch started talking to me about the Internet. I have previously owned up to being no tech-head. Still I could see right away that this development wasn't about technology (no matter how enthralling that technology might be), it was about creating a gigantic communications emporium, putting private citizens in touch with private citizens in pursuit of their specialized interests and enabling every business worldwide to be inexpensively in touch with the people who would be better off because of these business' offerings.

When I grasped this point, I experienced the same kind of epiphany which has graced my life before... and which I regard as a true sign of being in the right place at the right time, pursuing the right objective with the right people.

And so it has proved.

Nowadays we regularly hear from people who say things like, "I visited Worldprofit when it only had two advertisers... you've grown so big so fast," or "I've been watching you and you're doing it right, so I want to be a part," or "your malls are so sensibly arranged," or "how can you keep your prices so low?" These comments are gratifying, of course, but they are no surprise to us. Once the concept was clear to all concerned, the growth followed as a matter of course. With so much more growth to follow.

My Invitation To You To Be A Part Of It All

We have now reached the end of the first segment of our journey together. I have enjoyed sharing these ideas with you; I hope you have found them of value.

Fortunately, our journey together doesn't stop here today. No indeed! It can, indeed, be a journey we continue together for the rest of our lives. I invite you to continue our association and to help make it more and more profitable.

Here are the action steps you can do right now:

1) Dial 24-hour fax-on-demand (403) 425-6049 and get document #1 for information on getting a Web site in the Worldprofit Mall Complex. This fax-on-demand document is continually kept up-to-date with details about new malls, *etc.* Or, complete the order coupon that follows and e-mail, fax, or mail it back to Worldprofit with your Web site details. Your home page ordinarily is posted within 24 hours!

2) Use this same fax-on-demand number and get document #3 for details about my card deck. Use a card in my quarterly Sales & Marketing Success Card Deck to promote what you're selling and, of course, direct traffic to your Web site.

If you're not already getting my quarterly card deck, call (617) 547-6372 so you will.

3) Use this same FOD and get document #7 to become a Worldprofit Dealer. By using our easy-to-follow instructions, you can cash in on the stupendous growth yet ahead on the Internet by working with us. In the process you'll earn a LIFETIME COMMISSION each time anyone you refer renews their Web site. Or, complete the sign-up form that follows and e-mail, fax, or mail to Worldprofit.

4) E-mail us at webmaster@worldprofit.com and request your free subscription to my *Worldgram* newsletter. And tell your friends! I'll be happy to send it to all who want it — *free*!

5) Get your own mall at Worldprofit. Request FOD document #5 and get all the details you need to establish your own lucrative mall property in conjunction with the Worldprofit Mall Complex. There are literally thousands of subject areas available for your mall. Remember that when you associate yourself with Worldprofit, you are working with people who share your vision about making your mall the best of its kind, the most highly trafficked, and the most lucrative. In other words, you're working with just the kinds of people you need as part of your success team.

6) Put your publication in one of our malls and get your advertisers into your site. When you work with us, publishers, you work with people who understand your business; after all, we're in it ourselves! Call me at (617) 547-6372 to find out how to move at least part of your operations to the Web and how to maximize your profits while assisting all your advertisers to do better, too.

7) If you didn't get this book directly from me (thereby getting on my mailing list), call (617) 547-6372 to get a free subscription to my quarterly Sure-Fire Business Success Catalog, packed with hundreds of ways to make your business more profitable — now. Or write JLA Publications, P.O. Box 38-2767, Cambridge, MA 02238.

Last Words

When the celebrated 18th century historian Edward Gibbon finished his monumental *Decline and Fall of the Roman Empire*, he got up and took a turn in his garden. Later he turned that experience into an exquisite passage in his autobiography. As for me, I am concluding this book on a Sunday in June at 10:30 in the morning. It is hot and humid, the air is heavy. The town is quiet; indeed there are no sounds whatsoever except for the incessant hum of my computer, a sound so much my constant companion I no longer consider it at all.

In this room there are these factors: the present, the future, this computer, the Internet, you and me. We are now all bound together. I, for one, cannot wait to see what we make of these consequential elements, for as Wordsworth wrote:

Bliss was it in that dawn to be alive,

But to be young was very heaven!

Amidst all the exciting developments at this dawn of the Internet I feel very young indeed, awaiting with the keenest anticipation all that you and I will do together in this thrilling epoch not merely of our renewed lives but of our entire civilization and eternal swift-spinning planet.

ABOUT THE AUTHOR: DR. JEFFREY LANT

Millions of people around the world now rely on the sensible, hard-hitting, eminently practical business and personal development information provided by Dr. Jeffrey Lant.

He has founded 10 (and counting!) malls on the World Wide Web at http:// www.worldprofit.com. These malls include his *Worldgram* newsletter and *Worldprofit On-line Magazine*.

Over 200 publications and electronic data bases worldwide carry his "Sure-Fire Business Success" and "Qwik-Smarts w/ Dr. Jeffrey Lant" columns. He is also publisher of the Sure-Fire Business Success Catalog and quarterly 100,000 circulation Sales & Marketing Success Card Deck.

Author of 13 books, some of his popular titles include **Cash Copy: How To Offer Your Products And Services So Your Prospects Buy Them... NOW!; The Consultant's Kit: Establishing And Operating Your Successful Consulting Business; Money Talks: The Complete Guide To Creating A Profitable Workshop Or Seminar In Any Field; The Unabashed Self-Promoter's Guide: What Every Man, Woman, Child And Organization In America Needs To Know About Getting Ahead By Exploiting The Media; How To Make A Whole Lot More Than $1,000,000 Writing, Commissioning, Publishing And Selling "How-To" Information,** and **Multi-Level Money: The Complete Guide To Generating, Closing & Working With All The People You Need To Make Real Money Every Month In Network Marketing.** When Jeffrey writes a book, he sets out with a single mission: to make it the standard resource in the field, the benchmark against which all other books in that field are compared.

In his spare time, Jeffrey is an avid art collector, collecting Old Master paintings from the 17th through 19th centuries. Having earned four college degrees (including the Ph.D. from Harvard), he is also holder of four titles of ancient nobility dating back to the Third Crusade. As such his proper title is "His Highness The Prince of Tornavan."

Unique among authors, Jeffrey Lant's direct-access telephone number runs in every book, catalog, article, card-deck, audio cassette and on the World Wide Web, easily making him the world's most reachable author and business authority.

When you need help building your profit-making business, here's that number: (617) 547-6372, fax (617)-547-0061, e-mail: drjlant@worldprofit.com. Just be ready to do business!

Worldprofit Dealer Application

To: Future Worldprofit Dealer

From: Jeffrey Lant, PhD

You're undoubtedly aware of the exploding number of people with access to the World Wide Web. Right now, estimates range from a low of 30,000,000 people worldwide to a high of about twice that number — 60,000,000 people!

The number of people with their own Web sites — called home pages — is also extremely large. It is now estimated that there are about 18,000,000 home pages. The Wall Street Journal has estimated that within two-three years there will be over ONE BILLION Internet home pages and *USA Today* says simply, "Every business will have a Web site."

Up until now there was no good way for you to cash in on this explosive growth. Now there is. By becoming a dealer at Worldprofit!

About Worldprofit, Inc.

You may already know about Worldprofit. We maintain a large and fast-growing complex of 10 malls. More are already in development. These malls include the

- ✶ MONEY MALL
- ✶ MAIL ORDER MALL
- ✶ BETTER HEALTH MALL
- ✶ GIFTS MALL
- ✶ THE INFOMALL
- ✶ BUSINESS TO BUSINESS MALL
- ✶ NETWORK MARKETING MALL
- ✶ TOTAL HOME & GARDEN MALL
- ✶ HOME-BASED BUSINESS MALL
- ✶ THE CHRISTIAN MALL

When you access these malls at http://www.worldprofit.com, you'll find the Web sites for hundreds and hundreds of businesses worldwide… with more being added every single day thanks to our extensive marketing and promotional program and word-of-mouth referrals from our satisfied customers. You've probably seen our ads promoting the malls — they're everywhere! This is one very good reason why it's easy to sell Web sites at Worldprofit. People know who we are… and can easily access the malls to see for themselves just what they're like and just what they can have for their Web site.

Web Sites At Worldprofit Are Easy To Sell

It's easy to sell Web sites at Worldprofit. Here's why.

■ STATE-OF-THE-ART TECHNICAL ASSISTANCE. Our highly skilled technical staff provide advertisers with full professional Web site development. We offer free technical consultation during the entire set-up process. Advertisers can take advantage of our full spectrum of Internet capabilities including color graphics, electronic order forms, sound clips and advanced multi-media. We produce professional interactive Web sites with the emphasis on our customers getting results! We stay abreast of developments in the fast-moving Internet environment and translate these developments so that you profit from them. You don't need to know anything about technology... the Web... or even own or operate a computer. We do everything for you to make sure you profit now from current technology.

■ FREE SUBSCRIPTION TO OUR TWICE MONTHLY *WORLDGRAM* NEWSLETTER. We'll give every single person you sign up a free subscription to our twice-monthly *Worldgram* newsletter. This newsletter is packed with useful marketing and business-building information, including suggestions on how to create a money-making Web site. All they have to have is an e-mail address to receive the newsletter.

■ UNRELENTING MALL MARKETING & PROMOTION. We have the most aggressive marketing program in the Internet business. We know that people with Web sites want increased traffic. Here are just some of the ways we promote the malls to give it to them.

■ Jeffrey Lant's quarterly 100,000 circulation Sales & Marketing Success Card Deck. At least 60-70 cards per issue (that's 6-7 million cards!) promote the Worldprofit Malls in one way or another.

■ marketing in many other card decks. We run literally millions of cards every year promoting the malls.

■ quarterly 140,000+ Sure-Fire Business Success Catalog. Through *Worldprofit On-Line Magazine*. (You can access this at worldprofit.com to see for yourself. A new issue is added the first of every month!)

■ through two internationally syndicated columns, "Sure-Fire Business Success" and"Qwik-smarts w/ Dr. Jeffrey Lant." These columns reach over 1.5 million people monthly in over 200 publications worldwide.

■ through the *Worldgram* Newsletter.

■ through Internet search computers and newsgroups, and

■ by providing detailed marketing suggestions and recommendations to all Web siteadvertisers at Worldprofit.

Given all these promotional tools, it's no surprise that the traffic at Worldprofit goes up every single day by a substantial amount. Want to see how much? We prominently post a counter on our Web site at http://www.worldprofit.com — See for yourself!

■ REASONABLY PRICED PROFESSIONAL COPYWRITING ASSISTANCE. We know that advertisers may not be expert in creating client-centered home pages. No problem! Our expert copywriters can do it for them — at prices others just cannot (or will not) match.

■ LOWEST WEB SITE PRICES ON THE ENTIRE INTERNET. People are right to be interested in seeking value on the Internet. We provide it. Our prices are the lowest on the entire Internet... particularly when you consider the extensive promotion and demonstrated traffic we provide. The people you turn on to Worldprofit can have a one-year Web site with state-of-the-art fax-on-demand (so their prospects can get all the information they want by calling a central number and having it faxed back to them) for just about a buck a day That's right, just about a dollar a day. Given the fact that others charge hundreds, even thousands of dollars a month (and that additional per-lead costs are common), you can see now why the prices at Worldprofit are such a bargain... especially given our constantly rising traffic! We give advertisers high traffic and low cost... which is just the way they like it!!!

For these reasons, you'll find you don't have to "sell" Web sites at Worldprofit. Instead, just tell your prospects the facts and you'll discover just how fast they'll act to get their Web site... or sites; (many people take multiple sites).

NOW YOU CAN BENEFIT!

When you become a dealer at Worldprofit, you can easily profit from the explosive growth of the Web and the Worldprofit Malls in particular. Here's how...

→ we provide you with the marketing materials you need, including camera-ready flyer and ads in different sizes. Your camera-ready flyer comes complete with your LIFETIME DEALER NUMBER already printed on the form. Just take it to a quick-copy printer, get the forms printed in the color of your choice (yellow's always good), and you're ready to distribute them to your customers, as a package stuffer, in response to the ads you run, *etc.* It's easy!

→ if prospects call you to ask questions, answer them if you can; obviously the more you know about the Worldprofit Malls, the better. (That's why you should read our *Worldgram* newsletter and drop by the malls on a regular basis to see all the improvements we're constantly making.) However, if you can't answer some questions, no problem. Just refer your prospects directly to Worldprofit at (403) 425-2466, and we'll be happy to assist by providing the necessary information, in effect closing your prospect for you. Just make sure that prospect gives us your LIFETIME DEALER NUMBER so you get the credit!!!

Once your customers are ready to sign up, they simply send in the handy order form we provide (or e-mail us at webmaster@worldprofit.com or fax (403) 425-6049).

All forms and home page information go directly to Worldprofit headquarters for processing. Your commission check — 20% of the basic home page options and/or fax-on-demand options — is cut monthly and mailed directly to you. Nothing could be easier!!! You don't have to answer the prospects' questions... you don't have to set up their home pages... you don't have to consult with them on technical matters... you don't have to do the copywriting. We do all that... and you get a nice check every time you turn someone on to Worldprofit!

When it comes time for your customer or prospect to renew in either 6 months or a year, depending on the Web site option they originally selected, we'll cut you another check that same month as soon as they do. We make renewals easy not least because we stay in touch with all customers through the *Worldgram* Newsletter providing them with twice-monthly tips to improve their business marketing and especially their Internet marketing. This kind of contact pays off in high renewals — and more checks for you!!!

WHAT'S IN YOUR WORLDPROFIT DEALER PACKAGE

Here's what you get from Worldprofit when you become a dealer:

→ welcome letter with useful dealer information

→ free *Worldgram* Newsletter subscription to run without term. (You must provide us with an e-mail address at webmaster@worldprofit.com to get your subscription.)

- practical money-making report by Dr. Jeffrey Lant entitled HOW TO MAKE MONEY DAY AFTER DAY AS A WORLDPROFIT WEB SITE DEALER
- 8 $1/_2$" X 11" back-to-back camera-ready flyer with a space for your LIFETIME DEALER NUMBER
- camera-ready ads in various sizes. You can run these to get good, qualified leads.

"HOW MUCH DOES ALL THIS COST?"

We are familiar with other dealer programs on the Web that cost up to $3,000 and even require you to attend expensive training programs. Ouch! Not ours. Not us. You pay a one-time only processing fee of $100 US to become a Worldprofit Dealer. Then you're a dealer for life! Sell as many home pages as you want. Start today! Or whenever you're ready.

To become a Dealer, just provide the following information along with your $100 payment. Your complete dealer kit will be sent immediately upon processing.

——— PLEASE PRINT ———

Name _____

Company Name _____

Address _____

City _____ State/Prov_____

ZIP/Postal Code _____

day ph _____ eve ph _____

e-mail _____

If faxing your order with credit card, select: ❏ Mastercard   ❏ VISA

Card Number _____ expiration date _____

Signature _____ Print Name _____

Date of your order: _____

Please make my commission checks payable to: _____

If mailing, send with payment to Worldprofit, Inc., 9010-106 Ave., Suite 208, Edmonton, Alta T5H 4K3, Canada. If paying by check make payable to WORLDPROFIT, INC. U.S. dollar checks only please.

Questions: Call Mall Manager George Kosch at (403) 425-2466.

Remember what USA Today said, "EVERY BUSINESS WILL HAVE A HOME PAGE." Here's the easiest and most lucrative way for you to be a part of this incredibly lucrative marketing and communications phenomenon.

How To Get Your Web Site Home Page Today!

1 To start your account, mail/fax this order form and payment to Worldprofit, Inc., Suite 208, 9010-106 Ave., Edmonton, Alberta, T5H 4K3, Canada. Fax (403) 425-6049.

2 To get your Home Page materials to us, choose one of the following methods:

- Fax your camera ready information to us at (403) 425-6049. Your Home Page can be up in 24 hours, in most cases!

- E-mail the text you want included in your Home Page to: webmaster@worldprofit.com (IBM files only)

- Mail an IBM disk or typed 8 1/2" x 11" camera ready page to Worldprofit, Suite 208, 9010-106 Ave, Edmonton, Alberta, T5H 4K3, Canada

If you need copywriting assistance, we can arrange it for you. We have professional copywriters standing by.

If you have also selected the Fax on Demand service, mail your documents flat (maximum of 3) to Worldprofit at the above address.

MALL SELECTION (Please select the Mall of your choice) — Additional Mall selections are $50 each per year.

- ❑ MONEY MALL
- ❑ BUSINESS TO BUSINESS MALL
- ❑ NETWORK MARKETING MALL
- ❑ HOME-BASED BUSINESS MALL
- ❑ INFOMALL
- ❑ BETTER HEALTH MALL
- ❑ MAIL ORDER MALL
- ❑ TOTAL HOME & GARDEN MALL
- ❑ GIFTS MALL
- ❑ CHRISTIAN MALL

PAYMENT OPTIONS (Please Note: All Prices in US Dollars)

- ❑ **OPTION 1:** I want my Home Page to run for six months. Enclosed is $129.95.

- ❑ **OPTION 2:** I want my Home Page to run for six months and profit from the Fax on Demand service. $189.95.

- ❑ **OPTION 3:** I want my Home Page to run for twelve months and receive a FREE 60 character ad on the "InternetConnect" card (circulation 100,000; $90 value) $199.95.

- ❑ **COPYWRITING SERVICE:** $79.95 per page. (You must call to arrange.)

- ❑ **DELUXE OPTION:** I want my Home Page to run for twelve months and profit from the Fax on Demand service. $329.95. YOU SAVE $139.95! and will receive a FREE 60 character ad on the "InternetConnect" card ($90 value). Fill in your ad copy in the space provided below.

- ❑ **LINK OPTION:** I want a link to my existing home page for one year. My URL address is http://_____. $199.95 (All links subject to Worldprofit, Inc. approval.)

Put your *Free* 60 character ad here:

_____.

(We provide your URL address.) If you do not provide 60 character ad copy, we will write it for you.

REMEMBER, YOUR WEB SITE CAN BE AS LARGE AS YOU WANT.

If you are uncertain about the cost, call (403) 425-2466 for assistance.

I would like to enhance my Home Page with these optional features:

- ❑ Extra Page(s) – $20 each
- ❑ Order Form – $25
- ❑ Color & Features Pkg – $25
- ❑ Color Picture(s) – $40 each
- ❑ Color Background – $10

Please send your check or money order (make payable to Worldprofit, Inc.) to:

Worldprofit, Inc.
Suite 208
9010-106 Ave Edmonton
Alberta, T5H 4K3, Canada
Ph: (403) 425-2466
or Fax: (403) 425-6049

For faster service, use your credit card and fax this application to **(403) 425-6049.**

❑ Check ❑ Money Order ❑ MC/Visa

Card # _____

Expiration Date _____

Signature _____

Name _____

Company_____

Address _____

City _____

State/Prov _____

Zip/PC _____

Phone (   ) _____

Fax (   ) _____

E-mail address _____

Note: No advertisements of a sexual or offensive nature will be accepted.